The Congregation of the Humility of Mary had a long and enduring relationship with Marvin Mottet, first as a student and later as a valued friend. It was marked by mutual respect, affection and support. I think anyone reading about Father Mottet's life will be delighted with his whimsical spirit, inspired by his commitment to social justice and moved by the depth of his spirituality. Perhaps humility and love of earth created a shared humus-bond with CHMs. I am grateful to have known him and he continues to enrich my life.
Sister Johanna Rickl, President, Congregation of the Humility of Mary

"Marv Mottet was a man, more than any other I knew, who had a deep and profound spiritual life combined with a radical commitment to the poor and the courage to habitually engage in public action for justice. Often on the many trips I took to the Quad Cities I would stay at his rectory. His door was always open, and he always conveyed a warm sense of welcome. I often attended an early morning mass he said with a few of his parishioners. There was always a fervor, a humility and a sense of joy and gratitude in his manner. Even in ill health and obvious pain he seemed more concerned for others than for himself. He was like a Franciscan in his practice poverty. He drove old cars and wore clothes that had seen better days. We are to "love God with all out heart, all our soul and with all our mind, and to love our neighbor as ourselves. That's what Marv did, and he inspired me to try to do the same."
Greg Galluzzo, Founder of the Gamaliel Foundation

"Fr. Mottet (or Marv as he preferred to be called) was a prophetic giant who made conscious efforts throughout his life to seek out and encounter persons pushed to the margins of society and accompany them to wholeness. he was a priest pastor, prophet and friend. For me he was a valued friend who was always ready to consult, advise and when necessary, admonish. His cheerful demeanor and strong passion were unique and refreshing. The world is indeed a better place because of this holy and pastoral person."
Ralph McCloud, Director, Catholic Campaign for Human Development

"This book does a masterful job of capturing the essence of Father Marv Mottet, using his own words to tell his stories and convey his hopeful message for the Church and the world. He continues to inspire all of us at his alma mater, St. Ambrose University, where we are trying to live out our core values of wisdom, courage, service, and justice--all in the spirit of Father Mottet."
Dr Amy Novak, President, St Ambrose University

"Monsignor Mottet's life inspired us that knew him. May the labor of love undertaken by his dear friends, Art and Suzanne Pitz, inspire more people to appreciate his Christ-centered approach to justice and charity."
Deacon Kent E. Ferris, OFS, Director of Social Action, Diocese of Davenport

"Fr. Marvin Mottet was a humble, holy and soft-spoken person who dedicated his life to God and to serving mankind. Throughout his life he not only preached the gospel, especially the Spiritual and Corporal works of mercy--he practiced them. He bore witness to a rich tradition of justice articulated in the social encyclicals of the Catholic Church through his lifelong commitment to voluntary poverty, prayer, nonviolence, and hospitality for the homeless, poor, exiled, hungry and forsaken. His loving example was an inspiration to many and his good works live on. Fr. Marvin Mottet was truly a modern-day saint."
Bill Gluba, former Iowa State Senator and four-term Mayor of Davenport, Iowa

"Father Marv Mottet is an ordinary saint, as I explained in a column written in 2017, a year after his death. As editor of *The Catholic Messenger*, I devoted plenty of ink to my mentor who was an extraordinary advocate for social justice. In 2008, an immigration raid devastated the Postville, Iowa, community. The 78-year-old priest walked with a crowd through the streets of Postville in solidarity with the immigrants who endured separation from loved ones, loss of livelihood and an uncertain future.

Each interview with Father Mottet uncovered new insights about his tenacity and commitment to ministry, prayer, sacrament and social justice, the intertwining themes in his life's tapestry. His legacy lives on in the many programs and organizations he nurtured and in the Mottet Leadership Institute."
Barb Arland-Fey, Editor of The Catholic Messenger

HOW TO CHANGE THE WORLD TWO FEET AT A TIME

Lessons from the Life of Fr. Marvin Mottet

Suzanne Pitz and Arthur Pitz, Ph.D.

The events and conversations in this book have been set down to the best of the authors' ability. Some names and details have been omitted to protect the privacy of individuals.

Copyright © 2024 by Suzanne Pitz and Dr. Arthur Pitz, PhD

Publisher's Cataloging-in-Publication
(Provided by Cassidy Cataloguing Services, Inc.).

Names: Pitz, Suzanne, author. | Pitz, Arthur, author.

Title: How to change the world two feet at a time : lessons from the life of Fr. Marvin Mottet / Suzanne Pitz and Dr. Arthur Pitz, PhD.

Description: First paperback edition. | [Elmhurst, Illinois] : Professor's House Publishing, [2024] | Includes bibliographical references.

Identifiers: ISBN: 979-8-9896651-0-5 (paperback) | 979-8-9896651-1-2 (ebook) | 979-8-9896651-2-9 (audio book) | LCCN: 2023924116

Subjects: LCSH: Mottet, Marvin Alfred, 1930-2016. | Priests--United States--Biography. | Catholic Church--Clergy--Biography. | Human rights workers--Religious life--Biography. | Social workers--Religious life. | Christian life. | Christian men--Religious life. | Men--Conduct of life. | Social service--Teamwork. | Social justice. | Self-actualization (Psychology)--Religious aspects--Christianity. | BISAC: BIOGRAPHY & AUTOBIOGRAPHY / Social Activists. | RELIGION / Christian Living / Personal Growth. | BIOGRAPHY & AUTOBIOGRAPHY / Memoirs. | RELIGION / Christian Living / Social Issues. | BIOGRAPHY & AUTOBIOGRAPHY / Religious.

Classification: LCC: BX4705.M68 P58 2024 | DDC: 282.092--dc23

First paperback edition February 2024
Professor's House Publishing

To Emily Irene Jackson, our daughter,
who passed away after waging
a courageous health battle.
In her own way, Emily changed the world
at home and in Sierra Leone, West Africa.
Until the end of Fr. Mottet's life,
he prayed for Emily each day during Mass

Acknowledgements

Margaret Moser and Don Pitz persevered through the first draft of this book. Their exhaustive critique was as invaluable as their encouragement. They challenged me to question more insightfully, write more courageously, and think more deeply about readers of Fr. Mottet's book. My husband and co-author, Dr. Art Pitz, pieced together the timeline of Fr. Mottet's life and never faltered in his trust that we could write this book. It's handy to have an in-house history professor. He kept me from countless errors.

Short manuscripts by Fr. Mottet's sister Katy Bailey and his niece Theresa Mottet were useful. Several people who were close to Fr. Mottet read the manuscript and offered useful comments. We are grateful for insights from Loxi Hopkins, Theresa Mottet, Dan Ebener, Steve Goebel, Tim Collins, and Gina Howell. Mark Ridolfi, Managing Editor of The North Scott Press, edited the book from his journalistic perspective and made invaluable recommendations that improved readability.

The Two Feet of Love in Action image is used with permission of The United States Conference of Catholic Bishops.

Table of Contents

Preface

It seemed like I heard it, but I knew it was just a thought: "The book that needs to be written is Fr. Mottet's." I had no idea why or how, just that it was important. I admired Fr. Marvin Mottet, but I didn't know him personally. I heard him speak in 2008 when my husband Art and I attended the ceremony honoring him with the Pacem in Terris Peace and Freedom Award. In 2009, Art curated an exhibit at Putnam Museum on the civil rights history of Davenport, Iowa, and Fr. Mottet was one of his advisors. It was 2014 when this book stopped us in our tracks.

Since Fr. Mottet is well-known in the Quad Cities, we assumed someone was already writing his story, but deep inside we wondered if it might be our assignment. Art called for an appointment, and Fr. Mottet met us in the dining room at St. Vincent's Center, the headquarters of the Diocese of Davenport, Iowa, where he had an apartment. He said people had asked him to write his story, but he knew he never would. He joked that the book should be titled *How Not to Do It*. When we offered to write his story, he agreed without hesitating. I reminded him that we aren't Catholic, and he said, "Well, I can fix that." It was the first time we saw that twinkle in his eyes and the mischievous chuckle we came to love.

We knew about his role in the unique Davenport civil rights movement, but fifty years had passed, and his impact since then was vast. We didn't know that he was scheduled to die of cancer almost fifty years earlier or that he founded the Social Action Department of the Diocese of Davenport. We didn't realize that as a high school teacher, he and his fellow priests started so many social action organizations that they were nicknamed "the alphabet boys" because of all the acronyms. As his story unfolded, we learned that he led the early Catholic charismatic renewal in the Quad Cities and created the two feet model of social justice, which is now the standard national framework for Catholic social action. We were impressed that he knew Martin Luther King, Jr., Mother Teresa, Dorothy Day, and Cesar Chavez personally and had brought each of them to Davenport. We had no idea what a Catholic Worker house was, much less that Fr. Mottet started and lived in several of them.

We were charmed by his stories from Washington, D.C., where he directed the Campaign for Human Development and assisted organizations across the nation that were working to resolve the root causes of poverty and injustice. We knew very little about how he led Sacred Heart Cathedral in Davenport from the verge of bankruptcy to become a thriving congregation while he simultaneously renewed the church's decaying neighborhood. We had never heard of Quad Cities Interfaith, Interfaith Housing, or Café on Vine, all organizations he founded, that are still making a difference. We were especially surprised to learn that he conducted healing Masses and was an official exorcist.

From the summer of 2014 until two days before his death on September 16, 2016, we met regularly with Fr. Mottet to ask questions and listen, recording the interviews for later transcription. We also interviewed people who worked closely with him and knew him better than we did. We even met the beautiful girl he still loved in his eighties. I remember watching him walk down the long hallway from his apartment for that first interview. Even though he walked with a shuffle and was slumped a bit over his walker, he looked tall. He still had a lanky basketball player's frame, and his bony hands gripping his walker looked oversized.

In his eighty-fifth year when we began the interviews, the color had drained from the deep brown eyes of his youth, but they were still dark and clear. An inch-long vertical crease in the center of his forehead parted horizontal wrinkles that traced the arch of his dark eyebrows down to the sides of his eyes. He was bald, except for a fringe of gray hair. A brown spot marked the right side of his head. His gray beard and moustache were usually trimmed, but occasionally grew shaggy. As happens with age, his narrow nose had become more prominent, and it matched his strong jaw and chin.

Fr. Mottet wore old-style hearing aids in both ears. His rectangular-framed bifocals were often tipped up over his ears, probably to avoid the hearing aid wires. He punctuated his conversation with chuckles. His eyes lit up and a smile spread across his lean face when he remembered something interesting. When he felt strongly about something, he raised both hands and pointed with his index fingers. There were large purple-brown blotches on his hands and arms. He always wore a light blue long-sleeved shirt, often with the sleeves rolled part way to his elbows. The little black notebook he carried stuck an inch or so above his left shirt pocket. He always wore black rumpled trousers and large black shoes.

I was surprised that I immediately felt comfortable with Fr. Mottet, and I wondered why. I think it was because he was so unpretentious and nonjudgmental that there was nothing to be nervous about. Art and I quickly became attached to him, but not in a sentimental way. We trusted him and wanted to do the right things for him. It was a joy to take him to doctor's appointments or get his glasses fixed. We helped find things he misplaced in his room, which was always cluttered.

After he moved to Kahl Home, Fr. Mottet took increasing ownership of the interviews. He usually came prepared with notes in tiny script on scraps of paper and said, "I've had more memories." As memories do, one led to another and another, and his most-polished sound bites became familiar. He often told us things he wanted included in his book, and occasionally he mentioned something he didn't want in print.

The narrative of Fr. Mottet's life is filled with unforgettable characters: Woodcutter, the town drunk who lived at the Catholic Worker House; the O'Connor brothers, who turned him unwaveringly in the direction of social justice activism; Charles Toney, who rose from the welding department to administration at Deere and Company and led the Davenport Civil rights movement; and Fr. Geno Baroni, whose words Fr. Mottet carried in the little black book in his shirt pocket. He was as comfortable with prostitutes or congressmen in Washington, D.C., as he was with the Mayor of Davenport or the owners of the Vietnamese restaurant where we often ate lunch.

Fr. Mottet loved to tell stories. The lessons he learned along the way were harder to pin down because his habit of deflecting credit made it difficult to identify his unique contributions. Over time, he settled on ten lessons he wanted to pass on. As we listened, we began to realize that there are practical ways to change the world.

We enjoyed his stories, but we were always trying to understand why and how he did things and how he became the sort of person who could do them. We searched for clues and patterns. Seven years after his death, I'm still discovering them. I often say to myself, "Oh, that's what Fr. Mottet meant. He was right." This is Fr. Mottet's authorized biography. We can only provide an encapsulation of the details we recorded. The interviews were back-and-forth conversations. This book is written in that same style. It is mostly Fr. Mottet's lightly paraphrased words, but the sections in italics are added to provide clarification or context. We called him "Father" even though he was Msgr. Mottet. He laughed when he said, "We always use the 'f-word' around here." He called us "Art and Suzy." Art is the history expert. Most of the writing is Suzy's.

It's easy to spot problems and wish for a better world. In our best moments, we want to do something ourselves, but what? How? Who can show us the way, inspire us, and teach us the tricks of the trade? We need a mentor, someone believable who has done amazing things against the odds. Not enough money? Even though Fr. Mottet grew up poor and lived in voluntary poverty, millions of dollars flowed through his hands. He went from the dairy barn in Ottumwa, Iowa, to the White House and across the nation.

This book traces Fr. Mottet's life through four evolving stages: Playmaker, Organizer, Developer, and Healer. His life was filled with adventures, close calls, winning strategies, obstacles, miracles, healings, frustrations, divine guidance, and a couple of regrets. He was learning to the end and still expecting and praying for what he called "the greatest miracle of my life."

Photos, audio and video highlights, and copies of primary sources are available at fathermottet.com. His legacy is being continued through the Mottet Leadership Institute, and there is a push for his canonization. All royalties will be donated to the Mottet Leadership Institute and organizations Fr. Mottet designated.

PART ONE

Playmaker

How did a boy growing up during the Great Depression on a dairy farm in southern Iowa where Catholics were regarded as second-class believe that he could take on the world? How did he absorb the influences, gain the skills, and find the courage to become an effective activist?

Fr. Mottet was born in 1930 in the aftermath of the Stock Market Crash of 1929. Iowa was primarily rural, and the Depression hit hard. As banks failed, many farmers lost their entire savings, their homes, and their farms. Iowa was overwhelmingly Protestant with a small Catholic minority. The circumstances of Marv's childhood were traumatic, but instead of being traumatized, he was empowered. Why?

Part One introduces Marv and his family, their farm, his school, and the Catholic church in Ottumwa, Iowa. His character, leadership, and heart for justice took shape in Ottumwa, and he met the girl he still loved nearly seventy years later. As playmaker of his high school basketball team, he learned to set up the plays and not care who got the ball through the hoop. Then one day, Fr. Broderick came to the cornfield to offer him a chance to go to St. Ambrose College where his passion for social action flourished and his calling to the priesthood set the direction for his future.

Chapter 1

We Thought We Could

Take on the World

It was so unbearably hot. I was lying in the yard on my back when Dad and my older brothers came in with a wagon load of hay. It was loose hay in those days, not bales. We didn't have those modern conveniences. I was six years old. My sister Katy and I were born during the Great Depression. I was born on May 30, 1930, two years after Katy. Times were hard, but most people were in the same situation. It was thirty-five percent unemployment back then, and we think unemployment is high now.

My father, Clarence J. Mottet, was born above the bakery his family owned in Riverside, Iowa, on October 17, 1880. Dad worked on the Milwaukee Railroad before his family moved to Ottumwa, Iowa, around 1907. During the Depression, railroaders were better off because they had a good income, but he wanted something else. He said that a farmer once drove a herd of cattle through Riverside. He saw those beautiful Holstein cows and said, "Someday I want to do that."

Dad respected my mother, who everyone called "Gertie," and he set a good example for my brothers and me about how to treat people.

He never swore or cursed around us kids. He made up funny expressions. Instead of saying "B.S." he said "heiferdust."

Sometimes he talked German to the cows because he remembered some German words from his mother. One of the prayers he said every night before he went to bed was in German. He learned it from his mother but didn't know what it meant. When he finally asked, his mother said, "Well, it's a little child asking God to protect him through the night." He said that prayer for the rest of his life.

During the Depression, my mother's sister couldn't afford to pay for milk. I don't know if her husband was unemployed or what. We left them milk for years. When things got better, she paid us back at two dollars a month. Every month, my dad dropped my mother off at her sister's house while he did his other milk deliveries. That was her little social outing. They sat there and had some tea or whatever, and my aunt gave my mom her two dollars. Those two dollars went into the Christmas fund, so we always had something at Christmas.

I thought our Christmases were wonderful. Our parents tried to hide our presents, and we always looked for them. Sometimes my dad hid them under the hay in the haymow. We always got a red wagon. Part of our job was to haul wood into the house for the wood stove, and we needed the wagon for that. We went out all summer to gather logs and tree limbs. Then in the fall, a man came with one of those power saws to cut them up, and we had a big pile for the winter. Since there was no running water in the house, we also used our wagon every day to haul water from the well to replenish the supply in the house. The well was at least a city block from the house.

I'm Going to the Bank Today to Give Them Back the Farm

I remember my dad coming in at about ten o'clock at night from milking cows. He wanted to hear the news, so he ate supper by himself. He read the newspaper and fell asleep. He snored away with the paper over his head. In the winter, he stoked the fire at night with a big chunk of coal or a big log. Then he knelt to say his prayers. We could hear him whispering his prayers at night, and we could hear him shake the clinkers out in the morning and reload the stove to get it going. Dad might miss Mass once a year because of some emergency. When that happened, he took his prayer books and rosary into the "good room" and closed the door to make a holy hour.

Dad was well-read and involved in the Farm Bureau, which was important for representing the concerns of farmers, who faced terrible odds during the Depression. Dad was on a statewide committee called the Dairy Commission. Margarine, that was manufactured to look like butter, started coming into Iowa. The Dairy Commission got an Iowa law passed that margarine could not be made to look like butter, but it had to have a coloring capsule with it when you bought it. I was proud of my dad for taking that action. [1]

Founded in 1919, the American Farm Bureau Federation claims to be "The Unified National Voice of Agriculture." Its current issues include trade, regulatory reform, environment, farm policy, immigration reform, infrastructure, tax reform, and energy.[2] Clarence Mottet was a profound role model. At a young age, Fr. Mottet saw that an organization acting in the self-interest of its members had power to bring about change and that legislation is a vehicle for change.

The extension service was a big thing, and the county agent was a hero. He tried to help us farm better, and he had a modern car to haul us around to 4-H meetings where we met kids our own age. The government helped us survive the Depression. My dad would have canonized President Franklin Roosevelt.

All land grant universities, like Iowa State University, were required to have extension services throughout their state to improve farming and conserve the land. According to its website, 4-H is "America's largest youth development organization. . .4-H empowers young people with the skills to lead for a lifetime."[3]

Dad was French. In France, our name is pronounced "Mot-TAY," but we have always pronounced it just the way it's spelled. They weren't slouches. One Mot-TAY was a mayor. Another one ran a newspaper, and one had a grocery store. Both sides of our family came from Alsace-Lorraine, which was the doormat of Europe. As warring armies marched back and forth, Alsace-Lorraine shifted from one side to the other. You were French one day and German the next. We had cousins on both sides in World War II.

My mother's name was "Schwartz." A lot of our Schwartz relatives live in what is now France, like "big Julie and little Julie," the French relatives we are closest to. It was interesting, years later, to go there and meet relatives who looked just like our relatives in Iowa. They found us through the Sisters of Humility. Three Ottumwa Schwartz girls became Humility nuns, and our relatives had a picture of one of them. When our cousin became Mayor of Schmelz, Germany, he wrote the Mayor of Des Moines, Iowa: "We know those Schwartz girls are in Iowa somewhere. Can you find them?" The mayor sent his secretary to the Des Moines Library to search for that photo. She found it, and the library gave our relatives the information they needed to contact us.

My mother's family had a farm about a half mile inside the border of Germany. They went through a field and across what they called "the green border" to go to Mass in a little parish in France. I found the exact farm where my mother grew up because of a roadside shrine thanking God for their safe trip to America. We had a picnic out there. A stone over the door of a house read "Schwartz."

1936 was a bad year in the Depression. The weather was extremely hot and dry, and there was a drought. A lot of farmers in southeast Iowa lost their land. Dad came into the house one day and said, "Well, I'm going to the bank today to give them back the farm because we cannot make the payments." When he got there, the bank said, "We've got so many farms, we can't take care of them. If you'll stay on the farm, keep up the fences, and pay the interest on the loan, we won't foreclose." We didn't lose the farm, and our bank didn't fail or close its doors like so many banks did. The South Ottumwa Savings Bank is still in existence today.

People shared everything during the Depression. One time a poor woman with no teeth was visiting the cemetery next to our farm. After she visited the grave, she came to our place to ask for food. My mother sat her down and prepared her a meal. That was quite common in those days. When they came to the door, they got food. We were poor, but we were secure. We wore hand-me-down clothes from relatives and had hand-me-down newspapers, but we had plenty of food.

The Great Depression lasted until 1939 when the United States began mobilizing for World War II. It was the worst economic downturn in the history of the industrialized world. Prices dropped so low that many farmers went bankrupt. Between a third and half of all banks collapsed, and the lifetime savings of millions of Americans were wiped out. Most people who lived through the Depression were deeply affected by it, and some, like Clarence Mottet, never got over it.

We raised purebred cattle and paid our bills with milk. We delivered milk to the man who owned the hardware store, the bakery, the telephone company, the shoe repair place, and the grocery store. You name it. That's how we survived. My sister Katy said, "We never had money to spend like other kids, but we always had plenty to eat." Dad continued to deliver milk to customers even when they couldn't pay. He said, "Those children need milk." He was so honest that when he sold a calf, he pointed out the weak spots rather than the positive things.

My mother told me that Dad was doing very well until the Depression knocked his feet out from under him. He was kind of a dreamer, and he had big plans. He was well on his way until the Depression hit him. He planned to hire herdsmen to take care of the Holstein cattle and run the farm. Then he and my mother would travel the world. He wanted to produce a champion Holstein cow that produced the most milk and the most butterfat. Then he would put up a sign on the barn that said, "Wendover Dairy C.J. Mottet and Home of" the registered name of that cow. I was about ten or twelve years old when he told me that, and I remember making a vow, which you aren't supposed to do. I said, "I'm going to help my dad realize that." I worked my buns off because I knew my dad had never been able to reach his goals.

We knew the names and family histories of all the cows. The closest we came to that championship cow was Della. My dad and Wilb, my oldest brother, knew where to buy championship calves, and Wilb was always able to spot the best calf. My dad wanted to pick one, and Wilb said to pick the other one, so they bought them both. The calf Wilb picked grew up to be Della, the best cow we ever had. Della always had female twins and won the prize at the fair, but we never did have a sign on the barn with Della's name.

Wilb's actual name is "Wilbert." The seven Mottet siblings are Wilbert (Wilb), John (Jack), Lucille (Lucy), Paul, Mary Catherine (Katy), Marvin (Marv), and Bernard (Ben).

We had a large, fierce Holstein bull that was always penned up. He made so much noise and looked so mean that we were scared to death of him. When he broke out and started running around, we ran for our lives because we knew that farmers sometimes got killed by bulls like that.

I was next to the youngest of seven Mottet kids. Dad had twenty-two registered Holstein cows and seven milkers. On a dairy farm, the cows are milked twice a day. When we got old enough to sit on the milk stool, we were expected to help with the milking. I liked it because when it was cold, we warmed our hands up by milking the cows, and I knew it was a necessity. We chased cattle in the cold and wet and sometimes worked late at night. The barn was warmer than the house when all the cattle were in there. We didn't get a milking machine until after the war.

The consistent discipline of milking cows helped shape Fr. Mottet's character. As a child, he did what was necessary without complaining, and that pattern showed up throughout his life. He was used to discomfort, and he never shirked hard work.

14

Every morning, we drove the dairy cattle up the Bluegrass Road and south down a lane at the top of the hill for milking, and we brought them back again at night for evening milking. We ran barefoot up that gravel road like it was carpet. During the summer, we all went barefoot, but when school was about to start, we had to wear shoes so we could get used to them. Of course, we wore shoes when we went to church.

After milking the cows, we took the milk to the milk house. We had a cave where we cooled the milk and stored potatoes from the garden and pears from our orchard. Water ran into the cave from the well further up the hill. It was quite a farm in its day. We separated the cream from the milk in a cream separator because some of our customers wanted bottles of cream. My mother washed the bottles in a big vat and filled them with milk.

Dad delivered the milk to houses around town, originally in a milk wagon drawn by horses. The horses knew the route and when to start or stop. Later, he had an old panel truck with a sign on the side that read: "Wendover Dairy---C. J. Mottet prop." Wendover means "winding hills." Katy delivered the milk bottles to the porches. There was an extremely large family that couldn't pay. Dad said to them, "I'll leave the milk if you will wash the bottles," but they didn't even wash them. During the Depression, he helped a lot of people like that.

Wilb was always correcting us and looking after us. He drove the truck up from the milk house while our dad changed clothes before delivering the milk. Sometimes Ben, Katy, and I, the three youngest, climbed on the front bumper and rode up the hill. It was a stupid idea. Wilb found out what we were doing and chased us away. When we were little tikes, we had a two-wheeled cart, and Katy was running down the hill with Ben and me in it. Our old wooden silo was in danger of falling, so there were guy wires to anchor it to a fencepost in the barnyard. We were headed right for that wire. I don't know if we would have been decapitated or what, but Wilb ran out and lifted the wire. It could have been a terrible accident.

We had high ceilings, and we tacked an oatmeal box up on a door to play basketball with a rolled-up sock. It drove my mother nuts.

Throughout his life, Fr. Mottet credited his dad as one of three influences that led him into civil rights and social justice. It was the small things that mattered. He respected his wife. He prayed. He helped people in need. He dreamed and had plans. He taught his children to work and be responsible. In his own way, he was an activist and recognized the value of organizations that worked toward common interests.

The Rain on the Back Porch Tin Roof Would Sing Us to Sleep

As a child, I felt loved and secure. I had good parents, honest and hard-working. I was proud of the fact that we were a large family with seven children. One of my earliest memories is of my dad rocking Ben, who is eighteen months younger than me, and singing a little song. It went something like this: "Hush, be still as any mouse. There's a baby in the house. Not the doll, not the toy, but a bouncing baby boy."

I felt that kids who lived in town were sissies. They didn't have responsibilities or know how to work. By the time I was ten, I learned how to drive.

Wilb went to St. Mary's High School when he was a ninth grader. It was an all-boys high school and all city kids. He thought they were goof balls who had never had any responsibility. Wilb was a farm boy, who had to take over the farm and run the milk route one summer while dad was sick. He didn't do well at that school. His personality didn't fit in there, but later he went to Iowa State University on an academic scholarship.

During World War II, Wilb served in the U.S. Army in the South Pacific. We didn't have a tractor during the war because everything was rationed. We were horse and buggy. When Wilb came home, he was able to buy a nice Ford tractor, and we started farming the whole countryside. That is when we were blessed with indoor plumbing too.

Our farmhouse on the Bluegrass Road in Wapello County was two stories with bedrooms upstairs. The downstairs had a kitchen, the dining room, and what we called "the good room," which was never opened unless we had visitors. The good furniture was in there, and that is where my dad listened to the radio with his brothers and friends. When Pearl Harbor was attacked, our radio was broken, and we heard nothing about it until my Uncle John told my dad. I couldn't believe it.

We had heat in the kitchen and dining room. There was an old summer kitchen off the porch. The back room was the laundry room with a tin roof. The bedrooms upstairs were cold. My mother put bricks on the stove and wrapped them in blankets for us to take to bed to keep our feet warm under lots of covers. I slept in the same bed as my brother Paul. Dad slept in the other bed, and he raised the roof with his snoring. My mother and sisters slept downstairs. Our house was filled with crucifixes, holy pictures, pictures of saints, pictures of Jesus and Mary, and so forth.

Dad's brother John was a railroad engineer, and he helped my dad a lot. They had five boys, and we had five boys. They came out every Sunday and ran around the farm playing Daniel Boone. My dad and my uncles listened to the radio in the afternoon. If it was cold, they sat around the potbellied stove in the dining room and ate apples that we grew. I remember them listening to Fr. Coughlin, who sounded very eloquent.

Fr. Coughlin became a cult personality who was increasingly anti-Semitic and demagogic. It's surprising that Clarence Mottet tolerated Coughlin's views, since Coughlin relentlessly attacked President Franklin Roosevelt, but in the culture of that day, it would have been almost impossible for a good Catholic to criticize or disagree with a priest or bishop.

The cave by the house was for fruit, vegetables, and storms. My mother always lit a blessed candle during a storm to represent Christ, the light of the world. My dad had a friend who grew watermelons at a farm on the river. After the first killing frost, he knew he was out of business, so he let my dad get a load of watermelons for a penny a piece. When we came home from school on those hot September days, we went straight to the cave to break open a watermelon and eat until it was almost coming out our ears.

We picked wild blackberries. My mother's goal was to can a hundred quarts a year. We also raised chickens. Our black and white Bard Rock hens won the grand championship at the fair because we got old left-over cottage cheese at the creamery to feed them, and they got fat as pigs. The day we finished digging our acre of potatoes, my dad said before he left on his milk route, "I'll bring home a picnic of beer." That was about a quart, and we all got a sip of it. We only had pop on the Fourth of July.

We were poor, but we had a lot of blessings. When we asked our mother for money to do something at school, she said, "Look in Dad's pocket," and we rumbled around in his pocket to find a few coins.

When it rained, the water came over the end of the viaduct under the road and dug out a big hole where we swam. We got to come inside and rest when it rained. Two things sang us to sleep at night: the rain on the back porch tin roof and the thirty-two-volt generator my dad had in the basement to build up the batteries for dim lights in the house and the barn. We got electricity on Christmas Eve of 1941. The guy who put the lines up said to us kids, "The faster that goes around, the better it will make you feel." He was talking about the meter that showed how much electricity we used.

Ben said that Katy was "tougher than a crowbar." I was usually the peacemaker. After we milked the cows, Katy and Ben used to have boxing matches in the center aisle of the barn. They put rags in mittens, and I was the referee. Once when they were boxing, I tried to break it up. Ben threw a punch that hit me in the eye and knocked me out. That was Ben's last fight with a family member. He didn't realize he could hurt someone that badly. Ben later became a golden glove boxer.

Katy was freckled, and we used to kid her by saying, "A cow snorted right in your face." She was close to Dad, his baby girl. When she got married, Dad went out to the back of the church after the wedding and broke down. When we asked where he was, someone said, "He's in back of the church crying."

There were seven of us kids, and we were ready to whip the whole world. We never lost our dignity. I had that feeling from a young age. It started with my older brothers. I felt sorry for kids who were from small families. Even in those tough Depression days, I thought that if we held together, we could take on the whole world. I have never come to the place in my life where I doubted that was true. I've never questioned it.

Why Stoop So Low to Pick Up So Little

In the Schwartz family, all the girls were called by their middle names, so my mother, Margaret Gertrude Schwartz, was called "Gertie." She was a quiet woman, like many Germans, and I was always quiet like her. I guess I inherited more German than French. When the French showed up at a family gathering, it was just gab, gab, gab, talking all the time. She used unique sayings when we were growing up. If we weren't getting along, she would say, "Why stoop so low to pick up so little?" Occasionally she said, "Some people don't have enough sense to pour sand in a rat hole," or "Some women can throw more out of a spoon than a man can carry in a shovel." When I am praying the breviary, I often remember her saying, "The wicked grow like grass."

When I was seven years old, my mother almost died. The four youngest kids were sent off to relatives. At the hospital in Iowa City, she was delirious because of a high fever, and she begged them to cut her leg off. Her doctors told us she would live but be an invalid for the rest of her life. When she got home, she pushed a kitchen chair in front of her to learn to walk again.

When our mother got sick, Uncle Bill and Aunt Kathryn, who lived up the road from our house, stopped by and asked Ben if he wanted to come to their house for the summer. He hid behind Lucy's skirt and refused to go. He was afraid to leave home, but I spoke up and said, "I'll go." They told me to get my clothes. I had two pairs of overalls. I ran to get the one I wasn't wearing and jumped in the car.

That was an act of God because I was flunking first grade. I couldn't read, and my mother didn't have time to work with me when she was sick or in the hospital. Aunt Kathryn called the sister at the Catholic School and asked what she could do to help me. She said, "If he doesn't learn to read, he's going to have to repeat first grade." We walked up the road to a one-room country school and brought back arm loads of books, with permission of course. I read all summer, and that was the end of my school problems. Everywhere we went in the car, we read the signs. School was easy from then on. I went from flunking first grade to being valedictorian of my senior class.

I'll never forget the pain of receiving a postcard my mother wrote from the hospital because it told me how sick she really was. She was so sick and weak that her writing was scribbly. She was in the hospital practically dying, but she wanted to keep in contact with her kids, so she wrote that card. We have some pictures of her after she finally got out of the hospital. She was skin and bones, and she looked so weak.

The hardships of the Depression, nearly losing the farm, and his mother's serious illness that temporarily split up the family might have traumatized Marv. Instead, he was empowered. We wondered how. It wasn't simply a personal quality. He always said "we" when he talked about taking on the whole world. Success was contingent on sticking together. That was a clear pattern as his life moved forward. The Mottets were a typical Catholic family, though more devout than most. Respect and dignity seem to be keys. Fr. Mottet respected others and never lost his dignity.

Later, empowering others became the core of his life's work, and he knew that self-respect and dignity were fundamental to empowerment.

Chapter 2

We Knew We Were Second Class Citizens

Ottumwa was right on the Missouri border where there was a lot of anti-Catholicism. During the Civil War, Missouri was a slave state, and slaves escaped to the towns along the southern part of our diocese where there were Underground Railroad stops. Missouri farmers rode up on horseback with their shot guns to find slaves the farmers were hiding. Missouri was called "the buckle of the Bible Belt."

The "Bible Belt" referred to the area from southern Missouri to western North Carolina and from Mississippi to northern Kentucky. It was known for Protestant fundamentalism, or a literal interpretation of the Bible. The area was socially conservative and, based on biblical interpretation, strongly in favor of Jim Crow discrimination against black people. Protestants distrusted Catholics because they thought Catholics would be more loyal to the Pope than to the United States.

As Catholics, we always knew we were second-class citizens. We were a minority, so we really stuck together. There weren't many Catholics up and down the road where we lived. I remember a farmer who said, "These dumb Catholics come out and throw their seed on the ground, and they get a bumper crop." That same man said, "I don't have any use for Catholics, but don't you dare criticize the nuns at the hospital." People made fun of us. My older brother and sister went to the public school before there was a Catholic school. They came home and said, "The teacher criticized the Catholic Church in class today."

Despite the prejudice when I was a boy, I knew non-Catholics were our friends. Since we were looked down on, I had some idea what black people were going through. My mother remembered when the Ku Klux Klan burned a cross at St. Mary's Church in 1920.

There were many local Ku Klux Klan cells across Iowa. At that time, they weren't just anti-Black. They were antisemitic, anti-Catholic, anti-urban, anti-intellectual, and anti-women's rights. Although there were instances of cross burnings and vandalism, there is little evidence of physical violence.

My middle name is Alfred. My dad was so mad about anti-Catholic prejudice in the 1928 election that he named me after Alfred Smith, who ran against Hoover. My youngest brother was named Bernard Vincent Mottet. He was born on the feast of Blessed Mother, so it was clear what my mother had in mind with his initials.

My parents were devout Catholics. We got up to go to five-fifteen Mass on Sunday mornings before we came home to milk the cows, and we prayed the Rosary during Lent. I remember kneeling by chairs. When the little kids were snickering and laughing, my mom said to my dad, "Now discipline those boys."

I Was Laughing at a Cartoon in a Magazine

Our parents went to school through seventh grade, but they were concerned that we continue our education. It was common then in rural families, especially if you were a boy, to leave school to work in the fields when you hit eighth grade. Most of us kids went to St. Patrick's School, a three-mile walk from our home. Students at St. Pat's knew each other and were like one big family.

Catholics were less than ten percent of the population of Ottumwa, but we were proud of our school and the fact that the Catholic community really hung together. The public schools in Ottumwa wouldn't even hire Catholics as teachers. Sometimes they called us names like "cat lickers" and "mackerel snappers" as we walked past the public school on the way home. Once a group of public-school kids came as a gang to the corner at the noon hour, and they were going to beat us up. Sister Louise, our principal, went down and faced that whole crowd and sent them home while we were watching from the window. Then she let us out of school.

We belonged to St. Patrick's parish. The Humility nuns there were important in our life. At Mass on Sunday morning, the nuns marched over double-file and sat in the front pews. There were eight of them. They ran the hospital, which had a big influence, and we had them in class. A lot of them grew up on farms in Iowa. Girls from Chicago who came to Ottumwa Heights Academy or Marycrest College said, "These nuns are so down to earth." I remember Sister Louise Walsh, the principal, treating my dad with so much respect.

The Sisters of Humility of Mary, now located in Davenport, Iowa, operate Humility Homes and Services, which seeks to end homelessness in the Quad Cities area by offering housing opportunities and support services. Fr. Mottet took us to visit the Congregation of the Humility of Mary at their convent near St. Vincent's Center. The nuns were eager to show us displays of photos and artifacts from Ottumwa.

I've heard people who went to Catholic schools say the nuns were too rough on them, but I didn't experience that. They were farm girls, and they didn't beat up on farm boys. We were a persecuted minority. It was us and the nuns. They weren't famous for discipline, but they ran a tight ship. When you are teaching all boys, you keep discipline first, and you teach second. There were only seventy-five boys in the school. Three nuns taught, and the priests came for Latin and Religion. The Humility Sisters always said, "We're a demonstration school," because that is where they prepared the younger sisters to be professional educators. They said, "You have to be extra special because you're at the demonstration school."

My cousin Sr. Ann Therese was sixteen, and I was fourteen, but she was my teacher. She made me read a book. It was the first fiction book I ever read. I read a lot of spiritual books, but I was never great for fiction.

Ottumwa Heights, on the edge of town, was the cultural center for Ottumwa with a wonderful music program, an orchestra, and dancing. It raised the cultural level of Ottumwa. It burned down in fifty-eight. We were in class when the announcement came over the PA system: "Ottumwa Heights is burning down at this moment." The oldest nun was teaching boys I called "the hoods," rough guys. They were trying to console her, but she said, "Gentlemen, I would rather have the Heights burn to the ground than any one of you to commit a mortal sin." We were terribly impressed. When the Heights burned, it was totally destroyed. The Humilities went out to the air base and lived there for several years, and then they built a new place.

Ottumwa Heights was a four-story building that housed the Ottumwa Heights Academy and Junior College. It was the motherhouse of the Sisters of the Holy Humility of Mary with seventy-five resident nuns. There were also one hundred thirty resident students, who lost everything in the two-million-dollar blaze.

I went to Central High School, an all-boys school. We were so poor that we had none of the frills, just the essentials, but the nuns gave us a good education. That little school turned out a lot of guys who went on to be doctors, lawyers, dentists, college professors, and successful businessmen. One became a priest and was head of the Philosophy Department at St. Ambrose College. Another one had a doctorate in theology and became a Superintendent of Schools. I became head of a national program. That was all from a tiny little school.

It was three miles to school. We jumped out of bed and ran down to the road to look for cars that might give us a ride. If we got a ride, we would get there on time. If we didn't, I had a deal with the sister. I just walked in and knew I would automatically stay after school and do all my homework. That's one of the reasons I got good grades.

Catholic Central High School was on the fourth floor of what was originally St. Joseph's Hospital. The operating room became the typing room. I stayed out of there because I knew guys got in trouble in there. I wasn't going to go to college. I was going to farm, so I didn't take typing.

During my freshman year, my sister gave me a book on Fatima. and I wrote a report for the mimeographed school newspaper. The Blessed Mother appeared to three Portuguese children and predicted World War II, the communist uprising in Russia, and the efforts of communism to take over the world. She asked for prayer for peace. This had a profound influence on me, so I started a group that met at different farmhouses to pray the Rosary for peace. My dad said then, "He's going to be a priest."

It is unusual for a fourteen-year-old boy to organize adults from several households to pray for peace on an ongoing house-to house basis. It would still be an organizational feat. Young Marv didn't wait or hope that someone else would organize the community to pray. He acted. He was probably so matter of fact about it that it seemed natural to the families who got involved. They believed they were doing the right thing and making the world better. Understanding power and using it wisely became crucial to Fr. Mottet. The definition of power is "the ability to act."

I have a vivid memory from high school. One of our textbooks had a page about Catholic social teaching and papal encyclicals. I thought, "Isn't that interesting," and I carried that one page with me. It has had a lifelong effect on me.

This was the beginning of an enduring attraction to papal documents. The titles of papal encyclicals rolled off Fr. Mottet's tongue, but "Rerum Novarum" and" Quadragesimo anno" were like a foreign language to us. He studied encyclicals and took them to heart. They weren't simply concepts and rules. They were trusted guides that excited him.

One day at school when I was laughing at a cartoon in a magazine, Fr. Broderick came up to me and asked if I had ever thought about becoming a priest, I said, "No, why do you ask?" He told me that since I had a sense of humor, I might want to be a priest. I thought it was a stupid idea to connect those two things, but he planted a seed, and I didn't stop thinking about it for seven years. I went all through high school with a normal life of dating, dancing, and playing basketball, but I couldn't forget that Fr. Broderick was sitting on the sidelines thinking I could be a priest.

I was a poor farm boy, and priests were in another world. I thought my future was in Ottumwa. I planned to take over my dad's farm. In 1945, I was in a truck coming home from detasseling corn when the guy driving the truck said, "The atomic bomb was dropped in Japan." I thought he meant "automatic bomb." I had no idea what it was, but I learned quickly. That was the same year the civil rights movement started in Davenport, Iowa. I was fifteen years old.

They Called Him "Snowball"

As a Catholic, it was easy for me to identify with African Americans who felt second class. They rode the railroads up from the South to find jobs, which were often in the packing houses like Morrell and Company, the big employer in Ottumwa. You could always tell you were getting near the Morrell plant by the stench of warm blood, putrid waste, rancid fats, and disinfectants. The area reeked with a sulfurous and slightly metallic smell. African Americans lived in old houses along the river. When we drove past there, I saw those ramshackle houses with people living in poverty, and I thought, "That's not right," but it didn't all add up until I got to St. Ambrose. I think it is one of the reasons I got into civil rights.

Our family doctor was an African American, Dr. Gage C. Moore. African Americans were often lower class and poorly educated, but Dr. Moore changed the whole chemistry in Ottumwa. Since he couldn't rent an office, he bought the large white house across the viaduct at the foot of Jefferson Street hill. His family lived upstairs, and he ran his medical office on the first floor. When Jack, my number two brother, came back from World War II, our mother was sick again, but no one could figure out what was wrong. Jack said, "Go to that African American doctor." He probably said "negro" in those days. We didn't use the "N word" in our house. Dr. Moore diagnosed my mother's goiter on the first visit. He became a hero when we went for a basketball physical, and he said to my dad, "Don't work these boys too hard."

Dr. Moore was a Baptist, but on the last day of his life, he went to St. Mary's Church in Ottumwa to hear a Dominican priest preach about St. Martin de Porres, who lived in Lima, Peru and was half Black and half Hispanic. Dr. Moore came home, had lunch, took a nap on the davenport, and died, apparently of a heart attack. Thinking back, I realize that is one of the things that opened me up. I got into civil rights because of this African American man with credentials, a good education, and a competent reputation. I knew his family.

St. Martin de Porres showed up several more times in Fr. Mottet's recollections. He has become the patron saint for mixed-race persons, and of all those seeking racial harmony. He was well known in Peru for his heart for the poor and his devotion to the Eucharist and prayer. He gathered food and alms to give to the poor. He was also famous for miracles and healings, but he was ridiculed for being of mixed race.[4] Later, when Fr. Mottet worked with the Catholic Interracial Council, he considered St. Martin de Porres to be a perfect model.

My dad respected other people. An African American family came to bale our hay. He invited them in for lunch. They didn't want to take time to clean up for lunch, so they just thanked him. That stuck with me. There was a Jewish synagogue in Ottumwa across the street from what we called "Jew town," four or five stores run by Jewish people. My dad had good relations with Jewish people. He took in ducks and geese and traded them for overalls and things like that.

The Ballingall Hotel in Ottumwa was famous for its racism. They refused to let the famous singer Marian Anderson stay there. When The University of Iowa started using African American athletes ahead of its time, a joke went around Ottumwa that a plane went down in Africa, and it was an Iowa recruiter looking for athletes.

Every summer, we went to the Wapello County Fair at Eldon. We took Holstein calves from our herd, and we spent the money we won on school clothes. The farmers hired an African American teenager, to wash their cattle before the show. The farmers called him "Snowball." I thought that was unfair, but they probably didn't know any better. Snowball just kept working.

Fr. Mottet was eager to take us to Ottumwa to visit Ben Mottet, his only remaining sibling. Their easygoing mutual admiration was apparent. Ben drove us to the site of Wendover Dairy farm where they reminisced about the terrain and farm buildings that were no longer there. The farmhouse had changed, but it still stood on the knoll overlooking Bluegrass Road. We drove past sites of his childhood, including the community college that is now located where Ottumwa Heights burned.

On the return trip, he talked a lot about the importance basketball had in his life. He relished his basketball stories. It was easy to see that he was the playmaker of the team. He didn't think of himself that way, but he was still the playmaker later in the Davenport civil rights movement and throughout his life. He looked forward to a quick stop at Columbus Junction for his traditional pork tenderloin sandwich to eat in the car. His big treat was a carton of chocolate milk, which was always a favorite.

Give the Ball to the Guy Who Can Get It in the Hoop

I was the first of seven kids to go all the way through Catholic school. I went for one or two weeks to the public high school to play football. I went out there and busted my gut, but those other kids had been coached all through grade school, and I could see I wasn't going to be a football star. I knew I would always be an outsider. I came back to Catholic Central High School because I missed the community.

I went to a dentist across the street and upstairs from the pool hall. The dentist said he used to watch Msgr. Walsh, the founder of Catholic Central, walk two or three blocks from St. Mary's Church. When he walked in the front door of the pool hall, all the Central kids went out the back like rats. Our pastor called the pool hall "the community center." Everybody loved him because he had a social mentality and was ahead of his time. We were all poor, and he had an outreach to help families that were struggling.

I got some freshmen guys together and said, "Let's go down to the YMCA and get in a league to get a little experience since we don't have a freshman team." We had just learned in religion class about three saints from Cappadocia, so we said, "Let's call ourselves the Cappadocians. Nobody will know who we are." Our basketball team didn't even have a gym, but we got to the state tournament.

We eventually beat Bloomfield, which is on the Missouri border where it is so anti-Catholic. We practically had to fight our way out of Bloomfield. They hated Catholics. Fr. Broderick went to talk to the coach and the principal. He said, "We've got to do something about this. We've got to get along." We eventually became great friends. They came to watch our practice, which wasn't a good idea, but we went from being enemies to being friends.

One of my classmates, Hervey, was a real character, sort of a clown. He put out the high school paper with the frontpage headline "Pool Hall Burns Down 1,000's Homeless." Hervey had a deformed hand, but he was a good shot with the other hand. When we played in the state tournament, that guy with a crippled hand ripped the nets. He was a starter for us. He became a radio star in Kansas City and a friend of the Kansas City Chiefs. Once I was driving to the west coast with the radio on, and a guy was running a contest where the winner would get to spend a night in Ottumwa and visit the pool hall. I thought, "That's got to be Bill Hervey," and sure enough, it was.

It was a big deal when Central High was in the Iowa State Basketball Tournament. We were called "Gaels" because of the Irish background in Ottumwa. A headline before the state tournament read: "Good omen for the Gaels Playing Their First Game on St. Patrick's Day." We had quite a history of good basketball over the years. The Knights of Columbus raised the money to buy uniforms.

Our basketball coach was supposed to be a member of faculty, but we were too poor to hire a coach. In my senior year, Carol McDonald came to Ottumwa. He was in the Navy and stationed at Ottumwa Naval Air Station where they learned to fly small planes before they went on to bigger and faster airplanes. He was from the South, but he married a Catholic girl from Ottumwa and stayed. He was an excellent basketball player who had a basketball scholarship at one of those famous southern schools. Boy, could he rip the nets with a two-hand shot. He was only five years older than we were. After work at John Deere, he came with his lunch bucket to coach us at the Y. He was a wonderful coach. We called him "Mac." He never got paid a cent. He died this past year.

Mac taught us all the tricks that people wouldn't even think of, especially the pick and roll system, which was new then. First you stand in front of someone to block their movement, and then you roll out with the ball and do whatever you want to do. He really educated us, and that gave us confidence that we could go to the state tournament and stay with those other teams. You know, when you have confidence, you can overcome a lot of problems.

He had a system that made us smarter than the other teams. When the game started with the jump-off, our center turned his foot in the direction he was going to tap the ball. He tipped it to a guy who handed it off to a guard coming around so fast the other team couldn't recover, and he went down the court and scored two points. Sometimes I was the guy coming around, and sometimes I was the guy passing off. In our first game in Keokuk, I didn't know the pick and roll very well, and the crowd started yelling that I was using a body block. I learned the right move very quickly. We usually started a game with a two-point advantage. A famous Iowa City coach said it was the best pick-and-roll system he had ever seen. Coming from him, that was a big compliment to Mac.

"Dancing Donny Riley," one of our team members, was so fast that he could dribble the ball through any defense. He was the classiest guy. I wasn't the star. I'm an introvert, and I tend to be quiet. I remember Fr. Broderick saying, "You don't yell like all the other guys." I was tall for a guard, and I wasn't a good shooter, but I scored a few points. You could say I was behind the scenes. I looked for whether they were playing a zone or man to man. For the zone, we worked to unbalance them and shoot from the corner. We really worked together.

Fr. Mottet's role as the player who sized up the situation and initiated an effective plan of action was his sweet spot. He was good at it because he didn't need to be the one to take the shot, and he was tall. He knew his own strengths and weaknesses and those of his teammates. He was comfortable with his position behind the scenes. To him, the important things were working together and using winning strategies. Some of his top life lessons started with basketball.

Our coach was so good that we were one of the "the Sweet Sixteen" teams that got into the Iowa State Tournament. Teams from small schools were separated until the finals, and then they mixed them in with teams from the big schools. Sometimes a little team would knock off one of the big ones. We played an extremely good team that went on to be number two in the state. They clobbered us. That was partly because someone set us up for defeat by giving us false information. We had good shooters, and with the right information, we would have done well. A public high school beat them the next night by a bigger margin than they beat us, so we didn't feel so bad.

When we played our first sweet sixteen game, our coach was nowhere to be seen, and we didn't know what was going on. He was sitting up in the bleachers. The teams we beat along the way were so angry that they planned to publicly embarrass us by turning us in for having an illegal coach. We had Fr. Broderick sitting on the bench, and he didn't even know what basket we were shooting at. Mac came down at halftime and said, "They're saying up there that you're the worst-coached team in the state." We were playing Sioux City from western Iowa, and we knew nothing about them. Someone wrote a letter to our team telling us that Sioux City never plays a zone or a fast break, but that's exactly what they did. We were blind-sided, and our coach was up in the bleachers. If he had been there, he would have caught it right away. We had good shooters, and we would have done well against their zone.

The main thing I learned from playing basketball was teamwork. You can't get anywhere without a team. Our motto for the class of forty-eight was "to the state in forty-eight." That was a mistake. We should have said, "Win the state in forty-eight." I loved basketball because it was such a big part of our lives in high school, and it gave us a chance to go to other little towns in southern Iowa and meet new people. That was a big deal in those days. We got our pictures in the paper. One of the last was a picture of me falling down while the neighbor team ran over me. I still regret that we didn't get a chance to beat that team.

Since Fr. Mottet knew he couldn't get anywhere without a team, he focused throughout his life on recruiting the best possible team-players for each initiative he started. In the basketball photo he mentioned, he is in the thick of bruising action. He always wanted to be in on the action and didn't mind the bruises that often came with it. That photo is in the gallery at fathermottet.com, as are other photos mentioned in this book. Fr. Mottet was strikingly handsome in his youth, and he had a calm, serious look. The original photos are in the Diocese of Davenport archives.

In those days, Fr. Broderick hauled us around to play basketball all over southern Iowa. He could smell a vocation a mile away, which is one reason we had a lot of vocations to the priesthood from Ottumwa. I remember him bringing me home late one night after a basketball game. We walked into the house, and my mom and dad were sitting there after supper. My dad was reading the paper. I remember that scene like it was painted, like a photo. They were so peaceful, and I felt so secure. They chatted with Fr. Broderick a while. I felt protected because I thought, "I have a good example, and my folks are living their faith."

As point guard and playmaker of his winning Central Catholic basketball team, Fr. Mottet learned to use the tricks, set up the plays, and not care who put the ball through the hoop. These characteristics showed up throughout his life. By age seventeen, he was already a recognized and trusted leader and president of his senior class.

Chapter 3

You're Not a Victim--You're an Actor

It was a Friday afternoon in late August of 1948, and I was out in a neighbor's cornfield helping fill their silo. Fr. Broderick came out to the field. I wondered what on earth he was doing out there. He said, "Are you going to college?" When I told him I didn't know, he said, "You'd better decide. Today is Friday, and it starts Monday." He didn't say, "Are you going to seminary?" but if it weren't for Fr. Broderick, I'm sure I would never have been a priest. He said he was driving to Davenport on Sunday, and he had room for me if I wanted to go.

I talked to my dad, and he gave me permission, so I was in the car on Sunday. I was a walk-on at St. Ambrose College, not for athletics, but as a student. I had no place to stay, but I had three hundred dollars in my pocket, which was a lot of money in those days. It was a scholarship from a store in Ottumwa. Fifty years ago, room, board, and tuition at Ambrose was one thousand dollars. Most of the faculty was priests, who worked for fifty dollars a month plus room and board.

I had no place to stay, no job, no nothing, and I arrived at the very last minute. I thought I might study biology for a couple of years and go to Iowa State to major in agriculture and then stay with farming.

At that time, St. Ambrose was extremely active in social justice work. There were about three hundred fifty students. In the evenings, the priests ran labor schools to train working people and labor unions to be leaders. That especially impacted me because I grew up in a union home. Dad worked for the railroad for seven years and was a member of the Railroad Workers Union. The union never stopped sending him the union paper called *Labor,* and I had it transferred to me when I was in the seminary. The priests also worked for racial justice between Blacks, Whites, and Hispanics. They were doing everything they could to help poor people.

These things convinced me that my dad was right in how he lived. Before I went to Ambrose, I thought he should try to get rich instead of helping other people. In my senior year of high school, someone gave me a book called *How to Win Friends and Influence People.* At the time, I thought my dad would be better off if he did some of that stuff instead of helping other people. I walked onto the St. Ambrose campus with that attitude, and Ambrose screwed my head around in one semester. I learned that my dad was right, and that really set my future course.

The Little Red School on the Hill

With a few exceptions, we got social justice in every class. The faculty was made up of priests whose fathers worked in factories and were members of labor unions. Fr. Bill was called "the labor priest," and his brother Fr. Ed was the philosopher. They were scholars who read all the time. They had a humongous pile of books in the back pew of the chapel and stacks of magazines and newspapers in their room. Fr. Bill brought a copy of *The Catholic Worker* newspaper to class, and I started reading it. He said, "They're very good people, but they are pacifists." He was in the Marines during World War II, and he was no pacifist.

"The Catholic Worker" was a weekly newspaper, which began publication in 1931 to advance Catholic social teaching as an alternative to Communism. This was Fr. Mottet's first exposure to Dorothy Day, the co-founder of the Catholic

Worker Movement. At the outset of World War II, the newspaper advocated a form of Christian pacifism, which caused it to lose readership. It sold for a penny per copy and still does today, though it is now published only seven times per year. The publication of The Catholic Worker led to the establishment of Catholic Worker houses. Dorothy Day was a huge influence on Fr. Mottet's life, and he spoke of her often.

Fr. Bill O'Connor taught philosophy, but first he taught labor law. No matter what class you took from Fr. Bill, you got labor. In class, he hammered on ideas from great papal encyclicals, especially *Rerum Novarum*, which is often called "the Magna Carta of Social Justice." It defends the right of working people to organize in labor unions. We learned about those social encyclicals all the time. Both Fr. Bill and Fr. Ed went to graduate school at Catholic University, and they brought those ideas back to St. Ambrose.

Rerum Novarum was issued by Pope Leo XIII in 1891. He wrote: ". . .by degrees it has come to pass that working men have been surrendered, isolated and helpless, to the hardheartedness of employers and the greed of unchecked competition." Leo XIII warned of the injustices created by the reliance on the free market while at the same time warning of the dangers of state socialism.[5]

We were taught at Ambrose that the church lost the working class in Europe, and we could not afford to lose the working class in this country. In their labor schools at night, the O'Connor brothers taught union people about labor law and Roberts Rules of Order. They understood how the communists used these things to take over. Communists were experts in Roberts Rules of Order. They would drag out a meeting until enough people got tired and left, and then they were able to take over. The labor school taught workers how to counteract that. They learned labor law along with Catholic social teaching.

At the time, there were two labor unions in the Quad Cities that were controlled by Marxists. Fr. Bill worked with the FBI to get them replaced by legitimate unions. Charles Toney, an African American leader, helped him. The United Auto Workers came in and replaced one of those unions, but the Chamber of Commerce still called Bill O'Connor a communist, and they called Ambrose "the little red school on the hill." Ambrose faced a lot of stigmas and suffered financially.

Since communism is inherently atheistic, it is not surprising that the O'Connor brothers opposed communists so vehemently in Davenport. They managed to neutralize communist takeover tactics through their labor schools. Unfortunately, the term "communist" had already been weaponized against reform movements, and St. Ambrose College got its derogatory nickname.

After World War II, the labor movement in the United States shared goals with American communists, such as better pay and working conditions. Their overall influence on labor unions was negligible. While the labor movement was not associated with the communist movement, it did have a direct connection with the civil rights movement. Civil rights activists learned from the labor movement, especially the United Auto Workers, and used many of the same tactics.

Fr. Ed was kind of the godfather. You didn't want to disappoint him. He was such a nice guy, learned and holy. I remember walking with a bunch of guys when I was a freshman. They all lowered their voices until those priests walked by. I heard one student say, "Oh my goodness, that's Father Ed and Father Bill." We lowered our voices out of respect.

On weekends we had no money, so we took our dates to someone's house to discuss things like the social encyclicals or the liturgy. How square can you get? It was stimulating because it was cutting edge.

The atmosphere was exciting. There was so much action, so much thinking, so much planning. It was inspiring to be part of a movement. We knew the labor part was a movement, but racial prejudice got the civil rights movement rolling. The League for Social Justice, which was Ambrose faculty and students together, had done a survey in Davenport of racial attitudes and behaviors which was published as *Citizen Second Class*. It sounded like Tupelo, Mississippi, but in some ways, Iowa was a leader in civil rights.

Citizen Second Class *established that de facto discrimination against Blacks was systematically applied in housing, employment, medical care, veterans' organizations, and many other areas of society despite the fact that in 1868, the Iowa Supreme Court removed the word "White" as a qualification for voting and integrated schools. Unfortunately, those laws were rarely enforced.*

When I came to Ambrose in forty-eight, most of the students were veterans. The Navy had taken over the campus during the war, and the GI Bill was in effect after the war. There were barracks on the football field, and I lived in one of those barracks during my sophomore year. I often said that I learned as much having coffee with those veterans as I did in class because they had seen the world and experienced war. They were mature, and they were serious about changing the world.

Another significant person in my life was another student, John "Red" McAndrews. I was running the lunch counter at a pool hall downtown. Red came in, and we got to talking. He asked whether I had read a book titled *Fishers of Men*. I hadn't heard of it, but he told me to go to the library and get it.

I checked it out, and it changed my life. It was about the underground church in western Europe where the church had lost the working class by supporting the wrong side in the French Revolution. Fr. Joseph Cardijn started little groups of male and female workers called Young Christian Workers, and this movement spread all over western Europe. The main character knew what was right and was totally committed. I read what he did and the sacrifices he made, and it made me want to do that too.

Young Christian Workers had thousands of rallies across western Europe because of terrible working conditions in factories. Youth there took a test at the end of what we called "grade school." If they flunked the test, they went to the factory and not to college or university. The kids who went to the factories were losing their faith because of the physical and moral conditions, so Fr. Cardijn started working with them. He also went to Rome to see Pope Pius XI, but he couldn't get in. He was wandering around looking at the artwork when a door opened, and Pope Pius walked through with his entourage. Cardijn ran and knelt in front of him and said, "Holy Father, I want to bring you the working youth of the world." Pope Pius said, "You're just the man I want to talk to. Come into my office." Young Christian Workers became a great lay movement.

A lay movement involves people who are part of the church but are not ordained. Cardijn is famous for his statement: "Give me leaders and I will raise the world!" He established Young Christian Workers in 1912. According to its website, Young Christian Workers is "a movement run for, by, and amongst young people. We strive to ensure that all young people live life to the full. We live this active apostolate in our places of work and study and in the communities we live in. We do this through a process of reflection, enquiry and action where we reflect on our lives in the light of the Gospel and take action to bring about positive change in our own lives and the lives of our peers." Young Christian Workers has now spread to fifty-one nations.[6]

At St. Ambrose, I got into something called Young Christian Students, which was part of that international movement. Fr. Kamerick was the head of it. The idea was: "You're not a victim of circumstances. You're an actor. You're going to change the world." We used the observe, judge, and act method of social inquiry. Those are the three parts of St. Thomas Aquinas' prudent act. We met weekly to discuss the gospel and then take up some social problem that we worked on. When I was a freshman in Young Christian Students, we had a social inquiry about the initiation of new students. We were trying to get rid of the hazing and make new students feel welcome. I came back to Ambrose early for my sophomore year to oversee that and welcome new students. Instead of hazing, we had shirts that said, "Bee a Friend" because St. Ambrose athletic teams are known as "the Fighting Bees." We started the first day they arrived. That was our social change way back then.

Young Christian Students gave Fr. Mottet a disciplined and practical way to apply the gospel and make the world better. Students worked together to solve

Young Christian Students had a lasting impact on my life. I was living my faith, living the gospel. Our small groups were six or eight people with a priest or nun. We did an act of service every week. It gave me the cut of mind that I am an actor, not a victim. We asked, "What does Christ's teaching say, and what are we going to do about it?" We learned to agitate, but not irritate.

In my freshman year, the National Catholic Social Action Conference was held at Ambrose, and it took over the classrooms for two days. Maybe some of the other students stayed home, but I ate it up. I didn't know any better. I got acquainted with people who were already deeply in love with social justice, and it drew me in. It was real life— labor and race. My ideas about networking and building relationships started there.

We had a national Young Christian Students meeting near Davenport at Camp Abe Lincoln. That's where I met Matthew "Matt" Ahmann. When he got out of college with a social work major, he opened an office in Chicago called the National Catholic Council for Interracial Justice. About fifty Catholic Interracial Councils had started in the United States, and he pulled them together in one national office. Later, he helped organize the March on Washington, and he was in the front row with Martin Luther King, Jr.

> We are gathered to dedicate ourselves to building a people,
> a nation, a world which is free of the sin of discrimination
> based on race, creed, color or national origin, a world of the

sons of God, equal in all important respects; a world dedicated to justice, and to fraternal bonds between men. I am a Catholic. These are goals the Catholic community shares with all other Americans. As Catholics fought for their own rights as citizens, they now fight for the rights of Negroes and other minorities. [7]

I Wasn't Shy About Stealing Ideas

Fr. Mottet often referred to the lay apostolate, which is ministry carried out by lay people in the secular environment, not in the church. He referred to Young Christian Workers, Young Christian Students, and the Christian Family Movement as "specialized movements" within the lay apostolate. They were a way for the church to work for justice in the world long before Vatican II began to turn the church outward to engage with the modern world.

Young Christian Students and the lay apostolate really formed me. The national headquarters for these specialized movements was in Chicago, and I went to their meetings. Chicago was the place to go to find out what was happening. I met young priests who were working for social and racial justice. I heard their ideas and saw what they were doing, and I wanted to do those things. In Chicago, I got my first sense of how community organizing is done. Those leaders were organizing to make changes within the church and in the community outside of the church. They took the ideas that were bubbling up in Europe where they did graduate work and brought them home. You go from celebration of the Mass to work for social justice.

The Chicago church was thriving, and I was infatuated. They called those priests "Reynie's boys" because they were trained by Msgr. Reynold Hillenbrand. He tied liturgy and social action together and taught that people who participate actively in liturgy are personally renewed, which prepares them to go out and renew their homes, communities, workplaces, and schools.

In homilies, I often use a story about my dad as an example. After his dementia started, I was home from seminary, and we were standing in the back of the church. He shot up the front aisle and received communion first. There were a lot of people out in the aisle ahead of me. I asked him to stay right there while I went up to Communion. He said he would, but when I came back, he was nowhere in sight. My sister-in-law, who was driving to the ten-thirty Mass, picked him up blocks away. He thought the neighbors were starving to death, and he was headed out there to give them something to eat. In his senility, he was living out that theology perfectly by going directly from the Mass to serve his neighbor.

In Young Christian Students and the Christian Family Movement, people were living their faith and forming leaders. The observe, judge, and act process gave me a formula that we could use to figure out how to make changes. Someone said I am always looking for a formula, but I just learn from other people.

So much was going on, and it was exciting. The Catholic Interracial Council was taking off in Davenport at the same time I was learning about community organizing. I didn't know what I was doing, but in a dumb sort of way, I got ideas in Chicago that I thought could work in Davenport. I wasn't shy about stealing ideas and approaches that worked. The fast-food restaurants are always watching each other. The owner of a well-known restaurant told me that he looks through food magazines to steal ideas. That's the way I was about social justice.

Fr. Mottet honed what he called "stealing ideas" into a practical strategy for progress that he used throughout his varied career. He encouraged other organizations to steal his ideas.

Eating Hot Mexican Food and Drinking Cold Beer

In 1952, the Davenport City Council voted to clear Cook's Point for an industrial site. Cook's Point was a typical Mexican barrio, a two-acre site on the banks of the Mississippi River. There were no paved streets, sidewalks, electricity, running water, or sanitary facilities. Residents owned the small frame houses or makeshift shacks they built, but not the land, which flooded regularly and was close to the city dump. There was no comparison with the houses of African Americans by the Morrel packing plant in Ottumwa. Cook's Point was worse. About two hundred people lived there. Everybody had a garden to survive. When the City voted to clear Cook's Point, some of the residents were able to buy a few acres of land on the edge of Davenport.

St. Ambrose University students surveyed Cooks Point in 1949 and found 270 residents living in fifty-six homes. The Migration is Beautiful website in the Iowa Women's Archives of University of Iowa Libraries describes the harsh living conditions at Cooks Point and Holy City, the barrio in Bettendorf, Iowa, which adjoins Davenport. Despite their poverty, residents of the barrios lived in close-knit communities.

The League for Social Justice, made up of St. Ambrose faculty and students, decided to move the houses up to higher ground where the residents bought land. We worked together with the National Association for the Advancement of Colored People (NAACP). For several Saturdays that summer, we rode out there in a truck. We dug by hand with shovels and spades and moved dirt in wheelbarrows for foundations, cesspools, the road, and six houses. I don't remember how many students worked out there, but it was a dump truck load. Fr. Bill and the other priests were on board. It was the spirit of Ambrose. Some of the houses we worked on are still there today. I remember eating hot Mexican food and drinking cold beer after we worked all day Saturday.

I met and worked with African American and Hispanic leaders that have remained friends for the rest of my life. Ernie Rodriguez, who was born two years before me, grew up in a boxcar in Holy City in Bettendorf. His father worked in the Bettendorf shops. At one time or another, everyone spent some time on what was known as "relief" when the jobs didn't last. He grew up in tremendous poverty, but he had that same feeling that I did--we can change a whole bunch of things if we work together and get organized. Later, Ernie worked for me at the Social Action Department to form the Area Board of Migrants.

I met Charles and Ann Toney at Cook's Point, and we remained friends for life. When Hispanic friends came for lunch at Toney's house, they brought Mexican food, and that's where I came to love green peppers stuffed with cheese. What are they called? Poblanos, I think.

The person who deserves the credit for the Cooks Point project is Mary Terronez. She was an organizer at heart, even without being trained. She took a truck load of people down to the onion fields along River Drive and negotiated the workers' salary with the farmers and onion growers. At the end of the week, there was a party. That was important to Hispanics. Mary Terronez was a mover and go-getter. She was connected to the League for Social Justice and the National Association for the Advancement of Colored People through the Toneys, and she wasn't afraid to speak her mind. All those people were close friends.

Cook's Point made an indelible mark on me. I was happy doing that work. I loved it because I could see the results. We learned about social justice in the classroom, and then we went out and practiced social justice doing hands-on work. Years later when I travelled the country for the Campaign for Human Development, people asked, "How did you get started in this?" I said, "Number one my dad, number two St. Ambrose, and number three Cooks Point." We got our hands dirty. Those experiences ruined me for anything other than social justice.

What was that indelible mark? Fr. Mottet had little use for theories or talk that didn't lead to action and results. He saw for the first time, in Mary Terronez, the effect a skilled organizer can have. Cooks Point also reinforced his early preference for community-based action and the relationships that are formed in the process. "Dirty hands" was more than a description of the work. It was a metaphor for the powerful direct involvement he advocated. He said, "When you put your body on the line, people want to join you." It was part of the credibility he built through his lifestyle.

Chapter 4

She Still Lights Up My Life

Ottumwa was famous for vocations to the priesthood. The two major employers were Deere and Company and Morrell Packing Plant. During my summers in Ottumwa, I worked for both. I jokingly said, "One summer in a hog kill and you're ready to go to the seminary. There's gotta be something better than this."

I was in college when the Korean War broke out in 1950, and I expected to go to Korea. I had talked with Fr. Kamerick about switching over to the seminary, but I wanted to get military service out of the way first. He said, "No, that's no place to discern a vocation." By the end of my sophomore year, I had almost decided that I was called to priesthood. Priests like Fr. Broderick and Fr. Kamerick made a big impression on me because they were making a difference.

I was very attracted to marriage, and I had a wonderful girlfriend, Jeanne. I had my eye on her from the time she was fifteen. I think I met her at the Catholic Youth Organization. They had a dance every Sunday night, and everyone went. She was going with another boy, but we danced. That's how we met. Fr. Broderick used to say, "You're the best dancers on the floor." It was a slow two-step. I never did the jitterbug. I'm two years older than her, and I'm eight-five now, so she is eighty-three. She still remembers my birthday. She was the most beautiful girl in town and a saintly person who went to daily Mass and said the Rosary.

When Jeanne was fifteen, one of her lungs collapsed, but they didn't know why. She had no fever or cough. They took her to every doctor in Ottumwa trying to figure out what on earth it was. I walked all the way from the farm and across the south side of town to the hospital to see her.

When Jeanne visited the farm, she walked from town because there was no bus or anything. She had never ridden a horse, but we had a horse called Baldy that we rode without a saddle. Jeanne decided she was going to ride that horse. She was going along just fine, but suddenly Baldy stopped, and off she went. Another time, she leaned against the back of a trailer of hay, and fell when it broke, but she wasn't hurt. I remember her bringing a potato casserole out there so we would have something to eat when my parents were gone somewhere. She stayed at the farm for a week one summer. My sisters were there, of course. I got up early in the morning to do chores. Then I went back in to give her a good morning kiss.

Since I was the class president, I was the one who crowned Jeanne as homecoming queen. I asked her, "How big is your head?" before she knew she was chosen because I knew I was going to put that crown on her head.

One of the things Jeanne and I shared was our interest in Fatima. I told her about Fatima, and she told me about the Rosary. We used to say the Rosary on every date.

Choosing celibacy was a difficult decision to make. I tried to get it out of my mind, but God just kept bugging me. Jeanne and I talked about it many times. I had to think through scriptures that always haunted me. One was Matthew nineteen verses twenty-three to thirty. It says that if you give up one family, you will get a hundred more. I couldn't see how those two things worked together, but I found out later.

A Young Couple Sitting on a Bench Planning Their Future

Fr. Mottet had always remained private about Jeanne. Details gradually emerged, and we were, of course, intrigued. We located Jeanne through her Catholic Church in Kansas City, Missouri, and wrote to ask for an in-person interview. She was suspicious, so she called Father, and he encouraged her to meet with us.

We knew we were in love. During my first year at St. Ambrose, Jeanne came for a piano concert. We went down by the Mississippi River to sit on a bench, and we talked about getting married and having a family. She was already starting to have a feeling that I had a calling to become a priest. It was close to Valentine's Day during my sophomore year when I knew for sure I was going into the priesthood. I didn't think it would be fair to send her a Valentine, so I didn't. She was devastated. I agonized over how much that must have hurt her. Even Fr. Kamerick wondered how I could do such a thing. One time she said to me, "I didn't mean to, but I prayed you right into the seminary."

Their talk by the river was during Fr. Mottet's freshman year. Jeanne occasionally came to Davenport on weekends. During his sophomore year, he finally knew he was called to be a priest, so they had several months to sort through the emotions of being in love and wanting to be married but knowing that God might have other plans. Not sending a valentine was an inexplicable way to end their relationship, but they both understood what it meant and accepted it as God's plan. When they talked in their eighties, Jeanne said she knew he had made the right decision even though it broke her heart. That probably enabled her to move on quickly. Jeanne married in 1951 when she was eighteen years old.

In the second half of my junior year, I transferred to the seminary, and I lived in Irish Village, the third floor of Ambrose Hall. The peace I felt there was a sign to me that I was making the right decision. I looked out at the trees and saw the birds and squirrels and felt such peace after a couple of years of turmoil as I tried to discern my vocation.

Jeanne married Dallas Traxler, a veteran of World War II, and they had three boys. Dallas had been based in Italy where he flew fifty combat missions. A shell hit his aircraft and blew off the side sending debris into his eyes. He was awarded a bronze medal and a Certificate of Valor in Combat. He had surgery in a field hospital, but when he was older, he started to go blind. They went everywhere trying to save his sight. He was a few years older than Jeanne, and she was his caregiver for ten years after he lost his sight.

Years later when I was a priest teaching high school, Jeanne and her husband came to Davenport to visit Sr. Joanne Moore. We always said, "When God created Sister Joanne, He threw away the blueprints." She developed bone cancer, and they amputated one leg, so she walked with crutches. I used to kid her by saying, "I didn't know life could be so much fun with only one leg." While Sr. Joanne and I were showing Jeanne and her husband around, we walked past that place where Jeanne and I sat by the river. I remembered a young couple sitting on a bench planning their future. Later we visited a chapel where Jeanne and I had been to Mass many times. When we walked into the chapel, out of my heart came: "She is my gift to you, Lord." That was the price I paid. Sr. Joanne took us to a place overlooking the river for a nice supper. She asked me several times, "Do people think she is beautiful," and I said, "Yes." It was a high price to pay, but it was worth it. Jeanne told others that I made the best choice.

After Vatican II ended in 1965, some priests thought celibacy would change since everything else changed. I've read the history. Pope Paul VI took two things off the agenda at Vatican II: celibacy and birth control. Even seminary professors thought celibacy would be changed. When some young priests were ordained, they only planned to stay in the priesthood if that happened. A well-known priest in

Chicago claimed the average priest meets four or five women he could marry in his lifetime, so priests need to be prepared for that.

My relationship with Jeanne was my salvation. When young priests were leaving the priesthood to marry, I thought, "I've already given up the best girl in the world. Why would I want to go back? It makes no sense." I saw so many talented priests leave and sell insurance to make a living. What a waste!

The Second Vatican Council from 1962 to 1965, usually called Vatican II, was designed to bring the Catholic Church into the modern world. "No new dogma was issued, but the council transformed the church from an exclusive to an inclusive institution." It gave a larger role to the laypeople, updated the liturgy to be in the language of the vernacular, introduced the concept of religious freedom, and began dialogue with other religions. It also began the process of a historic reconciliation between the Catholic Church and Judaism.[8]

The Hardest Decision I Have Ever Made

Jeanne and I have seen each other about once every five years, and we exchange Christmas cards. My spiritual director was suspicious, and he kept a close eye on this. The first time I visited Jeanne and her husband in Kansas City, I took her a daily missal. It is quite a trick to use the missal, and she is the one who taught me. After Dallas realized how much this meant to her, he went secretly to the priest and took instructions to become Catholic without telling Jeanne. She never pushed him.

In the early eighties while I was at the Campaign for Human Development, some of our regional meetings were in Kansas City. I called her and asked her to go for dinner. She said, "I can't drive." I wanted one of her children to come, but that didn't work out. I said, "If you can't drive, and your children can't come with you, I can't go. That would be a scandal. There's enough scandal in the church." We were always very proper.

I was surprised when Art and Suzy told me they wanted to go to Kansas City to interview Jeanne, but I helped them arrange it. It is safe now for us to be connected. I have photos of her, and she looks like she will live to a hundred. It's strange that we talk on the phone at this late date. I always ask for her prayers. I told her I was sorry about the Valentine, but I was caught between a rock and a hard place. I even told her about that day when we walked into the chapel with Dallas and Sr. Joanne. She didn't know about it all these years.

She said on the phone the other day, "You broke my heart." It wasn't easy for me. It was the hardest decision I have ever made. I've never stopped thinking about it. Suzy asked me when I stopped thinking about the Valentine, and I answered, "Oh, about thirty seconds ago." We made a deal that if Jeanne ever gets to Ottumwa, I will go there to see her. Maybe it will happen for a high school reunion. I think that's where I saw her last time. She bought me a beer. She still lights up my life.

A little six- or seven-years old girl said to me, "Fr. Mottet, did you ever have a girlfriend?" I said, "Yes, I did before I became a priest." She wanted to know if I kissed her, and I told her I did. Then she asked, "What did you do with her after you went and became a priest?" I told her that God called me and that we are good friends still. She said, "No more kissing, right?" I agreed, and we laughed.

During the interview, Jeanne talked lovingly about her husband Dallas and her children and grandchildren, who were her delight. She was interested in details about Marv's life, and said she would always have a place in her heart for him. She admitted that he broke her heart, but she spoke warmly of him and said he could come and mow her grass if he'd like to. Problems with her hands kept her from playing piano, but nothing stopped her dancing. She said, "I don't care how fast they play the music. I can still dance. I always wear a long skirt. I love pretty clothes and pretty jewelry. I love all the modern stuff. I don't want to dress like an old lady. I don't feel like an old lady, so I'm not going to dress like one."

Fr. Mottet videotaped a message for us to take to Jeanne. In it, he said, "Sorry about the Valentine." Jeanne said it was nice to talk to Marv now, and in the message she recorded for him, she said, "Hi, Marv. The people you spoke so highly of are here. I really enjoyed them. I've told them things that will probably be censored. I've told them everything, and I especially want you to forget about the Valentine. I forgive you. I will pray for you, and you will always be a part of my heart. As ever, Jeanne."

Fr. Mottet wanted this story to be told, and Jeanne gave us permission to tell it. She even offered to give us dried flowers from the bouquet Marv gave her for the homecoming dance. They seemed too precious to take. Photos of Jeanne are posted at fathermottet.com.

One day Father said, "Suzy, you've reconnected us in our eighties." Jeanne passed away on August 24, 2017, less than a year after Fr. Mottet's death. Jeanne's obituary, which is available on the website of McGilley & Sheil Chapel, describes her as generous, hospitable, and "always making sure she was dressed to the nines before leaving the house." In addition to her passion for dancing, singing, and playing piano and organ, Jeanne was a eucharistic minister and held season tickets to the Kansas City Chiefs games.

PART TWO

Organizer

How did a quiet young high school teacher consistently end up in the center of action and develop the vison and relationships to become a successful organizer? How did he transplant avant-garde principles and tactics from Chicago to Davenport? How did his passion to develop leaders begin? How did he survive a deep spiritual crisis? How did he deal with catastrophic loss on the heels of his moment of opportunity?

Fr. Mottet never tired of telling stories about those days fifty years earlier when his friends, leaders of the Davenport civil rights movement, strategized, argued, and laughed at Charles Toney's barber shop. His stories brought those unforgettable characters to life. We had the privilege of interviewing two of them who were still living. The man in the background doing a lot of thinking, promoting ideas, connecting people, and writing agendas was Fr. Mottet. When we said, "It looks like you are still the one bringing the ball down the court," he insisted, "You give me too much credit."

His Chicago stories provided insights to his future direction and the keys to his success. He used terms like "avant-garde" and "cutting edge" to describe ideas that attracted and inspired him. In Chicago, he picked up principles and tactics for social action that worked for him like the pick and roll did in basketball, and he used them to become an effective behind-the-scenes organizer.

His years as a high school teacher provided opportunities to expand his horizon, but also included lessons in facing opposition that he would often need. In his stories about his students and his teaching methods, we got a glimpse of the man who would later develop leaders and organizations. His dark night of the soul and Sr. Catherine's miracle turned him in the direction of contemplative spirituality, which deepened throughout his life and sustained him in his final years.

The typewriter and mimeograph machine that Fr. Mottet used late into the night, were long gone by the time we interviewed him, but he had a flip phone and an old desktop computer that often gave him trouble. Until the last few months, he kept up with his email. His two extra-large rolodex trays were evidence of his vast personal network. Those cards were more than contact information. They were connections. He connected people with their interests, passions, and personal details he wanted to remember. He claimed he couldn't remember names, but he named a mind-boggling number of people who were part of his resource network.

Chapter 5

What's Important and What's Not

In 1952, I enrolled at Mt. St. Bernard Seminary in Dubuque. I didn't choose the seminary. The bishop did. It was a shock, like a bucket of cold water in my face. The seminary was on the conservative side. If you came from St. Ambrose or any of the Benedictine schools in the Midwest, you were considered too liberal. One of my goals in seminary was to avoid everything that would undo what I had learned at St. Ambrose and in Chicago.

Everybody had a nickname in seminary. We called the priest with a big scripture degree "Aunt Minnie Pearl." One day in class, he started criticizing St. Ambrose, the Davenport Diocese, and *The Catholic Messenger.*[9] I had it up to here, and I blew my stack. I don't know what I said, but I was out of control. He said, "That's more heat than light." My classmate patted me on the back and told me to cool down.

The church was growing like crazy in those days because of immigrants and large families, and we had vocations coming out of our ears. Rome encouraged every state to have a seminary. The *Summa Theologica* was our seminary curriculum. It is St. Thomas Aquinas' summary of the main theological teachings of the Catholic Church. It's about as good as you can get.

Back then, I was against anything Ignatian. Our spiritual director was a diocesan priest, who sat in the back and said, "Here are your points for today, point one, point two, point three." I could never figure out what he was doing. I thought I could pray if he would just shut up. In those days, I didn't know much about Ignatian practices, so the purpose of those points went right over my head.

Ignatian prayer practice is imaginative but disciplined. The most well-known Ignatian practice, the daily examen, is a set of introspective prompts or points: thanksgiving, petition, review, response, and a look ahead. Later in his life, he developed a deep appreciation for Ignatian practices.

My dad's death in my first year of seminary was one of the saddest moments of my life. It was the first death in my immediate family. My dad had Alzheimer's disease, which we called "hardening of the arteries" in those days. We noticed something was wrong when he disappeared. He went up the road, and a car picked him up and left him off at our driveway with a wrench in his hand. He said, "The cows are out. I saw them up the road." We drove up the road and asked where they were. He said, "Well, they were right over there," but we knew they couldn't be there. That was the first thing we noticed. Wilb said that Dad probably went through something like depression because he was so discouraged when the Depression ruined his dream. Wilb thought it affected him mentally, and he never recovered.

No place in Wapello County was secure enough to take our dad because he wandered away from home. The county home had closed, but the mental hospital at Mount Pleasant had a lock-up. When the Sheriff came to take him to the hospital, Dad thought they were taking him to a baseball game in St. Louis. He had just read a book about the Cardinals, and he talked about baseball all the way to Mr. Pleasant.

When I took my mother there for our first Sunday visit, he was lucid enough to know where he was. We brought his grandson, Michael, who was just four or five years old. Dad made over him like any grandparent would, but after that he said to my mother, "I didn't think you'd ever put me in a place like this." I felt so sorry for her because she was trying to do the right thing. After that first unhappy visit, he didn't know where he was.

My brother Wilb called in the middle of the night to tell me Dad had died. He got out of the facility, but they didn't know it, or if they knew, they couldn't find him on their large grounds. He was out overnight. It was so cold that he picked up pneumonia. The doctor said he dictated a letter to tell us Dad was very sick, but we got the letter too late. Wilb had to tell our mother about dad's death. The priest who anointed him was a friend of mine. He said Dad made the sign of the cross, so Dad knew that he was receiving the sacrament. He was seventy-two years old.

Since none of us were there with him, we felt like we had abandoned our dad at the end. When I walked into the funeral home with my mother to view the body, I felt such terrible pain. Here was the father of seven children, and he died all alone. We tried to make that up by being his pallbearers. Since the church at St. Pat's had been torn down, the funeral was at Sacred Heart Parish. The pungent stench of meat packing at the Morrell plant reaches that far. Wilb hired a photographer to get a picture of all of us together. It was 1952, and I was twenty-two years old.

In contrast to the pain, I realized that Dad's death added a new dimension to my life. Now there was someone in heaven who was looking down upon us and praying for us.

Operate Out of Cold Anger

One of the people I met at the seminary was Ed Chambers, who became a leader in community organizing. He and another guy took a year off before seminary to travel to western Europe. They came home with avant-garde ideas about liturgy, the monasteries, and the worker-priest movement. At the end of our first year, Ed got kicked out of the seminary after he asked too many questions about those things. The faculty turned him in to the bishop. We were lined up going to the chapel for tonsure,[10] which was the first step of the minor order, and Ed got called out of the line. He went back to the faculty room where his bishop said he was out. When we left the chapel, poor Ed was sitting in the back pew with his surplice off, and we knew what had happened to him. Ed went to Chicago where he got into community organizing and was trained by Saul Alinsky.

Fr. Mottet often talked about Ed Chambers. His book, Roots for Radicals: Organizing for Power, Action, and Justice, *is a clear and comprehensive presentation of community organizing principles.*

Saul Alinsky started as a criminologist. His study of neighborhoods led him to the back of the cattle yards in Chicago. He noticed there was less crime where neighborhoods were organized. Alinsky got churches and labor unions together for a meeting, and with these groups together, he said, "We're going to do something about this neighborhood. We're going to cut crime or do something about housing." They made a list of issues that were important to those people and chose one issue from the list. Then they started organizing about problems related to that issue. Alinsky learned this strategy from John L. Lewis, who organized the coal miners. A lot of community organizing came from labor unions.

Alinsky identified issues that were common to the self-interest of both churches and labor unions. When Fr. Mottet thought about the most important lessons of his life, one of his top-ten was: "You have to know people's interest and passion to get them involved."

Saul Alinsky is the father of community organizing. He wrote his first book in jail because when he travelled from Chicago to Kansas City, where he was organizing a Black slum, the Mayor of Kansas City had the police meet him at the train station and put him in jail. People condemn Alinsky today, but he gets a bad rap. His famous book, *Reville for Radicals*, is quoting our Declaration of Independence and Constitution.

There are a lot of myths about Saul Alinsky, and the Kansas City jail story may be one of them. When Fr. Mottet said Alinsky was quoting the Declaration of Independence and the United States Constitution, he meant that Alinsky's book espouses the same principles. Alinsky is considered an architect of the modern liberal left. He was blunt, passionate, and unsentimental. He knew and worked on projects with Communists in the thirties when "they did a hell of a lot of good work," but he never considered joining the Communist Party. When the Nazi-Soviet Pact was signed in 1939, Alinsky urged support for England and for American intervention in the war. Communists in Chicago turned on him and called him a warmonger. [11]

When Fr. Mottet said Alinsky "gets a bad rap," he was trying to set the record straight about Alinsky's liberal ideas. Alinsky's lengthy critique of liberals, in Reveille for Radicals *is scathing:*

> Liberals in their meetings utter bold words; they strut, grimace belligerently, and then issue a weasel-worded statement. . .They endlessly pass resolutions and endlessly do nothing. They sit calmly, dispassionately, studying the issue; judging both sides; they sit and still sit. . . Liberals have distorted egotistical concepts of their self-importance in the general social scheme. They deliberate as ponderously and as timelessly as though their decisions would cause the world to shake and tremble. . . The fact is that outside of their own intimate associates few know of or give a hang what these Liberal groups decide. They truly fit the old description that 'A Liberal is one who puts his foot down firmly on thin air.' (pp. 28-29)

I graduated from seminary in 1956 and was ordained at Sacred Heart Cathedral by Bishop Ralph Hayes. I wanted to go to the smallest rural parish and get lost. I was surprised to be appointed as a teacher at Ambrose Academy, which became Assumption High School two years later. It was a godsend. Teachers had freedom that parish priests didn't have. If you went to a parish and got under the thumb of a pastor, you were controlled. You had to be in at a certain time of night, and there were lots of things you couldn't do. I was able to go to summer conferences where I learned things that were cutting edge. More importantly, I had freedom to get in on the action of the Davenport civil rights movement. We started the Catholic Interracial Council in 1957, based on the legacy of the League for Social Justice.

I lived at McCauley Hall. It was good to live offsite from work. One of the problems of priesthood is that you live in a rectory, and you get no distance from your work. When I closed the door of McCauley Hall, I left work behind. I could be myself. The windows were open at supper time, and the whole neighborhood heard us laughing. Sometimes I laughed so much my belly ached. It reminded me of when Fr. Broderick asked me if I thought of being a priest because I had a sense of humor. Life at McCauley Hall was good times.

To earn enough money, I worked on weekends at a parish in Fulton, Illinois. On Easter Sunday in 1957, I drove to Ottumwa to give my mother a recording of Strauss waltzes, which she always liked. We went out to eat. After we got into the restaurant and sat down, she keeled over and fell out of the chair. I called the ambulance, and they rushed her to the hospital. She regained consciousness, but it was difficult for her to speak. She had another stroke on Mother's Day. She kept putting the rosary in her mouth, and we would take it out. That happened several times. Finally, I said, "Since she can't talk, she's trying to tell us to pray the rosary." We started praying the rosary with her. That was so important to her that her last breath in 1957 was when we finished the final prayer of a rosary. She had suffered a long time with congestive heart disease. A lot of people said the only reason she stayed alive was to see my ordination.

The first year after my ordination, I was called to a meeting in Davis Hall at St. Ambrose by Fr. Ed O'Connor, Fr. Bill O'Connor, and a small group of priests and faculty members. Charles Toney, an African American leader, who had been President of the local National Association for the Advancement of Colored People, and some Hispanic leaders were there.[11] Bill O'Connor and Charles Toney were very close. In fact, Fr. Bill brought Charles and Ann Toney into the church. The outcome of that meeting was the formation in 1957 of the local Catholic Interracial Council. It was partially a response to a group in the Quad Cities that included former Marxists. We needed to operate out of our own faith principles without constantly guarding against the influence of that other group. They asked me to be the chaplain and wrote a letter to Bishop Hayes to make it official.

The explicit goal of the Davenport Catholic Interracial Council was: "…the full realization of human rights and interracial justice in our area." It grew organically out of the relationships that had been established, and Catholic Social Justice teaching served as its core. Student participants came primarily from Young Christian Students. By 1963, all the seminarians at St. Ambrose were active members, but there was also an active involvement of the laity. Two Black leaders, Charles Toney and Bill Cribbs, were charter members. It was organized with a President, Vice President, Secretary, Treasurer, and a Board of Directors. Non-Catholics were welcome as members and some officers were Jews.[12]

Because of the younger crowd, we just took off. They called us "the young Turks." It wasn't just meetings. We were into big things like employment and housing. We put out a monthly newsletter and organized letter-writing campaigns.

"Young Turk" is an idiom referring to a young person who has revolutionary new ideas and is impatient to implement them. The Catholic Interracial Council was unique because in was interfaith, and the African American leaders were Catholics.

Most of what I did was behind the scenes. Other people, like Charles Toney, were out in front. I accepted responsibilities because I didn't know any better, not because I knew how to be a leader. Most of what I did was in a dumb way. I didn't even realize what I was doing, but I knew from Young Christian Students how to use Thomas Aquinas' three parts of a prudent action: observe, judge, and act.

Since I prepared the Catholic Interracial Council agendas after talking them over with Charles Toney, I emphasized statewide and national thinking. We organized letter writing campaigns to influence federal legislation. Years later in Washington, D.C., Congressman Jim Leach said in a meeting, "There's the number one letter writer of First District."

Fr. Mottet wrote and received substantive letters throughout his life. He believed in the power of speaking out in appropriate ways. Near the end if his life he identified "be a citizen lobbyist" as one of the ten most important lessons of his life.

Early on, we got an idea that came from Chicago--home visits. One reason White people looked down on African Americans was because they didn't meet them in their homes. We arranged for white people to go on Sunday afternoon to the home of an African American family who welcomed them. They had friendly discussions, and a lot of friendships grew out of that. Then we had African Americans visit the homes of White families. We had hundreds of home visits, and people saw this intermingling going on. Someone asked me how we organized all of that. No one took credit. We operated as a group.

That's how observe, judge, and act works. I observed the situation in Davenport. I judged that what they were doing in Chicago could work well here, and we acted on it. Since it was of value there, let's try it here. Just getting to know an African American family and listening to their stories is an education. That's what I advise people to do. When you realize what people are going through, you start thinking about what can be done.

A Young Christian Students group had started at Ambrose Academy a year or two before I was ordained. When I got there, the principal gave me the choice to coach a sports team or be in charge of Young Christian Students in addition to teaching. It was a no-brainer. Young Christian Students grew astronomically and spread all over the diocese. It was recognized nationally, and people came from all over to our study week. I had a typewriter and mimeograph machine in my room. I remember sitting up late at night to make up the social enquiry and scripture discussion for all those groups. Eventually ten or twelve priests each led a group, and I led two.

Each group met one night a week to reflect on the gospel and discuss how to change the world. According to Catholic social teaching, we are supposed to transform the social order. It is even in the Eucharist. Every meeting included the three parts of a prudent act: observe, judge, and act. When I wasn't working, I was typing all night to prepare for those thirteen Young Christian Student groups. At McCauley Hall, they were used to hearing me on the typewriter. I would have given my right arm to be the national chaplain of Young Christian Students, but God had other things in mind.

I was involved in the civil rights movement at the same time, so I also typed agendas for the Catholic Interracial Council. Charles Toney was clearly the leader. He and his wife Ann were organizers. They won an early civil rights case in Iowa. They walked into Colonial Fountain, an ice cream store near Central High School, on a hot Sunday afternoon in July of 1945. The owner refused to serve them. Charles asked her if she knew she was violating their civil rights, and she said she didn't care. The next day, Charles went to a Scott County attorney and asked him to file charges that the woman refused to serve him because of his race.

Charles knew the law and was willing to stand up for his rights. Two trials were held in criminal court with all-White juries. The woman testified at the first trial that she refused to serve them because Charles ridiculed her for being pregnant. Charles said, "You think in front of my wife I would ridicule you because you're pregnant?" Under pressure in the second trial, she admitted that she was opposed to the civil rights law and said that the Toneys should establish an eating place "for Negroes only" if they wanted to accomplish something. The woman was found guilty and fined one hundred dollars plus court costs of thirty dollars and seventy-fifty cents. Toney's victory was a first for Davenport.

When he was younger, Charles had a one-year scholarship at St. Ambrose during the Depression, but he ran out of support and got a job as a welder at John Deere. He was the first Black welder. Since he liked chemistry class, he applied for the chemistry lab at Deere and Company, but the guy who took his application laughed in his face. He took that experience with him years later when he ended up in management at Deere, but it took a long time.

Charles was intelligent, and he had a lot of experience. He was president of the Catholic Interracial Council from 1959 to 1969. With his leadership, we just took off. He was a problem-solver. African American kids felt they couldn't swim in the municipal pool because of the racism there, so he put a pool in his back yard. African Americans couldn't get their hair cut in a lot of barber shops, so he went to barber school and opened a barber shop in his home.

Charles said being a black man in the United States is like being six feet tall and living in a room five feet high. That's the best description of racism I've ever heard. When he moved his barber shop to a commercial site, he wanted to build a strip mall in that block, but Davenport banks wouldn't loan him any money. He said, "I can borrow money from the bank to buy a Cadillac, but I can't borrow money to start a business." I went with him to the Chicago loop to visit banks. Skyscrapers were all around us, and we were on time for the appointment, but we were unknowns. Charles didn't have a chance of getting a loan out of it. That was part of the discrimination.

After I started teaching at Ambrose Academy, Pope John XXIII decided that since the western Church was rich in both money and priests, every diocese should send volunteers to Latin America as lay missionaries called "papal volunteers." The Spanish teacher, who had connections in Latin America, arranged for me to go to Mexico, Columbia, Panama, and Peru in 1959. I spent about three months down there visiting our volunteers.

I got to be a bishop for a day when I was in the Altiplano in Peru. You have to prepare to go up to the high altitude, so I went up on a train, but I had to get out on a plane. The plane only came in once a day, and it was full. The guy handling the arrangements said, "I've got a bishop here who would like to get out of here tomorrow morning." They agreed. I was a bishop for a few hours, and I got on the plane. They are great on bribes down there.

I'll never forget a poor woman I saw walking around picking up sticks to create a fire to cook a meal. I thought about our stoves and how plentiful wood is in the United States. Those experiences burned into my memory. I thought I had a calling to stay in Latin America and be a missionary, but the bishop didn't get the message. He told me to come home and teach. I tried to get a lay person from outside the diocese to replace me, but I couldn't find anyone, and I figured my experience prepared me better for social justice work in this country. I didn't go into foreign missions in part because it was scary to think about leaving my home country for five or ten years and maybe never coming back. It was the right decision.

I had seen poverty in Ottumwa and at Cooks point, but the poverty, poor housing, and lack of opportunity in Latin America were such a culture shock that people said I walked around in a daze after I came back. In the United States, you can usually figure out what to do about a situation, but not down there. I saw Davenport differently. I was aware of the whole world out there, and the race problem became even more important to me because a lot of racism was against Hispanics. I came to understand other cultures and nationalities, and I became more international in how I viewed the world. I think exposure to news and media has helped more Americans realize that there is a whole world outside of the United States.

That experience in Latin America taught me what's important and what's not. Wealth and show, things like country clubs, are not important. Justice. That's what is important. I already knew that, but it became an even higher value.

Later, Fr. Mottet's personal slogan, borrowed from Pope Paul VI, became: "If you want peace, work for justice." When he selected the life lessons he wanted to pass on, he contrasted justice with charity. He said, "Charity can't make up for what is lacking in justice." He stressed the necessity to change the causes of injustice.

Back at Ambrose Academy, I was put in charge of the junior-senior prom. I went with the class officers to the Outing Club, a prestigious, members-only club where many social events were held. When I walked in, I said to the woman working there, "I'm from Ambrose Academy, and these are the officers of the junior and senior classes. We want to plan for our prom next year to be here." She stuck her nose up in the air and said, "Do you have an appointment?" For me the priesthood was a big step up. I could go where I wanted and so forth, but that experience taught me a lesson and added to my anger.

Every time I run into social injustices, I'm angry, but I operate out of controlled anger. I call it "cold anger." There is a lot of energy in anger. Organizers say to channel your energy, and don't waste it. I learned that from Ed Chambers. I grew up as a poor farmer. We drove by the country club, but we never set foot in it. I told the students about that as we were driving back to school. Later when I was pastor of Sacred Heart Cathedral, we had many events at the Outing Club, and I became quite comfortable there, but it was a shock in the beginning.

It Takes Very Few People to Get a Lot Done If You're Properly Organized

Several of the main characters from the Davenport civil rights movement passed away before our interviews, but Fr. Mottet made us feel like we knew them. Charles Toney, Jack Schneiders, and Bill Cribbs were the outspoken activists.

Near the beginning of our interviews, we talked with Jack Schneiders and Fr. Mottet together. Jack drove from Des Moines to St. Vincent's to work on Father's income tax return. Their easy rapport and mutual respect were palpable as they reminisced about Charles Toney and laughed about things that happened. Jack was still full of spunk and used coarse language. He wanted to make sure Fr. Mottet got the credit he deserved.

Saul Alinsky used to say, "If you're not having fun, you're on the wrong issue." Our civil rights work was exciting. We were thick as mud. We saw each other several times a week and kept in touch by phone if not in person. We were like family. One of the things people don't understand is that we had fun when we could.

Jack Schneiders, who was an Internal Revenue Service agent, was one of our White leaders who came out of the Christian Family Movement in 1962. Racism was one of their social inquiries, and they were eager to make a difference. Jack lived on Fourth Street where he never saw Black people, and the neighbors claimed there were no Black people in town.

Some people called Jack "the meanest man alive." When President Kennedy was killed, a man he worked with laughed and carried on. That same guy referred to Bill Cribbs with a slang term. Jack got him by what he called "the short side" and said, "We have to work together, but you say that again, and I'm going to hurt you." Unless it was the weekend, Jack always wore a suit and always dressed in black. People in the neighborhood thought he was probably armed. He was the intimidator, and people walked a big circle around him. Like a bulldog gets his teeth in you, he didn't let go until he got results.

Unless people lived through those times, they don't realize what it was like. The situation was so intense then that it was easy to get a press release in the paper. We used the media very intentionally. Jack was in and out of the newsroom all the time. He got to know them, and they called him on the phone when they wanted a statement.

The Black section of Davenport started on Eighth Street, so Jack and his wife Jean lived in an all-White section of Davenport. He didn't even have to drive through the Black section to get to his downtown office. Blacks were invisible to Whites who lived in neighborhoods like Jack's. Besides playing a key role in getting publicity for the Catholic Interracial Council, Jack became Vice President and then President in 1969 when Charles Toney stepped down. Jack Schneiders was especially important in getting Davenport's housing codes enforced and working with real estate agencies to get redlines taken down. Redlining is the common practice of denying application for housing loans in certain neighborhoods based on race even though the applicant is otherwise eligible.

Jack was at Charles' house all the time. He was involved in both the Catholic Interracial Council and the National Association for the Advancement of Colored People, so he knew what was happening. Jack's wife Jean did all the typing for both organizations, and Jack was Charles' right-hand man. When we were planning something, Jack knew which organization should take the lead. The two organizations worked together very closely, partly because of Jack.

We had a unique team, and each person had a special role. Charles was an extremely private person, but he and Jack became buddies. They both had thin moustaches. People in the neighborhood called them "the Toney twins." Charles was a handsome guy and a little vain. Jack's wife Jean said Charles got even more handsome as he got older. Charles called Jack's wife "Saint Jean." Jack left his wife and kids sitting in a hot car in front of Toney's house while he went in and talked for hours.

Jack and Jean were so into civil rights work that it was the center of their lives. On Saturdays, Jack went to properties in Davenport to make lists of what was wrong with the housing. He knew who the landlord was and what housing code was violated. Jean typed all those lists, and we mimeographed them. Jack was invited to speak at the Bettendorf Orbit Club, which was like a less-expensive version of

Rotary Club. They sat at two long tables. Jack spoke on taxes one time and on race the next. At one meeting, he told them about all those absentee landlords with their junk houses and how they jacked up the rent because people didn't have anywhere else to go. When somebody said, "I doubt that," Jack took the list and passed it down the tables. They pointed fingers, and soon the place emptied out. Jack wasn't invited back after that.

Jack kept meticulous records, which we needed for our newsletters. So many things were going on concurrently. He kept all the articles from three newspapers in manilla folders month by month. He had boxes and boxes of records. Jack eventually moved to Des Moines to work for the Internal Revenue Service there. President Nixon gave him a Presidential Award for Civil Rights. We felt sorry for him when he moved and couldn't get in on the action. He loaded all those boxes in a truck when he moved, and they sat in his garage for years. In 2009, Dr. Art Pitz curated an exhibit at Putnam Museum titled "Davenport's Civil Rights Movement: 1945-1974," and the museum wanted those records. Jack organized them by subject matter so people could follow what happened.

Fred Epstein, Vice President of the Catholic Interracial Council, was Jewish. He and his wife Ruth Epstein were board members. Fred didn't attend often, but he had a law degree, and we asked him for help on legal matters. Fred and Ruth were well-informed and delightful people. They owned KSTT radio, which was the hottest station in town. They had a call-in show that did a lot for civil rights. When I got cancer, Fred paid my airfare down to Houston to have surgery. Ida Kramer, another Jewish woman, was always around at our meetings and events. Jewish people were usually correct on social justice because they had experienced so much injustice. Some young Jewish people, who had experienced antisemitism, became community organizers. Many of the strong leaders, especially in the South, were Jewish. Some of them were killed in Mississippi during Freedom Summer in 1964.

There were others who helped us. Bernice Jones, a friend of the Toneys, rose from janitress to the position of Affirmative Action Officer at the Rock Island Arsenal. It was fun to be around her because she was a character. She could be strong on civil rights without turning people off. She let you know you were wrong with a smile on her face. Ernie Rodriguez worked with us. He later started the Area Board of Migrants and the Immigration Office. One of the first Black attorneys in town did a lot of legal work for us.

Fr. Mottet summed up the accomplishments of his lifetime when he said, "Everything important I have achieved came from relationships." Art and I are grateful that Bernice Jones and Ida Kramer, who both had remarkable stories of their own, were our personal friends. Bernice used the slogan "from the mop to the top" to describe her career, and she published her sayings in a booklet.

The Sisters of Humility weren't exactly open to the civil rights movement in the beginning, but they changed. One of the sisters worked at the Catholic Interracial Council and then left to start the Sixth Street Center, which served children. Two of the nuns taught in the worst public schools. They said, "We can't deal with families unless we get to know the children." They found a principal who would hire them, and they had great success in schools with a lot of African American students.

After Charles moved his barber shop out of his home to a commercial site, we did a lot of planning there. Charles had one chair, and Bill Cribbs had the other. The Cribbs family was a big name in town. With their landscaping business, they were able to provide jobs for people who came up from Mississippi. Bill Cribbs was active in the National Association for the Advancement of Colored People. At one of their meetings, two Nazis showed up with brown uniforms and swastika armbands. When they saw Bill and a few ballplayer-types up there in front, they left without saying a word. Back when Bill was playing football, they used to say, "Watch out for Cribbs. He will hurt you." Bill was so strong, he had to be careful when he was running the ball. He said, "I slowed down because these kids would try to throw a flying block. Hell, I could take out their rib cage, but that would really hurt them." He was also on the wrestling team, but because of racial discrimination, he wasn't allowed to wrestle publicly. A White student at Central High School was the state wrestling champion. Bill used to beat him every night, but not publicly.

Charles operated the barber shop after work and on Saturdays. A lot of people hung out there to hear all the conversations and be involved. I occasionally took other priests. Mexican American activists who were there learned techniques of community organizing in those sessions. We were always talking about the next project, the City Council, housing, employment, the police department, and things like that. Charles and Bill were movers and shakers, and people loved being around them. They were exciting people, always up to something and in the newspaper a lot. The strategizing and storytelling were always fun.

We didn't always agree. We had big arguments, especially about Vietnam and about Black Power. Charles wanted Blacks to have power, but not in the Black Power movement, which essentially said to Whites, "We really don't want you." He didn't agree with people like Malcolm X and Eldridge Cleaver.

You Gotta Hope the Knee Baby

Ann Toney's beauty shop was on the other side of the barber shop. Ann was born in the South and had Baptist roots. She was a fighter, but a kind person. Ann had a deep faith and was very involved. She was part Native-American, and she had lighter skin. You had to be careful what you said in their house. You couldn't insult Native-Americans.

A family who lived about two blocks north of the Toney's on Western Avenue went down south to Mississippi every other weekend with a station wagon to bring people back so they could get jobs. Mississippi was the worst state. All the immigrants from the South went to Ann's side of the shop. She heard all the latest about the South and told them how to operate in the North. She made a great contribution by keeping Charles informed of what she learned. We had trouble understanding the language of people who had just come from Mississippi. I remember hearing someone say, "You gotta hope the knee baby." Charles had to ask Ann to translate. "Hope" is "help," and the "knee baby" is the child that had just learned to walk and is always at the knee of the mother.

One time, Ann was embarrassed by my shiny overcoat. She didn't want the priest to look shabby and embarrass them in front of their friends, so she said, "You go down and buy a new black overcoat and charge the bill to us." I was floored, but I went to a store in downtown Davenport where they sold black clothing. When I told them to send the bill to the Toneys, they looked like they didn't believe me.

One time, we packed a big meeting down at City Hall where the mayor said something Ann Toney didn't like. She caused a stir when she said to him, "You are the biggest bigot in town." Bishop Hayes heard about it and was worried about how the publicity would affect the church. When I went to see him, he said, "Get your people under control." He was afraid of too much controversy. I explained that times have changed. We made him terribly nervous, but he let us go ahead. If anything appeared in a papal encyclical or a pastoral statement, he let me do it if he didn't have to give me time or money. I didn't ask for time or money, and it was the perfect setup.

The pool in Toney's back yard was one of the first private pools in Davenport. We had social gatherings around that pool. Even the novice Humility nuns came to swim. Those social gatherings were important. The Davenport civil rights movement was a political and economic movement, but it had a social and relational foundation. It didn't start that way, but that's how it developed as the friendships grew. I was down there all the time. They were family. My family was out of town, and their house was always open, like a revolving door.

When my sister Katy and her husband Virgil came to visit, I took them to Toneys, and they got to know each other. Virgil worked in management at Deere and Co. in Ottumwa. Later, after Charles became Director of Affirmative Action at Deere in 1972, the head honchos took him to Ottumwa to walk through the plant and do his equal employment thing. Virgil walked out of his office and said, "Hey man, they'll let anybody in here, won't they?" The management thought, "Oh, my God. This clown comes out of his office and embarrasses us." Charles turned around and said, "Hi, Virgil. How are you?"

The value Fr. Mottet placed on friendships dates to his experiences of community at Central High School, in Young Christian Students, and at Cooks Point. He often referred to "lifelong friends," and he didn't mind calling on them for help. "Lifelong" was a word Fr. Mottet used often. He carried ideas, and even pieces of paper, all the way to the end, not as memories, but as action items. A good example is Msgr. Geno Baroni's homily quote, which he always carried in the little black book in his shirt pocket.

When Ferguson, Missouri, blew up in August of 2014, people asked me for advice. I said, "The best thing you can do is get to know an African American family and listen to their stories, past, present and future." I've heard them all because I sat at the dinner table at the Toneys, and we swam in their pool.

Ferguson was a White-run city, but most of the population was African Americans, who were systematically subject to extortion by the White-controlled government and police. When a police officer shot and killed a black male, riots broke out there and elsewhere. The Federal Department of Justice investigated and forcibly changed the government and police of Ferguson to be more reflective of its majority population.

We Knew How to Get Attention

In the nineteen sixties, the Catholic Interracial Council was sending out fourteen hundred weekly newsletters all over the country. We had a hand-crank mimeograph machine, but the National Association for the Advancement of Colored People had an electric one that could turn out that many. They weren't just a sheet of paper. They ran twelve to eighteen pages and always had artwork on the front. We put the photo of the African American soldier, who carried a white soldier on his back out of the jungle in Vietnam, on the front cover of one issue. We sent it to every legislator in Des Moines with the question: "This African American soldier is saving a white man's life, but when he gets home, will he be able to buy a house north of Locust Street?" It got a lot of attention. Part of the genius of effective leadership is knowing how to get attention. You must get people to listen to you. We knew how.

They weren't afraid to say things that were shocking. The photo of the African American soldier is an example of gaining attention through agitation to get people to think about something in a new way. Catholic Interracial Council leaders used a variety of tactics to get attention, which gained them power to negotiate for change. They became adept at using media to achieve their aims. They used stories rather than abstract concepts. They focused on people and organizations that had the power to make the needed changes, and their approach was based on an understanding of the self-interest of those in power.

We weren't always successful. When something bad happened, like when snipers shot up Bill Cribb's office, we sent a letter to the head of the United States Department of Justice, but we got no response. Jack still has copies of those letters.

There were a lot of laws on housing, and we used them intentionally. We took laws created by the system and used them to oppose the system and get laws changed. An attorney friend showed us how to take a petition of five people to the Health Department and bring landlords in on bad housing. Examples were things like rats or the dump right in the middle of the ghetto on Gaines Street, which was especially bad when the river was up. One time a house burned down, and a Black guy died. Bill held a press conference and said, "You're trying to cook us all." That got their attention.

We made so many trips down to City Hall. Once they said, "We don't have any poor housing in Davenport." We went to them with a picture of a house about three or four blocks from City Hall with an electrical cord running from one house to another house. It was torn down quickly. Later I realized that we should have had one-on-one meetings with City Council members. They looked upon us as "the enemy," and we looked upon them as "the enemy," and there was no real conversation.

When a law about fair housing was passed by the Iowa legislature in 1967, one of the legislators said, "They're going to be bothering us all the time, so if anyone wants to make a complaint, they have to come up with a five-hundred-dollar fee." We had a big barbecue to raise money for the fee. Five hundred pounds of ribs were stacked taller than a person in a doorway at the barber shop. Anne had a connection at Oscar Mayer, and we got the ribs for thirty cents a pound. They had me in a chef's hat.

Later, when Governor Robert Ray came to the Black Hawk Hotel for an event, I asked him to get rid of that fee. He said, "I think we can live without that."

We got pretty good at fundraising. Jack joked that we didn't even know where some of the money we raised came from. When Jack went to one of the big realtors with his briefcase to raise money, the realtor said, "Are you here on business? How much do you want?"

Someone who wasn't part of our leadership picketed the office of one of Davenport's best-known realtors. The realtor claimed he wasn't as bad as we thought, but he was pretty bad. Jack thought he was a nice old guy. When Charles went to see that realtor, he said, "Young man, I don't agree with everything you've done, but I'm impressed with the way you went about it." He had lunch brought into his office for the two of them, which was a big breakthrough. He was impressed because we had banquets at the Black Hawk Hotel with people dressed in tuxedos and formal clothes, and he got good press coverage.

Deere and Company executives saw Charles on television and in the paper so much that they asked him to come into management. He said, "I'm doing pretty well out here on piecework as a welder." Deere was a leader in hiring, and they put him in charge of their affirmative action program. He gave the chitling test to people. He got local minorities hired and brought a lot of college graduates to Deere and Company.

The chitling test highlights cultural biases in testing. The test has been criticized as being insensitive and racially inflammatory.

We dealt with big issues during President Johnson's War on Poverty, which began in 1964. The local director of the Office of Economic Opportunity went to the Oscar Mayer plant and told them to take the government's training money, train low level workers for sixteen weeks, and then fire them. I think they ran that director out of town after that.

The rate of poverty in the United States was around twenty percent in the sixties. The Economic Opportunity Act of 1964 attempted to attack the roots of poverty and unemployment by providing job training, adult education, and loans to small businesses. As part of President Lyndon Johnson's War on Poverty, the Office of Economic Opportunity developed local Community Action Agencies that required the poor to have "maximum feasible participation" in planning programs. In 1967, the Green Amendment to the legislation gave elected officials authority over the Community Action Agencies and gave the poor a minority representation.[13]

Ambrose Academy became Assumption High School in 1959, and I taught there until 1966. While I was teaching at Assumption, an FBI man conveniently met me on the corner of Fourth and Brady. He was gathering information for Washington, D.C., and the Omaha Field Office. They wanted to know ahead of time when a march or event was planned. He begged to know what was going on because Omaha beat him up if something happened without him informing them. He wanted to know the names of all the people who were going to the March on Washington. J. Edgar Hoover, the first Director of the FBI, was trying to smear the civil rights movement and destroy it.

Jack Schneiders thought that FBI agent was a real friendly guy. He saw the FBI tapping his phone on a pole outside his house at eight o'clock at night. He got a phone survey about automobiles that went on for about an hour while he watched the guy out on the pole. Since Jack knew what they were doing, he used the call to bait the FBI or whoever was listening.

The federal government supported the civil rights movement by passing two major pieces of legislation, the Civil Rights Act of 1964 and the Voting Rights Act of 1965. However, the federal government also worked to undermine and control civil rights activists. The FBI spied on civil rights activists and waged a campaign to discredit black leaders.

Thanks to Charles, I integrated the Knights of Columbus.[14] A man I knew called me just before supper and asked me to speak because the scheduled speaker cancelled. It wasn't much notice, but he knew I always have something on my mind. I warned him they wouldn't like it, but he said, "Come and speak, and let the chips fall where they may." They didn't know what they were getting into. The Knights of Columbus in Chicago had blackballed a Black Notre Dame basketball star, and Charles was blackballed by the Knights of Columbus in Davenport. I told them about the basketball star, and then I read Charles Toney's pedigree without telling them who he was. When I said, "This guy was blackballed here," they were so upset that I thought I was going to have to fight my way out of there. They said, "You're always criticizing us. Why don't you join?" I told them I would join when the Black men do. I went home and asked Charles for a list of all the African American men who were Catholic. There was a full page, sixteen or eighteen of them. I put my name at the bottom. I called their bluff, and we all went in.

"Blackball" means rejection of a membership application to a club by secret ballot. The term doesn't necessarily connote rejection based on race, but Fr. Mottet had no doubt that the blackballing of Charles Toney was based on race.

Charles later integrated Crow Valley Golf Club. When he was blackballed there, he wrote to Lee Trevino, the big star of their golf tournament, and told him what had happened. Trevino told Crow Valley he wasn't coming. Charles also went to the management at Deere and Company, and they threatened to pull the Vice Presidents out of the country club. Crow Valley backed down and let Charles Toney in. He said, "This integration is getting expensive. I thought the Knights of Columbus was expensive, but Crow Valley is really expensive."

Young Communist Priests

I wanted students to know the teaching of the gospels and the church and be on fire for social justice. I wanted them to see that we can make a difference. We can do something to change the world. We can take it on. The class was on social justice, but students called it "creeping socialism." Once, I took students to City Hall. Their parents caused me a lot of trouble after they saw their kids on television at City Hall.

I often had outside speakers in my class, and I invited people on both sides of issues. Once I had a Jewish Rabbi and an Orthodox Priest speak to my class of seniors. I wanted students to get the whole picture and know I was open to all ideas. I had nothing to be afraid of. I would have invited a Republican. One of the speakers quoted St. Paul's statement that if you don't work, you shouldn't eat. After he left, I turned it around and said the Lord wants us to produce jobs for these people, and if racial discrimination keeps them from getting a job, we need to correct that. If a student objected to what I was teaching, I said, "Okay, next Wednesday you have the whole class to explain your philosophy." He would talk to his dad and come to class with a book or two. He was prepared, but the students took him on and shot holes in his argument. I didn't have to do a thing, and it was a good experience for them.

During Vatican II, I had students bring *The Catholic Messenger* from home. I divided it up and said, "Okay, who wants to report on this article?" Students raised their hands, and I put their names down.

They came to class and reported on the article. It was always current and exciting.

Students walked in with books by Ayn Rand, an atheist who believed selfishness is a virtue. I didn't understand capitalism until I read Ayn Rand. One kid went home and told his dad what I said in class. He had a classmate with him. The dad, a businessman, got so mad that the classmate said, "You better back off. Your dad is going to kill you if you keep pressing." Some people called us "the young communist priests," but we were just running Young Christian Students groups. We were teaching things that previewed what would come out from 1962 to 1965 in Vatican II.

I also taught my students moderation in drinking. My French dad said, "We had wine at two meals a day: lunch and supper. We would have it today if we could afford it." I taught them to drink with food like Europeans do and not like Americans who just chug it down without food.

I remember a humbling experience with one of my students. I was preaching social justice and rights for African Americans, but I used the expression "I'll Jew you down." The student came to me privately and told me Jewish people don't like that statement. Out of the mouth of youth comes wisdom. He was socially involved with young Jewish people and knew they'd object to that expression. I never used it again. You learn from young people.

They had some tricks. During the Hungarian Revolution, which began in 1956, a Hungarian refugee came to our school. One of the students took him aside and explained how to say good morning to the principal. It was "You're full of shit" or something like that.

I read that adolescents are influenced by slogans and advertising, so I got a professional sign painter to create signs that I hung in my classroom and around the school. I started a bookstore so they could buy paperbacks. It was an extension of a bookstore in town, and I was their top salesman. When my students went to college, their professors were surprised how many books they had read.

Observe, judge, and act. It is a certain cut of mind. Three of my students went to the legislature in Des Moines with that mentality, and they were some of the most effective people there.[15] A couple of students went into the City Council, and they were prepared. Several Assumption students became college professors. Bill Gluba, who became Mayor of Davenport, is a good example of the difference a teacher can make. He wasn't an outstanding student at Assumption, but he played football. When he went to St. Ambrose College, his Political Science professor turned him on, and he went on to graduate school at the University of Iowa. He lectured in Government at St. Ambrose and was elected three times to the Iowa General Assembly. I made calls for Bill when he ran for congress against Jim Leach in 1988, but he was defeated.

My student Greg Cusack became National President of Young Christian Students. He went to Georgetown University in the department that trains diplomats and State Department people. His dad wasn't sure he should go there, but I said, "Greg, you let other people make the money, and you make the decisions that change the world." His dad looked at me like I was crazy, but we're good friends. Greg was elected to the Davenport City Council in 1969 and then to the Iowa House in 1973.

One of my outstanding students was Michael Ceurvorst. That's a Belgian name. His dad ran a meat market, and they started the Belgian Village restaurant where I like to eat. They had twelve children, and they were all smart. Mike sparkled with brilliance. After he served in the Army, he used the GI Bill to study in Germany. Later, he ran the U.S. Consulate in Stuttgart, Germany. When I visited my cousins in Europe, I took a carload to visit him.

I'm proud of my students. Jim Anderson worked at the FBI. He was a Democrat and against the Vietnam War, but he put the handcuffs on Daniel Berrigan, who burned draft files, resisted arrest, and ran off on a wild chase across the country. Jim told me he was just a cub scout in the FBI, and they sent him out to arrest all those people. Later he helped put Vice President Spiro Agnew away for corruption. Jim said it was pure accident that he found the evidence of Agnew's corruption.

As a high school teacher, Fr. Mottet aimed successfully to develop leaders who could change the world. His focus on Young Christian Students, his teaching methods, and his spiritual influence produced what Michael Ceurvost later described as "a shared, communal enterprise." When Fr. Mottet was eighty-three years old, Council 10 of the League of United Latin American Citizens held a surprise event to honor him. Michael Ceurvorst, then a retired diplomat, wrote in a letter his sister read:

> "The friendships we formed — literally in prayer, scripture, and heated topical action-oriented discussion in our homes — bonded a group of us in a way that has persevered over 50 years, even as our lives developed in different locales, jobs, professions, and even convictions. We learned that life is more than about our achievements, that we are intimately involved in realizing the gospel vision wherever we were or are, and that this is a shared, communal enterprise. We learned to pray together and separately; a habit important in a lifetime of development."

Chapter 6

Go Out and Change the World

In 1963, I studied Spanish for three months at the Center for Intercultural Formation in Cuernavaca, Mexico. I returned to Davenport just before the big March on Washington. Since very few people could go to Washington, D.C., the Catholic Interracial Council arranged a march in Davenport in late August of 1963. I didn't have anything to do with it because the march happened right after I got home from Cuernavaca. We marched from St. Anthony's Church down the hill to the bandshell at LeClaire Park. People from African American churches on the hill joined us. Two thousand people came. That was a big crowd for Davenport and quite a victory for the Catholic community. I said, "This is what religious processions should be." We had a sign for every parish except one that didn't participate. John Howard Griffin, the author of *Black Like Me*, gave the major speech, and the pastor of St. Mary's Church spoke about his experiences. A minister said, "That guy could read the phone book, and it would be eloquent."

The Highlight of My Life Was the March on Washington

In 1963, Martin Luther King, Jr. invited all the civil rights groups to come to Washington, D.C., to march on the capital. It was called the "March on Washington for Jobs and Freedom." I had never been to

Washington, D.C. Six of us drove from Davenport, five men and one girl, Carol Gross, an Assumption High School student who would be involved in Freedom Summer in June of 1964. Charles Toney and Bill Gluba were there. The guys all got off work late in the afternoon. We jumped in the car and drove all night to get there. We were told to have a sign on our car so the police would let us through. We arrived at about ten o'clock in the morning, and the march had already started.

A quarter of a million people were there. It was the biggest march in Washington, D.C., until then. We jumped right into the crowd. We walked down the street carrying our nine-foot "Catholic Interracial Council of Davenport Iowa" sign. Anyone from Iowa who was standing along the curb joined us, so our group gradually grew. We were in front of a large crowd from Birmingham, Alabama. They were all African Americans, and most of them were dressed in overalls, which became the uniform of the Poor People's March.

In 1967, Martin Luther King, Jr. started the Poor People's Campaign, sometimes called "Poor People's March," to meet with government officials to demand jobs, unemployment insurance, a fair minimum wage, and education for poor adults and children. The organization, which is still active, now calls itself the "National Call for Moral Revival" and works on fourteen policy priorities.

Reporters came by and asked, "Father, how many people have you got here?" I was tempted to turn around and say, "Well, I hate to estimate a crowd," but I said, "We've only got nine people here." One reporter said, "Oh, Davenport, Iowa. That's where Bix Beiderbecke was from." That was the first time I ever heard that name. He was a famous trumpet player from Davenport, who died in his late twenties. A seven-kilometer race in Davenport commemorates him each year. Charles Toney knew all about him, so he talked with the reporter.

We were right up front at the Lincoln Memorial when Martin Luther King, Jr. gave his "I Have a Dream" speech, and we knew immediately that it was a historic speech. People ask me how it felt. I was thirty-three, a dangerous age. Christ was crucified at that age. It was such a meaningful experience that it was the highlight of my life. There was so much love and harmony between the people, Black and White, and from different parts of the country. If someone stepped on another's foot, they said, "Oh sorry, I didn't mean to do that." It was such an uplifting thing. When the twenty-fifth anniversary of the march took place, I was back in Washington, D.C. I went down to watch, but it was nothing compared to the original event. It didn't have the crowd or the spirit. You can't recreate a once-in-a-lifetime experience.

And as soon as that speech was over, we jumped into our car and drove all night to get home because all the guys had to go to work the next day. When we pulled up at Assumption High School, I walked into the classroom fifteen minutes before the first class, and I had an interesting experience to talk about. The march gave me the impression of a religious experience. There was so much understanding among the people and a feeling of unity. Everyone was friendly. It seemed like we were witnessing a great religious procession for justice, peace, and unity for the whole world. I was deeply moved by that experience.

Fr. Mottet drew hope and inspiration from people who did things to change the world. Hearing Martin Luther King, Jr.'s "I Have a Dream" speech from his place near the front of the throng on the National Mall imprinted him with passion for a better world. His dad was a dreamer, and Fr. Mottet was attracted to dreamers, but he was only interested in dreams if there was a plan to make them happen.

In 1964, after studying four or five summers in the Chicago area, I got a master's degree in theology at Dominican House of Studies in Riverside, Illinois. I lived in a rectory that was south of the home of one of the mob bosses. When I drove by his house with my brother, I said, "This big crook can buy a house here, but an African American saint couldn't rent a house."

I learned so much during that time. I met priests who were doing great work for social and racial justice, and I wanted to do what they did. In Chicago, Msgr. Reynold Hillenbrand gave the most important speech I've heard in my life. He spoke on institutional change. A lot of people think food baskets will change the world, but they're wrong. Msgr. Hillenbrand put the liturgy together with social justice and institutional change. If you try to do institutional change and social justice without this liturgical understanding, it doesn't work. The connection is essential, and without it, social justice work goes off in wacky directions. I saw it as the way apply gospel teaching to the secular order and avoid the mistakes of atheistic communism and secular socialism.

By "institutional change," Fr. Mottet meant changing the root causes of social and racial injustices rather than addressing the symptoms. He believed lasting change was possible only by getting at the real problems. Institutional change became the cornerstone of Fr. Mottet's thinking. It built on the "cut of mind" he had adopted in Young Christian Students. Observe, judge, and act gave him a practical way to apply the gospel and change his world, at first in small ways. The concept of institutional change linked with liturgy gave him a broad principle that served as his guidepost. For Fr. Mottet, liturgy was both the driving force and the guardrail for his life's work.

It is right there in the Eucharist. First, you offer the bread and wine, and you ask Holy Spirit to come down and change this into the Body and Blood of Christ. The people receive the Eucharist. Then you pray over the people that they will be the church and go out and transform the world. "Go, the Mass is finished" doesn't mean go out and have coffee. It means go out and change the world.

Msgr. Hillenbrand's life-changing speech prepared me for the rest of my work. In 1969, I set up the Social Action Department at the Davenport Diocese office based on institutional change, and I used it all the time in my work at the Campaign for Human Development starting in 1978.

In Chicago I also learned one of the basic tools of community organizing, the one-on-one interview. I knew from Dale Carnegie that you need to remember people's names because it's music to their ears, and it gets their attention, but you also need to know a person's interest and passion. You reveal just enough of yourself to keep the conversation going while you get to know the person, especially their values. At some point, you make people see the difference between what they claim they believe and what they're doing. That's what agitation is, but agitation is not irritation.

The one-on-one interview became Fr. Mottet's primary tool for organizing, fundraising, and developing leaders. It was as ingrained as observe, judge, act. As a result, his contact network had far more depth and richness than the names and numbers in his rolodex trays. When he chose his top-ten lessons, one of them was: "You have to know people's interest and passion to get them involved."

I Got Martin Luther King, Jr. and Mother Teresa Through Personal Connections

My interest in papal documents goes all the way back to my Young Christian Students days. The last encyclical written by Pope John XXIII, was *Pacem in Terris,* which means "peace on earth." It came out following the 1962 Cuban missile crisis. During the crisis, the Pope facilitated secret communication between President Kennedy and Nikita Khrushchev, Premier of the Soviet Union. The encyclical was the inspiration, beginning in 1964, for the Catholic Interracial Council to award an annual Pacem in Terris Peace and Freedom Award.[16] It wasn't all about publicity. It was one more chance to get our message out and educate the community. Its purpose was to honor people who worked for peace and freedom.

Pope John XXII didn't facilitate secret communications, but he did play a role in averting catastrophe during the Cuban missile crisis. In October of 1962, American spy planes discovered that the Cuban and Soviet governments were building bases in Cuba for ballistic nuclear missiles that could reach most of the United States. Through back channels, President John Kennedy urged John XXII to speak out, and the Pope drafted a message that appeared in newspapers around the world. The headline in Pravda, the official Communist party newspaper, quoted Pope John XXIII: "We beg all governments not to remain deaf to this cry of humanity." This gave Soviet Premier Khrushchev a way to withdraw and be seen as a man of peace. The United States made concessions, and Khrushchev agreed to withdraw the missiles. The Pope's intervention was one of many factors that averted the crisis, but Khrushchev publicly expressed his gratitude to the Pope.

The Pacem in Terris Award added a lot of work on top of everything else we had to do, but it brought famous people to the Quad Cities. I worked through friends to get most of the early recipients to come. The people I met were so humble. They didn't brag about themselves. They talked about their work and their ministry. I have so many memories of the people who came for the award, but I'll only mention four: John Howard Griffin, Martin Luther King, Jr., Dorothy Day, and Mother Teresa.

Pacem in Terris *called for an end of the arms race, a reduction of weapons stockpiles, and banning of nuclear weapons.* Pacem in Terris *put Catholic social teaching into a global context based on common good that was accessible not just to Catholics, but also to non-Catholics and people of other faiths. It emphasized human rights and obligations, which included social and economic rights in addition to civil and political rights.*[17]

Fr. Mottet invested a great deal of effort over many years in the Pacem in Terris Awards, and it was something he was proud of. Giving honor was important to him. The recipients were all people who were changing the world, the kind of people he sought out.

The first Pacem in Terris Award in 1964 went posthumously to President John F. Kennedy. We read a letter from his widow Jacqueline Kennedy during the ceremony. John Howard Griffin, the author of *Black Like Me*, also received the award and spoke at the ceremony. He knew the Toneys and had stayed in their home. He and I clicked and became good friends. Griffin opened doors for me and provided inside information. He was quite an intervener. The FBI called him when there was an uprising in a city because they knew he had the trust of both Blacks and Whites. When they sent him into a Black community, he helped the FBI and police understand what was going on there.

In 1959, John Howard Griffin underwent medical treatments to darken his skin. For six weeks he travelled the South personally experiencing and documenting Jim Crow segregation. He was shocked by the level of prejudice, oppression, and hardship everywhere he went. In 1961, he published Black Like Me *to tell his story.*

We got Martin Luther King, Jr. to Davenport in 1965 through my friend Matt Ahmann. I called him in Chicago and asked how we could get King to Davenport. Matt said, "He owes me a big favor because I delivered all those priests and nuns down in Selma to march with him. I'll try to get him for you." He called King's assistant, and we got Martin Luther King, Jr. to come. It was during a historic flood in the Quad Cities, and one of his assistants, who saw the news about the flood, called at midnight from Los Angeles to say he didn't think they should come. I said, "There's no problem. We took your word for what was going on in Selma. You take my word for what's going on here. The airport is high, the bridges are high, and the Masonic Temple where the ceremony will be held is up on a hill."

He came, and it was a tremendous experience. His life was being threatened every day. People mocked him, even his friends, so he needed bodyguards. We hired policemen to guard him, and he had a police escort from the airport to Davenport. The Davenport police met him at the foot of the bridge. We had a dinner at the Masonic Temple, one of the biggest places in Davenport. He said, "You can tell we're making some progress when a Catholic Interracial Council gives an award to a Baptist minister named Martin Luther King, Jr., and it takes place in the Masonic Temple."

That brings up a lifelong regret. Matt Ahmann asked me to go to the march from Selma to Montgomery in 1965. He was trying to get all the priests and nuns he could, but I was working in a parish in the Rockford Diocese on weekends. I had such a sense of duty and couldn't get anybody to take my place, so I didn't go to the Selma march. Later Matt called me and said, "Did you see the news about that beating when they crossed the Edmund Pettis Bridge?" I regret that to this day that I didn't go to Selma.

When the film *Selma* was released, Art and Suzy took me to see it. I love crab legs, so we had dinner at Red Lobster before the show. I didn't talk much after the film. When we got back to Kahl Home, the doors were already locked, and I had to call for help to get in.

Some people believe Dorothy Day was the most important American Catholic. During the Depression, she usually stopped in Davenport when she was travelling the Midwest because she had a lot of friends at St. Ambrose College. On one of her first visits, a priest on campus gave her his car to drive home. In 1972, I knew she was passing through, and I called the woman who travelled with her to invite Dorothy Day to receive the Pacem in Terris Award. She accepted, and I got a group of Catholic Interracial Council people together and met with her in the dining room at St. Ambrose. At the time, the award was a necklace. I tried to put it on her, and it fell on the ground. She said, "That just proves that I shouldn't have it."

Dorothy Day is one of two of our awardees who is up for canonization, and there will be more. Six of them got the Nobel Peace Prize. I went to her funeral in New York. Her coffin was homemade, a simple pine box, and the pallbearers were her granddaughters. Her staff went around the neighborhood to the churches and asked for candle stubs. They put them all together and created that big candle. It was so appropriate.

Dorothy Day was a major influence in Fr. Mottet's life. Along with Peter Maurin, she founded the Catholic Worker houses. Fr. Mottet started and lived in several of them. He followed in her spiritual footsteps when he went to Washington, D.C., and prayed a prayer like hers in the same place where she prayed. He talked often about his desire for her to be canonized.

The thing I noticed about Dorothy Day and Mother Teresa was every time they opened their mouths, wisdom came out. When Mother Teresa came for the Pacem in Terris Award in 1976, we had a simple supper at Assumption High School. Before that, the ceremony was in hotels, and the hotels made all the money. As Mother Teresa walked down the hall, a young lady ran out and said, "Mother Teresa, I'm so and so. I've been writing to you." Mother Teresa said, "You ready to go?" When the young lady said she would go and pack her suitcase, Mother Teresa said, "If you need to pack your suitcase, you don't belong in the order." That was the end of that.

Two years later, when I went to Washington, D.C., to work for the Campaign for Human Development, Mother Teresa wrote me a letter thanking me for working among the poor. That letter is one of my prized possessions. I have it framed on the wall. When Mother Teresa was invited to the Reagan White House, a meal was served, but to teach them a lesson, she never ate a bite.

I Felt Like I Had Died and Gone to Heaven

One day while I was teaching, a pain came into my gut. It was excruciating. At first, it was diagnosed as colitis. Dr. Motto said, "Give me a week-long schedule of your life." I told him I went to bed at eleven o'clock and got up at five. I ran Young Christian students with thirteen groups and worked on civil rights with the Catholic Interracial Council. I taught high school and worked in a parish on weekends. I was trying to save the whole world in ten years. Dr. Motto said, "It's no wonder you're sick. You're trying to do the work of three men," but I loved all of it. Dr. Motto was a good counsellor. He said, "Learn to recognize the signs that you are getting too tense. Go out to dinner or go to a movie. Relax." I learned to do that, and it was very helpful. I also had to learn to pay attention to the Holy Spirit.

Fr. Kamerick taught me to report to the bishop every year to tell him what I was doing and ask for permission for the next year. I went to Bishop Hayes in 1966 and said, "I've been teaching adolescent boys for ten years. I would like to work with adults, and I want to work in the Davenport area so I can continue to work with the Catholic Interracial Council." I don't know if I said it, but I felt that if you work with adolescents all day, you start thinking like them. When I gave a homily on the weekend, everything was in educational mode and broken down to a high school level of understanding.

Bishop Hayes said, "Well, young man, I'll have to be careful where I put you," but he didn't put me anywhere. The appointments came out and my name wasn't on the list. He was eighty-one years old, so he probably forgot. I had already moved my books out and given up the weekend job I loved. I called Msgr. Dingman, and related all these things to him. He was kind of the inside man who understood our mentality and told us how to operate within the structure of the Church. He already knew about it, and there was nothing he could do. That began my dark night of the soul.

The dark night of the soul concept dates back centuries in written accounts of mystics and visionary figures in several religions. It is usually described as a passage through a wilderness into new understanding and opportunities. Sometimes the dark night lasts for years and reoccurs later. Fr. Mottet's year-long dark night experience was relatively short. He never again experienced anything like it. It left him open and ready for things that were about to happen.

It was painful that people called me and my fellow priests "young Communist priests" when all we were doing was running Young Christian Students. I felt like I was under a cloud because of the views of parents and administrators. I knew we made Bishop Hayes nervous, but he let us go ahead if what we were doing appeared in a papal encyclical or church document. Later when Bishop O'Keefe came, he told me we made all the bishops nervous.

During that dark night, I had a hard time praying. Someone taught me to play three chords on the guitar, and I put songs to music the best I could. I celebrated Mass at the Humility novitiate on Tenth Street, which was a big outlet for me. I could celebrate Mass every day and preach to those novices and their directors. I transferred recordings onto a large tape of the Bible, especially the New Testament, and I listened to that while I was driving. It was one of the ways I kept my sanity. The only way I could pray was with those few guitar chords.

I knew what it must feel like to wake up in the morning and think, "I married the wrong person. What future is there?" I told my oldest brother how I felt. The Chancellor and Assistant Chancellor at St. Ambrose commiserated with me. I was so arid. Dry. The scriptures, those recordings, and the Mass saved me. I took a part-time job in the Peoria Diocese on weekends, and that helped. I learned later that my students didn't know I was in that dark night.

It is tempting to think that Fr. Mottet was depressed as a response to job dissatisfaction, but he didn't talk about his experience in emotional terms. His description was entirely spiritual and framed in terms of loss of direction, purpose, and sense of God's presence. He didn't say he was sad or unable to carry out his responsibilities. I don't recall Fr. Mottet ever saying he was depressed.

Bishop Hayes retired in 1966. Bishop O'Keefe from Minnesota was appointed to replace him and installed in 1967. I went to his welcome reception in January at the Black Hawk Hotel. The first chance I got, I asked him for permission to move into the ghetto. I would still be teaching, but I would have those Black community relationships. He said, "I know why you want to do that, but I'm not giving you permission." At least he understood.

One night, I was driving home from the Toneys with Bishop O'Keefe, and he said, "I would like to have you go to graduate school and study social work." When he said that, it was the end of my dark night of the soul. I felt like I had died and gone to heaven. He told me I could take courses at the University of Iowa that summer or go to conferences on social and racial justice. It was an easy decision. I wanted the summer off to go to those conferences. That's how I got all the avant-garde ideas, things on the cutting edge.

Fr. Mottet's hope, direction, and purpose were restored almost instantly. He knew that God had intervened, and he could see a way forward that was far beyond the request Bishop Hayes had ignored.

Chapter 7

The Lord Can Do Anything He Wants--Tell Him to Go Right Ahead

In 1967, I enrolled in the Social Work department at the University of Iowa. It was my first time in a secular university, and it was fun. I wore my collar the first few days so students would know who I was. Everybody had to introduce themselves. They said, "I'm so and so," and they said whether they were married. I said, "I'm single, and I intend to stay single." They all laughed. I had to let them know because there were women in the class. After that, I bought the loudest red shirt I could find. I went to an event where one of the faculty members said, "That's about as red as it can get." I wanted to make a switch from black. I was older, and I had a lot of experience. I was elected president of the class, which surprised me.

During my graduate school days, I took a couple of carloads of students to march for fair housing with Fr. Jim Groppi in Milwaukee, Wisconsin. Fr. Groppi rallied a group of young African American men, who marched along like soldiers to protect the protesters. When a police car came, the marchers were trained to stand in front of the car and look the policemen right in the eye until the next group of marchers arrived. That was his way of keeping them safe. We marched through the white neighborhoods where there was so much hatred. People threw whiskey and beer bottles from tall buildings, and they crashed on the street. I was so tense the next morning I could hardly get up or walk. I think they saved their worst for priests and nuns. The Justice Department said that Groppi's disciplined marches kept Milwaukee from having a riot. The marches resulted in a city ordinance for Open Housing in December 1967. Groppi later dropped out of the priesthood.

Ed Chambers started Saul Alinsky's training school in Chicago in 1968, and I attended the first session along with some graduate school classmates. Some of Alinsky's work turned me off because there was so much bad language. Alinsky was used to raising hell wherever he went, but he taught agitation, not provocation. Agitation is getting a person to think about something in a new way by bringing up objections and things they never thought of before. It takes a lot of training. When I went to Alinsky's school, he didn't say any of the things conservatives always accuse him of. I thought he was down to earth. He received the Pacem in Terris Award in 1969.

Ed took over when Alinsky died. He turned community organizing into a profession with good training and a decent salary. One of his main points was the distinction between private relationships and public relationships. This is one of the least understood keys of organizing. Private relationships are family and close friends. You stick with them no matter what happens. If they go to prison, you visit them. If they become alcoholic, you try to help them heal. If they are in another political party, you argue with them. Private relationships are permanent. Public relationships are with politicians, corporate executives, mayors, governors, and so forth. In public relationships, there are no permanent friends and no permanent enemies. This distinction enables you to work together on issues where you have agreement. The distinction between public and private relationships is one of the most important lessons I learned, and it seems to be the hardest thing for Americans to understand. Not distinguishing between public and private relationships makes progress difficult.

The distinction between public and private relationships gave Fr. Mottet a way to sort through ethical controversies in a practical way and get things done. He was almost always pragmatic. That doesn't mean he ignored the ethics of issues or didn't take a stand, but he avoided the all-or-nothing approach that often leads to stalemate and stops progress. Near the end of his life, when I pressed him for his top-ten lessons, he listed "You must distinguish between private and public relationships."

Sliding into Home Plate

I was ordained for eleven years and in graduate school for social work when I got sick and went to the hospital. On my thirty-eighth birthday, Dr. Motto came in and said, "You've got colon cancer. It has metastasized, which means it has spread from the original site to the lymph system. I can't tell you how long you've got to live, but maybe six months. I've had people live longer than that." I was reconciled to the idea that I was going to die, and I knew it was best to have all my funeral arrangements made. Dr. Motto was sad to tell me, but I consoled him. I said, "Doctor, it's easier to die for Christ than live for Christ. I know. I've been trying." I had a good life up to then.

When Dr. Motto told me I had cancer, the image came to mind of a baseball player sliding into home plate. I laid in that hospital bed and thought, "I'm going to see the Lord face to face in a couple of weeks." At a retreat the week before, a thirty-seven-year-old priest was taken to the hospital with a stomachache. He had surgery, was full of cancer, and had three weeks to live. I thought I had three weeks, and the message that stuck in my head was: "Use the time you have. You never know how much time you have coming."

The doctor came a few days later and said, "I expect you to get out of here in a couple of weeks. I want you to go home, wear your loudest shirt, and thumb your nose at everybody. Then you come back to the hospital, and I'll start you on chemotherapy."

I was very peaceful. One of the scriptures that came to me was in Romans 8: "Nothing can ever separate us from God's love." *(Romans 8:38-39)* For a long time, I was haunted by another scripture that says that if you give up one family, you will receive a hundred more. *(Matthew 19:29)* I wondered how that could be. A "Family Only" sign was on the door of my hospital room, but I had no family within three hours. When I had the surgery, no family was there, but they came later from Ottumwa. After a while, the whole church walked through the door. Soon the nurses were saying, "If cancer doesn't kill him, all the visitors will." They had to change the sign to "Family Only. Absolutely No Visitors." That taught me the lesson that if you are celibate in the church, you belong to every family. The church is your new family of faith.

My sister talked to the doctor and asked how long I had. I knew I was a dead duck as far as he was concerned. I called Sr. Joanne and told her I needed to talk to her. She knew right away that it was bad news, and she came. Since I was in graduate school, I had no place to live. She invited me to live at Marycrest College. They taught home economics in the basement of one of the halls in what they called "the model apartment." They put me there. I had a bedroom and a bathroom, and I was the model.

I remember going to St. Ambrose to have dinner with priests who were close friends. They were talking about the Vietnam War. They felt politically powerful, and I felt so vulnerable. I felt powerless. I knew I could die any day, and I felt so close to eternity.

The plan was for me to take all the chemotherapy I could for six months. If I was still alive in November of 1968, I would go to Houston to Dr. John Stehlin, a famous surgeon who practiced "aggressive medicine." They open you more often and cut out more. Dr. Stehlin seemed to be successful with it. He was the number two man at MD Anderson Hospital. He had movie star patients and his own TV program.

Sr. Catherine's Miracle

On Thursday, August 15, 1968, the Feast of the Assumption of the Blessed Mother, I was asked to take Mass at the Carmelite monastery in Bettendorf. I only knew one sister there and had never been there for Mass. I had lost a lot of weight. I thought for sure I was dying, and I looked like it, but I went. By Sunday night, I had terrible back pains, and I wound up at the hospital. Every breath was like a stab wound. I couldn't get pain medicine because my doctor was out of town. I learned that I had pneumonia with pleurisy because the chemotherapy lowered my blood count and made me susceptible to pneumonia.

That week, I got a letter from Sr. Catherine at the Carmelite Monastery. She wrote: "It has been revealed to me in prayer that you will be completely healed via faith." I wrote back: "Sure, I believe the Lord can do anything he wants. Tell him go right ahead." I asked her later what happened. At communion, she had a deep experience in the presence of Christ that lasted for three days. Every time she tried to pray, all she could think of was me and my illness. She said, "Lord, I'm contemplative. All I'm supposed to be thinking about is you, and when pray, all I can think about is this sick priest. You must want me to pray for him." She prayed for three days. Every time she opened the Bible, it was to a complete healing. She thought that was what the Lord was telling her, and she wrote the letter.

I was at Charles and Ann Toney's house for dinner with Fr. Barry McDermott. He asked if I was going to Houston to Dr. Stehlin, and I said, "Barry, just get off my back. I won't call him." Then he walked over to the phone and made that call. The person in Dr. Stehlin's office said, "Have your doctor send the records down." I was scheduled to go to Houston in November. I thought I would be coming back in a box.

Before I left for Houston, the Catholic Interracial Council had a rally in Davenport. At the end of the rally. I was on the stage with Cesar Chavez, who was famous for organizing the farm workers and the grape boycott. As we chatted, I said, "I'm going to Houston tomorrow for cancer surgery." He turned to his aide and said, "Write that down." I stayed at John Howard Griffin's house the night before my surgery.

When I was in the hospital on Thanksgiving Day, in walked Cesar Chavez and two or three farm workers. That was tremendous loyalty. The Catholic Interracial Council supported his grape boycott, and he repaid the favor by visiting me in the hospital.

Fr. Mottet placed great importance on friendships. Two famous men, who had become his friends, were there in Houston when he needed them. Both were Pacem in Terris Award recipients. Griffin was the author of Black Like Me, *and Chavez was an influential civil rights activist and founder of the United Farm Workers.*

Dr. Stehlin opened me up from stem to stern and found no cancer. They gave me a clean bill of health. When John Howard Griffin broke that news to me, I said, "That's Sr. Catherine's Miracle." It was the Feast of St. Catherine, and Griffin was in Mass while I was in surgery."

The opportunity that ended Fr. Mottet's dark night of the soul seemed to be cut short by a terminal cancer diagnosis, but he felt peaceful. When Dr. Stehlen found no cancer, it was completely unexpected, but Fr. Mottet talked about it as though it were perfectly normal. Sr. Catherine's miracle had a profound impact on the rest of his life. His tell-the-Lord-to-go-right-ahead trust never faltered. A Quad-City Times article in September 2005 quoted him as saying, "Life becomes precious, friendships become precious, time becomes precious. That's the way we should live, with one foot in eternity, but it's hard to do." [18]

A nun, who was a nurse at the hospital, brought all her nurses to my room for Mass when she got off at three o'clock. I had to lie in bed since I had a laparotomy. My whole stomach was cut open. One of the sisters came in and said, "Do you think this a proper place to have Mass?" I answered, "This is where all the suffering is going on. Yes, I think this is appropriate."

My experience of the power of prayer started me into the healing ministry, and I've been in it ever since. I'm convinced that the Lord wants a lot more healing to go on. Healing is an answer to prayer. Anyone can pray. We all should, especially parents for their children and children for their parents. I've also learned the power of the Holy Spirit in our lives. When He went back to heaven, Jesus promised He would send the Holy Spirit. That's how He works in us and through us today. After the last supper, He said, "You will do the same and even greater works than me." That is only because we are given the power of the Holy Spirit. Jesus was one person who lived thirty-three years and travelled only as far as he could walk, about forty-five miles in any direction. Today there are millions of Christians, and we have all kinds of modern conveniences. The Holy Spirit works through people. He transforms people so they can go out and transform the world.

While he was in the hospital, Fr. Mottet started growing a beard, which he had for the rest of his life. His miraculous healing gave him a renewed sense of empowerment. His understanding of the Holy Spirit's power was about to deepen along with his opportunities to change the world.

PART THREE

Developer

How did a local activist scrambling for money end up with national influence and millions of dollars at his disposal? How did he later restore and transform a large inner-city parish and neighborhood? How did he make a successful transition from activist and organizer to developer of organizations and leaders?

After his miraculous cancer healing, Fr. Mottet's world expanded exponentially. The lessons he learned deepened and accumulated. Although his focus shifted to his role as developer, he was always the playmaker implementing strategies, and he still operated with the mindset and skills of a community organizer. Once Fr. Mottet learned a lesson, he used it for all it was worth all the way to the end. He saw his gradual shift to developing people and organizations as a natural and practical way to change the world.

From 1968 to 2005, Fr. Mottet faced his greatest challenges. Fast-paced developments happened concurrently on multiple fronts. When he talked about his exciting life as a priest, this is what he meant. Until 1978 when he left Davenport, he was involved in the Catholic Interracial Council, the new Social Action Department of the Diocese of Davenport, the Catholic charismatic renewal, social action initiatives that spread beyond Davenport, the startup and funding of Catholic Worker houses, and the founding of Senior Iowans and Project Renewal. He recruited remarkable people and developed effective teams, and he conceived the two feet model for social justice that became the social action paradign of the United States Conference of Catholic Bishops.

While he is in Washington, D.C., from 1978 to 1985, he led a multi-million-dollar national organization while he simultaneously started and lived in Catholic Worker houses. He exemplified his two feet model through his solidarity with poor people and his lifestyle choices. He traveled the nation educating groups and raising funds to develop organizations that worked for institutional change.

In 1985, he returned to Davenport where he lived the rest of his life. He experienced miracles, opposition, heartache, and more health problems, but he still called Sacred Heart Cathedral and its decaying inner-city neighborhood "the luckiest thing that ever happened to me." His preference for interfaith action showed up in the multiple organizations he founded that still operate today. His twenty years at Sacred Heart were bracketed by the pain of the clergy sex abuse scandal.

Chapter 8

It's Amazing What You Can Do

When I came home from Houston in 1968 with a clean bill of health, I wanted to go to work. I missed the cycle of the two-year program at University of Iowa, and finishing would take a long time. I was on fire with Vatican II, which ended in 1965, and the avant-garde combination of social justice and spirituality.

After Bishop O'Keefe's installation in 1968, people in Davenport wanted to know about his plans. He said, "My plan is to implement Vatican II. The Church is moving. We're moving from in-house out into the world." His statement was a wide-open door for me. After Vatican II, priests tried to get religious lay people to transform the social order through the special movements. Today we get them into church and make them lectors, deacons, music ministers, and youth ministers, but we should be training them to transform the social order and work for justice and peace.

When Fr. Mottet said he was "on fire," he meant he was inspired, energized, and convinced he was headed in the right direction. He was like a man driving a high-performance car, and the light had turned green. The Vatican II directive for the church to reach out into the world and Bishop O'Keefe's readiness to implement it in the Davenport Diocese seemed like the perfect setup for him.

In his first year in Davenport, Bishop O'Keefe put out an annual letter on civil rights focused on housing. I knew the tricks of the trade, so I sent it to the *National Catholic Reporter*, and it went nationwide. A bunch of realtors called Bishop O'Keefe and said, "Why are you writing about this?" They put pressure on him. I got a call from a priest friend in St. Paul, Minnesota, who said, "What did you do to Jerry O'Keefe? He was the chancery mouse around here, and now he's sending letters on civil rights and getting national publicity." It's true that Bishop O'Keefe was usually very quiet, but a priest who worked with him in Minnesota gave me a warning: "If he ever gets the idea that you are a nut, you've had it."

Housing has always been an issue. Davenport realtors got a law passed to require a sixty percent vote for authorization of any federal housing. It's hard to get fifty-one percent, let alone sixty percent, so the Catholic Interracial Council tried to change that law. I went to the president of the Iowa Realtors Association to talk about repealing the law. I started by telling him that my part-time job as a college freshman was scrubbing floors for him. He was so surprised that he said, "I won't support this, but I'll not fight it."

There were probably other reasons for the realtor's position, but the floor-scrubbing story is an example of Fr. Mottet's reliance on relationships, and it seems to have worked.

I sent a lot of letters, but personal contact is better. In the early days of the Catholic Interracial Council, we weren't politically smart. We packed the council chamber with people, which was good, but we didn't meet one-on-one with the aldermen. It was hard to compromise when we didn't know their positions and self-interest. Personal contact is better. You need to know the right people to talk to and then go talk to them personally. You make an appeal based at least partly on their self-interest and passion.

Priests earned about fifty dollars per month, but we worked weekends in a parish, which meant we could afford a car. We went to a doctor who gave us free medical care. When I was ordained in 1956, the diocese had no retirement policy, but a priest's dad, who was in the investment business, gave me good advice: "If you just set aside ten dollars per month, you'll be surprised how much it will grow," and it did.

Since Bishop O'Keefe turned me down in 1968 when I asked to move into the ghetto, I decided to hire a nun to work there, and I needed to pay her salary. My mutual fund had grown to fourteen thousand dollars on my small consistent investment, and I cashed it in to hire the nun. That blew my retirement account.

The Catholic Interracial Council still had some of the money we raised at Martin Luther King, Jr.'s banquet, which gave me the courage to hire the nun. I told the Humility sisters what I wanted to do, and they found a nun to work in the ghetto and represent the Catholic Interracial Council. She lived in the basement apartment at Charles Toney's house. The nun I hired, along with a lay woman, started the Sixth Street Center in a big empty building that had been a grocery store. She invited all the neighborhood kids to come. They also worked with the parents.

I spent all that money, but it was a wise investment. Everybody else worked as volunteers, which proves you can do a lot with volunteers and a small amount of seed money.

Throughout his life, Fr. Mottet was able to start with a little and do a lot. He called the amount of money he needed to get started on a project "seed money." It sounds risky, but it always worked for him. It wasn't magic. He worked hard and had help from his friends.

Like I Had Been Stabbed with a Sword

While I lived in the model apartment at Marycrest College, I made a cursillo, the first one in the diocese. A team of people came from Dubuque and other towns. The cursillo gave me a new prayer life. The Bible opened up, and I felt like reading it all the time. Scripture wasn't history. It was a love story between God and His people.

In the summer of 1967, I started reading about the charismatic renewal and learned some of the background. Starting in 1889, an Italian nun wrote several letters to Pope Leo XIII about her concern for unity and the renewal of the church. Just before the turn of the century, she asked him to invoke the hymn "Veni Creator Spiritus," which means "Come Holy Spirit." He dedicated the next century to the Holy Spirit.

On January 1, 1901, the Pentecostal movement broke out in the United States, not in a Catholic church, but in a Methodist Bible school in Topeka, Kansas. A young woman there said, "Look in the Acts of the Apostles. They prayed in tongues. Why don't we pray for those gifts?" They did, and they received the gifts. A Black minister from Los Angeles was there. He went back home and rented a little warehouse on Azusa Street. People experienced the gifts of the Holy Spirit, and Blacks and Whites prayed together. That was unheard of at that time. The news traveled, and people came from all over the world. That went on for three years with three services a day.

Mainline Protestant churches opened up, and then the Catholic Charismatic Renewal started in Pittsburgh at a Catholic college dedicated to the Holy Spirit. Some of the faculty went to a weekend retreat for faculty and students, and the Holy Spirit showed up in power. The Catholic Charismatic Renewal spread all over the world. It was electrifying. There are now at least two hundred million Catholics who have received the baptism with the Holy Spirit.

At first, I thought it was crazy. But I went to a Full Gospel Businessmen meeting at a hotel in Davenport. As I walked in the door, two women who were fallen-away Catholics said, "You can't be saved in the Catholic Church." I just laughed at them and walked on. The next day three or four people showed up to apologize. They said, "That should never happen at our meetings." I made a lot of friends at that Full Gospel Businessmen's group.[19] They were so happy a priest showed up. They stormed heaven praying for me.

About that time, I went to a summer conference in Chicago. The participants were in a swimming pool during a break. I asked a Canadian Jesuit scripture scholar if he believed people were receiving the gifts of the Holy Spirit. After a long pause, he said, "Yes I believe it." That opened me up. I thought that if he believed it, it must be real. A Davenport woman, who had received the baptism of the Holy Spirit at Notre Dame, started a little prayer group at her house in Davenport. I went there, and they prayed like crazy for me.

An ordained Methodist minister from Des Moines was the person who prayed over me for the baptism of the Holy Spirit. She got the list of all the Catholics who had made the cursillo. She knew we were sitting ducks because cursillo brings you right up to the baptism of the Holy Spirit. She came to my office to talk, but I said, "This isn't a very good place to talk. You come to where I live at Marycrest College." When she came, I had five reasons why I didn't need that. I said, "I'm baptized. I've been confirmed. I spent four years in a seminary, and I have years of theological training. I am an ordained priest." I kept resisting. Finally I said, "Besides, it's hillbilly theology."

She said, "Have you got a Bible? Open it to Second Corinthians, chapter one." I started reading the passage, and I couldn't finish it because I was convicted by the Holy Spirit of spiritual pride. I stopped. It was like I had been stabbed with a sword. I can't remember what happened after that, but I got two or three words in tongues.

After Jesus' resurrection and before his ascension into heaven, he told his followers to wait for the baptism with the Holy Spirit. (Acts 1:5) It is considered a starting point for using charismatic gifts. When Fr. Mottet talked about his baptism of the Holy Spirit, he was not referring to a once-in-a-lifetime experience, but to a filling with the Holy Spirit that was ongoing.

The Apostle Paul went to Athens and tried unsuccessfully to match wits with the great philosophers. He learned his lesson. When he went to Corinth, he simply said, "I came to give you the good news of Jesus Christ and the power of the Holy Spirit." He used the term "the convincing power of the Holy Spirit." *(First Corinthians 2:4)* The greatest revolution in the Catholic Church would be to understand the convincing power of the Holy Spirit. The Holy Spirit can change lives and get people off drugs and alcohol. Holy Spirit can heal. Eastern churches never lost this, but the western church lost it. We need to re-discover the gifts of the Holy Spirit and pray for healing. There will not be a new evangelization unless there is a new Pentecost.

Pope John Paul II began using the term "new evangelization" in 1983, and it was extended by Pope Benedict XVI. It has three qualities: new means, new expressions, and new ardor. The new evangelization calls Catholics to be unafraid of the old, unafraid of the new, and courageous in following the Holy Spirit. Pope Benedict XVI emphasized the need for profound intimacy with God.[20]

The charismatic renewal was interfaith from the start, but the biggest group that shows up at international meetings is Catholic. We are indebted to Protestants. We need to be filled over and over. It is an ongoing process. I pray in tongues every day, not just in urgent situations. It's just automatic for me. In the car when I'm driving is a perfect place.

You Look Like You're Living in Considerable Comfort

When I first got cancer, everybody thought I would become a Trappist because I spent so much time at the Carmelite and Trappist monasteries. I thought I was very close to eternity, and I went there to pray every chance I had.

While I lived at Marycrest after my surgery, a nun from Ottumwa told me about an Ignatian retreat she made, and I knew I needed to make one even though I had been against anything Ignatian. In a dream, I was instructed to call a priest in Des Moines about making a retreat. He was a young Jesuit, who had just been through surgery himself. When he came out of surgery, the only scripture he could think of was Micah 6:8: "What doth the Lord required of thee, but to do justly, and to love mercy, and to walk humbly with thy God?" Micah is the prophet of social justice.

That priest directed me to Fr. Gene Merz, and I made my first three-day retreat. After that, I made a retreat with him at least once a year. It was wonderful. When Fr. Merz moved from Des Moines to St. Paul, Minnesota, I travelled there for retreats with him. He was my spiritual director for thirty-five years.

My life was full of opportunities and challenges, but I scheduled one day a month for complete privacy at the Carmelite monastery. The Russians call this practice "poustinia." You go for twenty-four hours and take nothing but a jug of water, a loaf of bread, and your Bible. You read scripture and pray. I went in with questions about what direction we should go, and I came home with answers. I've been asked how the answers came. Some people get a word of knowledge, but I got a hunch, just an idea that it would be alright to go a certain way.

In 1968, I moved to the rectory of St. Joseph's Church at Sixth and Market, and I said, "Lord, I have only one night that I haven't committed, and I'll give you that." I asked the pastor if I could start a prayer group, and he said, "Yeah, go ahead. I have nothing against prayer." It was a crack in the door, but I'm sure it was the talk of the town. It was the second prayer group in the diocese. The first was at the Catholic Students Center in Iowa City. I called a group of people I knew from social and interracial justice work. Quite a few were

Hispanics or people who worked with Hispanics. We sang songs and read scripture in the living room at St. Joe's. We always prayed for healing. A bunch of seminarians from St. Ambrose came, but it was mostly social workers and people in social ministry. Out of that first group, three young men went to seminary.

At the beginning of each meeting, I read from the book of Hebrews: "In the early days I spoke to you through the prophets and so forth, but now I speak to you through Jesus Christ." *(Hebrews 1:1-2)* Then a nun from the Carmelite Monastery gave a teaching. It was very ad hoc. Later we developed a six-week course. Psychologists say it takes six weeks to change your ideas and change your life.

We welcomed people of all denominations, and some ministers occasionally came. They were amazed that Catholics got into charismatic renewal. The Humility Sisters started a house of prayer on Tenth Street, and half a dozen people went there to spend a weekend. They asked for the gifts of the Holy Spirit, and their prayer was answered. When they came back, we became more charismatic. We sang a lot and prayed in tongues.

Eventually, we outgrew the rectory, and we met in the sanctuary of St. Joe's parish. One time, a Protestant minister came, and after the meeting he said, "I appreciate your music, but I realize how anti-Catholic I am." The sanctuary had the old Catholic altar with a facade and statues of the saints and things like that. Sometimes people from the parish came and sat in the back pew to listen. I imagined they were saying, "What's that strange group up there doing?"

Steve Goebel came as a conscientious objector in 1968. After a week, he still hadn't found a place to stay, and I was trying to scrounge up money for him. Finally, I said, "You can stay with us at St. Joe's rectory."

So much was happening in 1968. The anti-Vietnam war movement, which began three years earlier, led to massive protests after the Tet Offensive. Public disillusionment grew as costs and casualties mounted. Anti-war demonstrations with up to one hundred thousand protesters took place. Vietnam war protest songs were popular.

Forty thousand young men were being drafted each month. The Selective Service System included the classification of "conscientious objector," a person who is opposed to military service on the basis of beliefs. In 1968 and beyond, many young men, who were opposed to serving in the Vietnam war for reasons of conscience, were placed by local draft boards in the Selective Service Alternative Service Program for a period of twenty-four months. They worked in jobs that had to make a meaningful contribution to the national health, safety, and interest. Fr. Mottet saw an opportunity to change the world, and he took it. He created a conscientious objector program that had twenty young men serving throughout the diocese. He had big plans for what could be accomplished. Steve Goebel was one of those conscientious objectors.

St. Joe's was the old St. Kunigunda's German-Catholic parish on the west side. It was old style and rundown. Steve was from a big family in a small town where he shared a room with two of his brothers. The rectory seemed spacious and comfortable to him. I still laugh about the day Steve said to me, "You look like you're living in considerable comfort here." I was trying to live humbly in what was probably the most modest rectory in the diocese, and it was still too good.

A week after Steve moved into the rectory, I said, "By the way, Steve, I'm going to have a prayer meeting on Sunday. I would like you to come. It's a charismatic prayer meeting." Steve had been in graduate school at Notre Dame when the charismatic renewal exploded there. He heard about the "Holy Ghost freaks with tongues of fire," but he stayed as far away as he possibly could.

From time to time, over two hundred people came to that prayer group. People came at a time of crisis when they were hurting. They came to get the encouragement and the energy they needed to go on. When they came, they signed in with their name, address, and phone number, and those lists are still in my files somewhere.

When I arrived at St. Joe's parish, everything was locked up. They kept everything perfect. The church was perfectly clean. The altar vestments and utensils were perfectly clean, but there was no outreach in the neighborhood, which had runaway poverty. Later, healing Masses started from there and went out to four or five parishes, but St. Joe's parish never opened like I always hoped. That parish would have thrived, but in the end, we closed it and sold the property.

What was happening was so powerful we thought it would spread to every parish in Davenport. That was a mistake our leaders made. We divided our leadership and spread it too thin. Still, our prayer group at St. Paul the Apostle has been going on for thirty-five or forty years.

We realized that charismatic renewal and the St. Joe's prayer group were one more way for Fr. Mottet to develop leaders and change the world. We interviewed Steve Goebel and heard his story about the prayer group.

> I'm living in the rectory. I have no money. I have no car. I don't know anybody in town except a couple of nuns. Am I going to say, "No, I'm busy?" I went downstairs to his charismatic prayer meeting. It was the first one, and about twelve people were there. It was nice, but I was a little uncomfortable. Nobody had done anything strange yet, but at the end of the meeting, one of the nuns turned to me and asked if I would like to go to the prayer room to be prayed over for the baptism of the Holy Spirit. It was so put-offish, but I couldn't explain why. I wanted to figure out why I didn't want to be part of this, so I left with several books from the book table, and I started reading. That changed my life. I had a personal experience with Jesus Christ. I had been raised a good Catholic. I was in the choir. I was an altar boy. I was at daily Mass. I had all the right trappings, but I did not have a lively awareness of the Holy Spirit's work in my life. That occurred simultaneously with Marv's impact on me in terms of changing the world. Later I did want to

be prayed over, and eventually I became a leader of the charismatic prayer group.

I didn't change my mind when Bishop O'Keefe refused to allow me to live in the ghetto. I had to have credibility. I knew that if I really cared about people who live in poverty, I could not live in prosperity, so I changed my lifestyle. I didn't take a vow of poverty because we are warned against taking vows. As Pope Paul VI put it in 1976, "Modern man listens more willingly to witnesses than to teachers, and if he does listen to teachers, it is because they are witnesses."[21] Because of my experiences in Chicago, I wanted to live in a Catholic Worker house.

Fr. Mottet's decision to live in solidarity with the poor was a personal choice, not a principle by which he judged others. We asked him once what he thought about our big, lovely house. He said simply, "Keep it."

A few other people were interested in a Catholic Worker house. A Notre Dame student was excited about a house that was for sale, but I didn't have money to buy a house. Instead, the owner of Republic Electric gave me a house at 806 West Fifth Street in west Davenport. He was happy, and so was I. In 1976, I raised the rest of the start-up money for the first Catholic Worker house, and I stayed there for a year. Eventually, I had to stop raising money for Catholic Worker houses because I needed money for social action programs. We didn't know any better. We were on a roll.

When we opened that first Catholic Worker house by the railroad track, it filled up in twenty-four hours. A whole subculture of people was homeless and just getting by. Once you open a center, word spreads. Our first guest at the house for men on West Fifth Street was Woodchopper, the most famous drunk in town, a great big guy. He lived in a camp on the riverbank and begged at St. Mary's convent. He rang the doorbell and ordered a sandwich or something and then looked in the window to see if they were coming with the sandwich. The housekeeper at St. Mary's had a special table and chair on the back porch where she fed homeless people.

When Woodchopper lived at the Catholic Worker house, he was sober for a year. He saved up his money and then went to the bars to buy everybody a drink. "When Woodchopper drinks, everybody drinks," he said, and he bought for the whole place. He claimed he got the name Woodchopper when he worked for Joe Kennedy, the president's dad. Kennedy made a lot of his money by importing Scotch whiskey, and Woodcutter's job was splitting oak for barrels of Scotch. When Woodchopper didn't show up one Christmas morning, I looked for him in all the bars in downtown Davenport. At first, I was surprised they were open, but people were in there. It was their second home, a social center. I found him and brought him back.

Woodchopper was something else. He had a Catholic background and came to Mass all the time. He was just part of the community. After I came home from Washington, D.C., in 1985, he died. We had a funeral Mass for him. Everyone in town knew him. People had so many stories. His death made the newspaper.

Bill Cribbs pointed out to us, near the end of his life, that Fr. Mottet didn't judge people. That made it possible for him to live in Catholic Worker houses in Davenport and later in Washington, D.C., and to befriend drunks and prostitutes, as well as well-known politicians. The core of his observe-judge-act cut of mind was judging situations, not people. Later in his life, when he faced unyielding opposition, he judged the actions, but not the people.

Chapter 9

Food Baskets Will Not Do It

In 1969, Bishop O'Keefe gave me permission to start the Social Action Department. People criticized him for it, but it was the perfect opportunity for me. Shortly after I started the Social Action Department, he made a decision that surprised a lot of people. He put Catholic Charities, which had a forty-year history, under the new Social Action Department. Catholic Charities fought that decision. A letter in *The Catholic Messenger* asked what qualifications or credentials I had. The writer knew I hadn't finished my Master of Social Work degree. I understood what was going on, so I didn't answer the letter. Catholic Charities missed the whole ball of wax in the sixties. I knew the future was not in charity. It was in justice.

Fr. Mottet's objection to Catholic Charities was that they provided services but didn't address root causes. He was fully committed to working for institutional change. If root causes don't change, the world doesn't change. This was his first fight, and it was a long one. A few years later, his two feet model showed how charity and justice work together.

I argued for institutional change with the Catholic Charities people in our Missouri, Iowa, Nebraska, and Kansas region, but they were the head of their empires. They were the big stuff in their dioceses. I argued that we needed to get to the cause of poverty and work for justice. Charity won't do it. Food baskets won't do it. It was an uphill battle. When I went to a Catholic Charities conference in Chicago, I walked into a room full of cigar-chomping monsignors who were cursing the war on poverty. I had my fill of it. I came home and told Bishop O'Keefe, "We're headed in the right direction. Let's go ahead."

"War on Poverty" is the unofficial name for legislation that was part of President Lyndon Johnson's Great Society, which expanded federal government roles in education, health care, and poverty reduction. Johnson introduced this concept in his State of the Union address in 1964.

When I started my job at Social Action in 1969, a priest who taught sociology at Ambrose, warned me about the woman in charge of Catholic Charities. He said, "That woman has run off a priest and two lay women with Master of Social Work degrees, and she'll run you off. I advise you to fire her as soon as you can."

Catholic Charities primarily handled adoptions, but because of abortion and birth control, adoptions dried up. United Way[22] hired a consultant who recommended a merger of Catholic Charities with Children and Family Services, which was a public agency. The bishop and the chancellor of St. Ambrose thought we wouldn't be good neighbors unless we went along with the United Way study, so I became the bad boy of Catholic Charities. Children and Family Services agreed not to send people for abortions, and we merged the staff. The Director of Children and Family Services took over as Director of the new Family Resources,[23] which is now a multi-million-dollar agency serving a large area of Iowa and Illinois.

According to their website, Family Resources' mission is "Supporting successful lives to build strong communities." The agency provides a wide range of services: survivor services, mental health and counseling, comprehensive care coordination, foster group care, foster and adoption, and after care services for youth who age out of foster care.

The woman in charge was mad. Running Catholic Charities is one of the biggest jobs in the diocese. Firing her was the most difficult thing I ever did. Her lawyer took action against Bishop O'Keefe. Several bishops were former Catholic Charities directors, and she got them to put the heat on Bishop O'Keefe for giving so much power to United Way. I still carry wounds from my fights with Catholic Charities.

I worked closely with my superiors, so it was all in order. They already had things against that woman because she didn't know how to work in the church. She planned things without their approval and then sprang it on them. I knew I had to get rid of her, but I walked on eggshells. Later, when I was recruited for a job in Washington, D.C., and Bishop O'Keefe had to give his approval, he said, "Anyone who can fire that woman can handle the job."

If You Want to Win a Race You Get the Best Racehorse You Can

I started the Social Action Department in January of 1969, and we hit the ground running. Our office was on the first floor of 410 Brady Street. I hired Betty Anderson to be our secretary. When we opened the door on the first day, I saw a bouquet of flowers, and I said, "Oh, someone's congratulating us for opening Social Action." Betty kept quiet, and I didn't find out until years later that her husband always sent her a bouquet of flowers on the anniversary of their first date.

Our interview with Betty Anderson was delightful. By then her husband had died, she had remarried, and her last name was Torry. Her quick mind and sense of humor matched Fr. Mottet's. It was easy to see why they worked so well together. They were both gentle, get-things-done people who valued results, not drama. They understood and respected each other. They both loved the work and thought it was fun. Betty said her memory was failing, but her recollections were vivid, and she charmed us.

We got our clearest picture of the beginning of the Social Action Department from Betty. She clearly enjoyed reminiscing about what it was like:

I worked with him from February of 1969 to October of 1992 or 1993. I have a blanket with the dates embroidered on it. I had never met Fr. Mottet, but one day he called me on the telephone. The bishop had asked him to consider opening a new department to serve people in need, but it wasn't a set thing yet. He sat by my Methodist pastor at a meeting and told him he needed someone to help him open a new office. He didn't have the faintest idea where to go. My pastor said, "I know someone who could do it, but she is very happy where she is." He gave him my name.

I didn't want to change my job. I was in the travel business, and I had moved up rapidly. The owner liked me, and I had a flare for the business. I loved it, but I knew I had to meet Fr. Mottet and think about it. We arranged to meet at the building where the office would be, an old building in downtown Davenport with no place to park. It wasn't for me. I got there before he did, and I was knitting a baby sweater. He walked in, looked at me, and said "Are you expecting?" I wasn't. He showed me around a big bare room with a dirty back room. The downstairs was a dirt floor. This was crummy stuff. I thought, "Well, poor people are used to this, and maybe we are trying not to be snooty."

He told me I would be his secretary to take telephone calls and whatever. I said I would go home and think about it, and by the way, what is the salary? It wasn't enough, so he had to get permission to give me more. I said a prayer and went to bed. You can't force it. I don't know why I felt I should do it, but I did, and I became the secretary to Marv Mottet. When I said yes, my husband was stunned, but whatever I wanted was fine with him. I told Marv I wasn't going to work anywhere I didn't have a place to park, so he arranged with the priest across the street at St. Anthony's for me to park in their back yard. That priest wasn't happy about it, but Marv got him to do it.

We rounded up some second-hand furniture, and we started out. We had this terrible old building with the toilets down wooden stairs--just toilets and dirt. You had to tell everyone when you were going down so they wouldn't come down on you. When you were on the toilet, these huge cockroaches came out, and I just hated them. It made me sick to my stomach. I wasn't going to step on them because I couldn't stand that crackling noise. I remember one coming at me lickety split, and I heaved a loose brick on it. I didn't hear the crack, so I knew he was digging in the soil. I went upstairs and said to Father, "You have the biggest feet. You need to go down and step on that brick." I made a little chart to put on the door. It had different sizes of cockroaches, and you were supposed to mark how many roaches you killed and what size. We all had fun with that one.

I learned one thing about Marv right away. He can't do what most women can do, which is multitask. He needed to concentrate on what he was doing. I found a glass or metal wall so we could cordon him off, and he could have privacy. I checked the phone, and if it was somebody he didn't need to talk to, I did the nasty stuff.

If something is wrong and needs to be fixed, Marv doesn't sit around and wait for somebody else to fix it. He does it. I'm sure I learned a lot. When you are with someone almost daily, it just seeps in. We always had something going on, so I never thought of it as work. I couldn't wait to get there. He gave me the opportunity to use the values I had for the benefit of other people, and he gave me free reign. I don't ever remember him bawling me out. Once or twice, we disagreed on how a newsletter should be done or something like that. A lot of times we added to each other's suggestions.

When I started the Social Action Department, Bishop O'Keefe kept calling us "social service," and I said, "No bishop, its social action, not social service. It's observe, judge, and act. We are going to get at the causes of poverty." I hired Frank Rhomberg, who had a background in business and worked with him and Betty Anderson to set our goals. The older priests said, "Don't make the mistake of the social gospel." I asked, "What's the mistake?" but I knew they meant the idea that we can create the Kingdom of God. It's important to understand that we cannot. We can cooperate with it or oppose it. Anything we do to work for peace and justice is contributing to the Kingdom. We cooperate with God's purposes by working for justice, peace, unity, love, and charity. We oppose the Kingdom of God by being selfish, violent, warlike, or hateful.

A couple of ladies loved to go to garage sales, but Betty couldn't stand them. We told them to buy things people might need, and we stored them in a garage. Then we sent them out to look for empty apartments at reasonable rates. This really helped people in Davenport because we were pushing for affordable apartments where they wouldn't get killed overnight.

Some people tend to see a big picture, and some people can only see part of the picture. We could see the big picture and what things had to happen to make that picture. Maybe it was because three of us were Chicago-ites. When we got something started, it was so exciting to see it peel off. Somebody else would start one like it. I worked with other agencies. It didn't make sense not to. If we had an extra table and somebody over there needed a table, we gave it them. When we had extra chairs, we made sure another agency got the chairs.

Our strategy was to research, plan, develop, and spin off. We didn't want to control the thing. We wanted someone to take it over. When we started a program in another diocese, we wanted an organization there to take it over. Someone asked me why they didn't just start it themselves. There could be lots of reasons. Maybe they didn't see the possibilities. When new things were starting in the diocese, we paid their phone bill for the first year. A little thing like a phone bill might stop their operation. We helped them get started, and then they could raise the rest of the money.

Fr. Mottet didn't claim altruistic motives for his sharing of resources. It was a practical strategy that made sense, advanced their goals, and contributed to God's Kingdom. One reason he was able to launch so many successful ventures was that he had no proprietary hold on things he started. "Observe, judge, and act" deepened to become "research, plan, and develop." "Spin off" was the multiplier effect.

Some people think God always gave me the right people at the right time, but it's not that simple. If you want to win a race, you choose the best racehorse you can, the person with the most experience or ability. I kept that in mind when I hired people. I looked for a doer, not a talker. Betty Anderson had a business background, and she was a whiz. I never found anybody who could match her. Betty, Frank Rhomberg, and I were like a wheel with three spokes. If one of us was missing, the wheel had a bump. We had planning meetings at Betty's house out in LeClaire. I said, "Frank, I'll dream up the dreams, and you figure out how we can do them." Frank went to the library and got a bunch of books on planning, which I would never have thought of.

Everybody in our office had cancer. I had it first, so I said I gave it to Frank.

To have a good team, you must give people freedom to use their talents. It's the same as on a basketball team. Get the ball to the guy who can put it through the hoop. Once when I had lunch with Frank Rhomberg, I said, "I feel like I'm holding you back." I probably was at the time, so I tried to turn him loose and let him use his talent. So much was happening. My day each month at the Carmelite Monastery gave me time to pray about all those things.

When Fr. Mottet became Executive Director of the Social Action Department, he was no longer the quiet man in the background. He was out front leading the way. He reveled in the opportunities, the action, and the people he recruited. He was proud of his ability to put together a team. That probably started when he suggested that his freshman classmates in Ottumwa start a basketball team at the YMCA. His ability to attract committed and effective people who could work together made him an effective organizer and developer. At the end of his life when he identified his most important lessons, he said, "Everything important I have achieved came from relationships."

When You Put Your Body on the Line People Want to Join You

I needed someone with a Master of Social Work degree, and I got lucky. After Vatican II, a lot of nuns wanted to work outside of churches. I knew a nun in Chicago who worked in a placement program for nuns. When I called her, she said, "I had just the person you need in here yesterday. I'll see if I can find her and send her off."

It was Sister Concetta Bendicent. She was raised in Chicago. Her mother died when she was about two. Concetta and her brother always looked out the window of their apartment and waved when their dad got off the train from work. Her brother fell out of the window and was killed. Concetta was five when she watched her brother die, and her dad put her in the Guardian Angel Orphanage which was operated by the Poor Handmaids of Jesus Christ. In 1969, Concetta was working at the orphanage. She thought they should reach out to the large number of Hispanic people who were moving into the neighborhood, but instead, they just built bigger walls. She took her problem to her spiritual director who said, "You gotta get out of here because this can drive you crazy." That's when she went in to see the Sister I was about to talk to.

Sr. Concetta came out to Davenport for her interview with a carload of nuns. I interviewed her, and I knew right away I wanted to hire her. She had that Chicago spirit and was impressed by the same things that impressed me. Since I was a relatively young priest hiring a young nun, they had warned her to be very proper. Concetta was a beautiful woman. She looked young, but I knew by her papers she was fifty.

She was a kindred spirit. We saw eye to eye. She could not have been better.[24]

Shortly after she arrived in 1970, Sr. Concetta got together the senior citizens who lived above the storefronts downtown after they lost their farms. They sat on benches along the street, and the nuns stopped and talked to them. We teased the nuns about propositioning all the old men in Davenport. The men talked about their problems, things like: "We can't cross the street because the yellow light turns too quick, and we're caught in the middle of the street."

Concetta got the Knights of Columbus, which was nearby, to have a weekly lunch for senior citizens. It was a simple meal of soup, a sandwich, a Twinkie, and a cup of coffee, but it was just what they needed. They were separated in those apartments, and they needed socialization. That lunch brought them together. Every week the noise got louder as they got to know each other. When a priest from Des Moines visited, I took him there. He said, "The Kingdom of God is in there." I thought it was a great insight. The people came together and enjoyed each other. They had love for each other, and they were eventually going to make some changes.

That is how Sr. Concetta started Senior Iowans, which later became the Commission on Aging for Senior Iowans. At that time, the Scott County Commission on Aging was what I call "a talking group." They accused Sr. Concetta and her two volunteers of organizing the dirty old men in Davenport. Seniors had less than fourteen seconds to cross the street at the traffic light they complained about. We brought grade school kids there, and they couldn't get across. We timed them.

Then we went to the city council to get this changed. A ninety-one-year-old blind woman, who walked with a cane, was one of forty or fifty elderly people who packed the chamber that normally had the four council members and maybe a newspaper reporter at a big table. We recommended a change in the traffic pattern, and the council members muttered to themselves around the table while they considered it. Our blind woman said, "Would you please speak up!"

They adjusted the timing of the traffic light. That was a small institutional change. We got our first Campaign for Human Development grant to spread the Senior Iowans model around the diocese.

Senior Iowans eventually became the Quad Cities Center for Active Seniors.[25]

After Sr. Concetta was in Davenport for a while, she said, "Whatever you've got, I want it." It was the baptism of the Holy Spirit. A verse in the Old Testament says there will be a day when ten people will grab the hand of a Jew and say, "Take me to your God. I've heard great things about your God." *(Zechariah 8:23)* I think that is how we should be as Christians. We should make people want what we have. As Pope Francis says, "Don't be a sourpuss."

Sr. Concetta attended our prayer group at St. Joe's, but she got cancer and had to leave for treatment in Chicago. A doctor friend in a hospital where she had worked gave her radioactive material to attack the cancer. When I visited her in the hospital, she looked like a corpse. It was like you could close the coffin door, but she rebounded and came back determined to give the rest of her life to the poor. I'll never forget what she said when she came back: "I left to go to the hospital in Chicago, and you were just a prayer group. I came home, and you're a community."

In 1972, as Sr. Concetta crossed the Centennial Bridge from Rock Island to Davenport, she saw church steeples two blocks apart, St. Mary's and St. Joe's. She said, "What really is the presence of the church in that neighborhood. What kind of presence is there?" As she walked to work, four or five children sat crying on the railroad track in front of what later became Nazareth House. She asked them what was wrong. When they said their dad was dying, she went into the house. He was having an epileptic attack. She helped the kids and then walked a block further where she found an elderly woman in a partially-burned-out house with rain coming through the roof. She knew that instead of building fences, you've got to reach out to people, so she got a little house in the neighborhood where she could serve the elderly and the children. She named it Project Renewal, and it is still there today.

At one time, Project Renewal had five houses with volunteers. People said, "You run that like a religious order." We had daily Mass in one of the houses. Concetta didn't want a lot of the administration. She organized Project Renewal with a one-and-a-half-page description she passed out. She tried to keep things simple.

Sr. Concetta was an excellent social worker. Multi-problem families drove me nuts. It was hard to know where to start. Concetta could take it apart one problem at a time, and she just picked at it. We got a ramshackle house. Several nuns from the Poor Handmaids came out for the summer and cleaned it out, fixed it up, and made it operational. The key idea for Concetta was presence. She was very impatient with the Poor Handmaids because the nuns had pantries full of food, but they were surrounded by hungry people. She insisted that her nuns not live above the people in the neighborhood and that what comes in the front door must go out the back door. She said, "You are not a social worker coming from the outside. You're the next-door neighbor." I worked closely with them and rented a house across the street. I helped people with their gardens and helped them buy houses.

Sister Concetta called her house "the Vine." In the first month, four young single women came to volunteer. The dudes in the neighborhood saw this and knocked on Concetta's door at midnight. They asked, "Hey, is this the Vine Street House?" There was a house of prostitution a block away on Vine Street. She slammed the door and called me the next morning to say, "We gotta change the name." I teased them about that, but I was great at thinking up names. We named it "Nazareth House." Mother Teresa stayed at Nazareth House when she came to receive the Pacem in Terris Award.

Carol Malinowski, a nice Polish girl, came from New York as the first to volunteer at Project Renewal. Three other volunteers came in a month. Carol became a very dear friend, and eventually her parents came and lived in a second-floor apartment next door. It became "the upper room." People are amazed that volunteers just came, but when you put your body on the line, people want to join you. It's contagious. Most volunteers were from Iowa, and they lived in the five houses we had. They all had part-time jobs to support themselves while they worked at Project Renewal.

Sr. Concetta had survived one cancer battle, but later, she had another cancer. Her order in Chicago sent a small hospital plane to take her to one of their two hospitals in Chicago. As she was taken on a stretcher from Mercy Hospital to the airplane, she reached out her hand to the social worker, whose name was Joe, and said, "Joe, someday we'll work together." I was so impressed. She had all her belongings in a little case about as big as my computer. I will never forget that. That's living simply.

According to cemetery records, Sr. Concetta died in 1979 at the age of sixty. By then, Fr. Mottet was in Washington, D.C.

Chapter 10

We Were Planning a National War on Poverty

In 1969, we offered work placements to twenty conscientious objectors through the Alternative Service Program. We had big plans for them. We only had part-time salaries for a couple of our conscientious objectors. We told the others we would cover them if they got a part-time job to support themselves and worked a minimum of twenty hours per week on what we wanted them to do. Those guys lived in poverty. They had to rent an apartment and so forth. They didn't make enough money, but it was good medicine for them.

Our twenty conscientious objectors worked with the poor all over the Davenport Diocese, which covers twenty-two counties. We sent them out to find needs. Our plan wasn't to build an empire. We intended to research, plan, and respond. That is basically the same thing as observe, judge, and act. They researched the needs of the poor. Then they planned a response and developed a program. It could be for the elderly, the homeless, adolescents, or anything they identified. We also assigned our conscientious objectors to other agencies. Their research led to senior citizens organizations, legal aid, and homes for adolescents in several counties. We started or helped start twenty-five programs around the diocese.

A lot of adolescents were in county jails. Our conscientious objectors interviewed them in the jails and came back with a report about what the kids said and a plan for how to help them. Sr. Concetta knew the Franciscan Brothers in Chicago, and we brought them out to help. People wonder how I got the Franciscan Brothers here, but they prayed about it, and they came. Each group home was an independent corporation. We made a down payment on a house and then raised the rest of the money.

Franciscans are the religious order started by St. Francis of Assisi. They are known for their service, humility, peacemaking, and contemplation based on ideals of poverty and charity. True to his goal to recruit the best people for the job and turn them loose to use their talents, Fr. Mottet relied on the experience and expertise of the Franciscan Brothers, who worked among the poor in Chicago. The residential homes they set up were like half-way houses for adolescents who needed help.

The colonel in charge of Selective Service came from Des Moines to check on us, and he was pretty upset with what we were doing. I could never remember his name, so I called him "Colonel Flyswatter." After a while, he realized we had a heck of a good program. We were planning a national war on poverty. We thought President Carter planned to start up the draft. If he had done that, we would have started a national program based on the Davenport plan, but he went to a volunteer army instead.

With a little creativity, Fr. Mottet's program met the eligibility requirements of the Alternative Service Employer Network, but the conscientious objectors assigned to Davenport were probably more empowered than what was considered normal.

All the time I worked in the Social Action Department, I went to the Carmelite Monastery in Bettendorf and continued the contemplative spirit of poustinia. Lay people urged me to get out of social action and focus on pastoral ministry because the charismatic renewal was so powerful. That pressure was hard because I was so deeply into social action. People's lives were being changed through charismatic renewal, so I considered it. It was unusual for a person involved in social justice work to be in the charismatic renewal. People didn't see how the two fit together. I have always considered myself a bit of a freak along that line, but one does not survive in social justice work without a strong spiritual base.

While I struggled with this conflict, Ezekiel's vision of dry bones became a blueprint for my future work. A local priest and twelve men who were neighborhood leaders started a religious community. They asked me to come and give a talk. I read about the valley of dry bones in Ezekiel 37 and applied it to their situation. In the dry bones story, the Holy Spirit breathes the spirit into people.

I made a thirty-day retreat in Canada with a critical question: should I stay in social justice work or get out and focus on charismatic renewal? The answer was to stay in social action, go deeper, find the spiritual roots, and share them with others. I knew my future direction. It prepared me perfectly for my later work in Washington, D.C., where I would help bishops write letters, create an education program, speak all over the country, and hold press conferences. After my thirty-day Ignatian retreat, I became more contemplative.

Like Dorothy Day, Fr. Mottet wrestled with how to fully integrate his spiritual values and practices with his work in social action. His Ezekiel 37 blueprint enabled him to do that successfully. He thought it was the only way to be effective in social action. This was so important that at the end of his life when he tried to identify ten life lessons, he said, "Be a contemplative in action." The pattern for the rest of Fr. Mottet's life was "Go deeper, find the spiritual roots, and share them with others." It enabled him to evolve from an organizer to a developer and vastly expand his reach.

Msgr. Jack Egan, "Mr. Social Justice," was a friend of mine. He was our big hero while he was in Chicago. He was an Irish street fighter. He went to Notre Dame and raised a lot of money. While he was at Notre Dame, he called his social action friends together to start the Catholic Committee on Urban Ministry (CCUM), which we called "seecum." It grew fast, and several leaders came out of it.

One of the priests who came to those meetings at Notre Dame was from Cairo, Illinois, which they called "Little Egypt" because of its hard racial history. He told us about people who shot bullets through his rectory windows. About thirty of us were in the group, and Jack asked, "How can we help this priest survive?" We brainstormed about what we could do to help him. I don't remember what we came up with, but that is how Jack ran those meetings. People like Geno Baroni and Jim Groppi were there. Geno became important to me in Washington, D.C.

Jack tried to hire me a couple of times, but I could never work for him. He was too high-powered and intolerant. He was a pastor in south Chicago during the block busting when realtors scared the white people out with threats that housing prices were dropping. They bought houses dirt cheap and then sold them at exorbitant prices on contract sales to African Americans. Jack got a bunch of Jesuits together to form the Contract Buyers League. He brought in an organizer to train them how to get ordinances to stop the block busting. That training gave birth to some of the largest organizing networks in the United States. One of the best known is the Pacific Institute of Community Organizing, which works up and down the west coast and in the South.

"In 2004, the Pacific Institute of Community Organizing changed its name to People Improving Communities through Organizing to reflect its national reach. Today, this organization and its affiliates raise $40–50 million a year, which supports the work of 44 affiliated federations working in 150 cities and towns in 19 states plus the District of Columbia. Affiliates organize around a host of issues including police reform, disrupting the school-to-prison pipeline, eliminating food deserts, and raising the minimum wage, as well as campaigns centered on job creation, affordable housing, combating racism, and immigrant rights." [26]

Because of my cancer detour, it took a long time to get a University of Iowa graduate degree. While I lived at the Catholic Worker house, the Dean of Social Work heard about me and knew that my studies were interrupted by cancer. He said, "We've got to get that guy a degree." I told him about the credits I got at Notre Dame and the research our conscientious objectors did. He said, "That's better than anything you'll get at the University of Iowa. Just write up what you've done in social action and supply that as your graduate thesis." I finished in 1975 without going back to the University of Iowa. I went to Bishop O'Keefe and said, "Remember when you sent me off to graduate school several years ago? I've finally completed it." He wanted to have an article in *The Catholic Messenger*, but because it took me so long, I was too embarrassed to let that happen.

I've Never Had It Not Work

The next Catholic Worker house I started was the Dorothy Day house. Someone gave me the house. That isn't unusual. I got at least seven houses that way. Someone asked how I got so many houses, and I said, "Out begging." The next question was: "What's the difference between fundraising and begging?" I said, "They are the same thing." For a year, I lived in the Peter Maurin house, which was run like a Catholic Worker house. We took people off the street, and they lived there. I helped start another Catholic Worker house in Fort Madison, Iowa.

I started a lot of things in the same way. I bought on contract, made the down payment, and then sent word to my friends about what we were doing. They sent money. I called the money for the down payment "seed money." We also wrote to organizations, and we got most things paid for quickly. We started with the seed money, took possession, and believed we could come up with the rest of the money. I've never had it not work.

One of Fr. Mottet's most important lessons is: "Be fearless in asking for favors." Sometimes he said, "This is what I would like you to do," but often it was a request for money. Over time, he learned who, when, and how to ask. Money was a tool he needed to help the poor, and he was unintimidated in asking for it. Millions of dollars flowed through his hands in Washington, D.C., and later in Davenport, but the blue shirt he wore for many of our interviews was tattered and

I even bought a truck that way. One of my former students worked at a bakery shop on East River Drive. He said, "I've got a truckload of bread if you can come and get it." I needed a truck, so I went to the Ford dealer. When I went in to see him, I said, "I live at the Catholic Worker house. We take in homeless people off the street. I'm not asking you to give us anything, but would you sell us a truck at cost so I can get free food for those people." He was glad to get rid of the truck, so he offered to sell a truck at cost plus what it cost to fix it up. I had a bumper sticker on that truck that read "Robin Hood was right." When people passed me, they honked and waved. Later, I had a bumper sticker that read "If you want peace work for justice." That became my motto.

That's how the Social Action Department operated. If we could get a thousand or five thousand or ten thousand dollars, we used it to start something bigger. We always put a few thousand dollars of seed money in our budget and managed to get it approved. It is amazing what you can do with a small amount of seed money and a few volunteers. We were able to start so many programs.

In 1976, I set up a non-profit corporation, Thomas Merton Corporation, Ltd. Its purpose was to simplify administration and make it quicker and easier to start new things. It wasn't easy to get 501(c)3 status in those days, but I did it. A woman in Congressman Lane Evans' office facilitated it. Thomas Merton Corporation was an incubator. Other programs could start using it right away instead of going through that long process. One funder had already said, "I'll give you money when you get your own corporation."

501(c)3 is a U.S. tax law provision. It grants exemption from federal income tax to nonprofit organizations that exist for religious, charitable, scientific, literary, or educational purposes.

Eventually we bought a house on Vine Street that became the Thomas Merton House, and I lived there until I was called to Washington, D.C. When I read Thomas Merton's *The Seven Story Mountain*, I said, "This guy gets it. He knows what is going on in the world, and he is praying about it. He is tying together problems in the world with prayer." Merton's point was that he was supposed to pray for the world, but in the monastery, they were kept from the news and forced to pray all the time. He didn't even know that the atomic bomb was dropped on Nagasaki. Merton was a close friend of John Howard Griffin, and they met at Merton's hermitage. I got my reports about Merton from John Howard Griffin.

According to the Thomas Merton Center, Merton was "the most influential American Catholic author of the twentieth century. . . He wrote over sixty books and hundreds of poems and articles on topics ranging from monastic spirituality to civil rights, nonviolence, and the nuclear arms race. . . For his social activism Merton endured severe criticism, from Catholics and non-Catholics alike, who assailed his political writings as unbecoming of a monk." [27] Thomas Merton exemplified one of Fr. Mottet's top life lessons: "Be a contemplative in action."

Merton was a hell raiser as a kid. His parents were artists. He went to school in Europe and spent a lot of time in Paris. He said he learned Romanian in bed. He had a conversion experience in the huge European cathedrals. When he went to New York City, one of the people he met with was Dorothy Day. They often met for lunch, and he considered going into the Catholic Worker movement. Instead, he wound up at the Abbey of Gethsemani, a Cistercian monastery in Kentucky. The rest is history. His first book, *The Seven Story Mountain*, is the story of his conversion. He wrote to intellectuals all over the world and was one of the greatest mystics of the century.

At the end of his life, he went to the East to explore what we have in common with Buddhists and other eastern contemplatives. He gave his talk, and when he went to his room to take a shower, he was electrocuted by a short in the fan. He didn't show up for his next lecture, and they found him dead on the floor.

John Howard Griffin was a professional photographer, and he had loaned his camera to Merton. When he heard about Merton's death, he cabled immediately to say, "Do not open that camera. It is mine." Griffin worked in his dark room developing the last scenes Merton had taken. Griffin had heard the story of Merton's dream about a harbor and a boat, which was probably a dream about his death. The last picture he took out the window was a harbor and a boat. I think he was one of the most important people of the twentieth century. He was right that you need to know what is going on in the world to pray for the world.

The Tricks God Plays on You

In 1972, the Social Action Department started Legal Aid. It was our first big project, so we thought of it as our first baby. Poor people, especially African Americans, had no legal leverage and couldn't get a fair hearing in court. Frank put that together while I was in the hospital, and he had a sign up in the front window when I got home. Law students came from Iowa City to get a little experience, and lawyers from Davenport advised them. Many of the people who came for legal assistance were Black women. So many forces were destroying Black families, and Black women had no one to turn to.

That same year, I hired Ernie Rodriguez, the Hispanic leader I worked with at Cooks Point and in the Catholic Interracial Council, to start the Area Board of Migrants. It functioned as an immigration office. The first year, one thousand people came for help, people living in fear and anxiety. We were the only office between Chicago and Omaha. We worked on housing for tomato workers in Muscatine, but when we strengthened the Iowa housing laws, Illinois got most of the labor contracts. We improved a law in one state, and it got worse in the other state. To address the root causes, we had to work on both sides of the river.

We worked out a plan for the Area Board of Migrants to be funded jointly by the Davenport Diocese in Iowa and the Peoria and Rockford Dioceses in Illinois. The original budget was $30,000, ten from each diocese. It was tough to get this approved. The bishop of Peoria wasn't familiar with the problems of migrants. I remember the bishop of Rockford saying, "This is a long way to drive to spend ten thousand dollars," but it was a lot of money to us.

To protect agricultural workers, the Iowa Department of Public Health had a Migrant Labor Camp Program that requires permits for housing for seven or more migrant agricultural workers. Chapters 81 of the Iowa Code specifies rules for shelters, water supply, and other basic labor camp conditions. The Illinois Department of Public Health had a similar set of laws and rules. The Area Board of Migrants worked to improve migratory labor housing laws in both states. The work of the Area Board for Migrants is now carried out by the Diocesan Immigration Program.

United Way wouldn't fund the Area Board of Migrants, so I still designate my United Way contribution to Quad Cities Interfaith and Project Renewal, and I say, "Shame on you for not funding the Immigration Office." I get my licks in there. The Immigration Office is the busiest office in the diocese today. Second is Social Action. Third was my office, but that's not true anymore. I'm not there.

Not everything we started worked. Before I went to Washington, D.C., we set up an organization to sell homes to minorities. Bill Gluba, who was in real estate then, said, "It takes me ten times as much work to sell a house to a poor person or an African American as to someone else," so we formed and funded our own organization. After it was going, I talked to the leader of Churches United, who was a friend of mine, and he said, "Why don't you let me take that, and we'll run it through Churches United?" They sold a few houses, but it never developed. It died while I was in my first year in Washington, D.C. They did the best they could, but it died for lack of perseverance or dedication. I would not have let it die if I had been home.

A Franciscan nun, who taught French and spent summers in France, came to tell me about her meeting with Jean Vanier, the founder of L'Arche, which cares for men with mental disabilities. He was from a famous Canadian family and was a ship commander in World War II.

When Vanier spoke in Clinton, even our Archbishop went to hear him. I happened to walk into the hall as he walked in, and everybody thought I was with him. After I listened to him, I was sure we should start L'Arche in a wing at St. Vincent's. It had been an orphanage and then an adolescent treatment center. The bishop was a gentle and quiet person, but when I went to him with my idea, he said NO in the loudest voice he has ever used. He had his mind made up to use St. Vincent's as the diocesan headquarters and a residence for retired priests. He had a short fuse and could lose his cool and get very angry in a staff meeting, but he was back to normal in less than a minute.

Sister Concetta and I went to Canada to visit Jean Vanier, and we spent an afternoon with him. We learned that he sometimes quoted this scripture: "Go and do whatever is in your mind." *(2 Samuel 7:3)* I was certain we were going to have a L'Arche community in Davenport, but we still prayed about whether to go ahead. When that scripture came up in one of the Advent readings, I thought it was a confirmation, and I told Concetta that we should go ahead. We intended to buy a house on Corporate Boulevard. It was a beautiful home with gingerbread decoration. It was my ideal house for L'Arche, but the county supervisors wouldn't approve it.

I complained to the Lord. I said, "We've been praying about this. We've been discerning it. What's happening?" Nothing worked, so I let the Franciscan nuns start it in Clinton. I learned a lot from that decision because they now have two or three houses in Clinton. Protestant churches got involved, and it became more ecumenical. At the twenty-fifth anniversary celebration, the head of the Franciscan nuns and I both said, "This just proves it's God's work, not ours."

Clinton was the right place for L'Arche, and Davenport was the right place for Project Renewal. I learned discernment. God is going to have His way, and you have to be open to the Holy Spirit and the tricks God plays on you.

Shortly after Vanier's death in 2019 at age ninety, L'Arche released an internal report stating that Vanier, under the guise of giving spiritual guidance, engaged in "manipulative and emotionally abusive sexual relationships with six women in France between 1970 and 2005." Fr. Mottet died before any of this information became public.

By 1977, the Davenport Catholic Interracial Council had done what it could do. All the main civil rights legislation had been taken care of in Iowa and nationally, and the Pacem in Terris Award was going well. Because of the growing Black Power movement, we decided to put the Catholic Interracial Council to bed.

The Davenport Catholic Interracial Council, the largest civil rights organization is Iowa, was instrumental in getting housing and employment ordinances passed in Davenport and, to some degree, in Iowa. It worked cooperatively with the National Association for the Advancement of Colored People and became the dominant civil rights organization in Davenport. This avoided the competition and cross-purposes that happened in other cities. After Martin Luther King, Jr. was assassinated, riots broke out in one hundred cities, but not in Davenport, largely because of the work the Catholic Interracial Council had already done. Through their efforts, the Davenport Human Relations Commission got a budget and power to enforce ordinances and was eventually reconstructed as the Davenport Civil Rights Commission, which has subpoena power and still exists. Bill Cribbs was the Civil Rights Commission's first full-time director, and he was able to successfully resolve several discrimination issues.

A paper titled Citizen Second Class—and the movement to change that in America's Heartland *by Dr. Art Pitz tells the civil rights history of Davenport in detail. The paper is available at Putnam Museum, the African American Museum of Iowa, or from the author.*[28]

One Foot Charity and the Other Foot Justice

I was at a meeting in Iowa City around 1977, and Msgr. Madsen said, "I need a one-page statement I can put in front of an average parishioner, and they'll understand the connection between charity and justice." One day when I stood on the railroad track on the corner of Fifth and Warren by Project Renewal, I got the idea. Next door was a multi-problem family in all kinds of poverty, and I thought:

"That's the answer, one foot charity and another foot justice." I'm sure it was a gift of the Holy Spirit. It takes two feet to walk. It takes two feet to keep your balance, so charity and justice go together. I developed that and took it to Washington, D.C., with me. Steve Goebel said, "It's too bad you didn't copyright that. You would be a rich man today."

I had someone draw two feet, and I added all the things on institutional change and justice on one foot and immediate emergency aid on the other foot. You must do both. The value of charity is that it gets people in an immersion process. They find out how serious the problem is and realize how much poor people are suffering. People who get involved in charity have the chance to see the urgency and the possibilities of what can be done. That's like dipping your toe into the water, but justice is doing something about the cause. That's institutional change.

At first the drawing was big shoes like mine, but a woman on my staff said, "Those are men's feet. You should put toes on there so it could be male or female." On one foot, I listed all the organizations that worked for justice, like Bread for the World, Pax Christy, and the Catholic Committee on Urban Ministry and gave their addresses and phone numbers. I kept adding to it all the time. On the other foot, I listed charity, things like food pantries, soup kitchens, and Catholic Worker houses.

This was the origin of Fr. Mottet's signature two feet model of social justice. Charity has an important role, but Fr. Mottet always prioritized institutional change. The model is a clear conceptual framework that lends itself to graphic imagery. The United States Conference of Catholic Bishops has adopted a graphic titled "The Two Feet of Love in Action." Both feet have toes. The orange foot on the left side represents social justice, and the green foot on the right side represents charitable works. The social justice foot lists seven ways to remove root causes and improve structures. The charitable works foot lists seven ways to meet basic needs and aid individuals. The path the two feet walk is the Kingdom of God. The two feet model didn't end Fr. Mottet's tension with Catholic Charities, but, over time,

I was appointed to the National Committee of the Campaign for Human Development, but I barely knew what it was. I received cartons of promotional materials, and I didn't know what to do with them. They were supposed to go to the priests in parishes, but I took them to a meeting about Vatican II where there were hundreds of nuns. I gave those materials to them, and they took them wherever they went. God takes care of his dummies, so it was the best things I could have done because nuns have so much influence.

The National Committee was around thirty-five Catholics with social justice backgrounds from different parts of the United States. We reviewed grant applications from around the country. I read hundreds of them. I called a lot of the people who wrote grant applications to ask how they did things and whether it worked. If something worked, I stole the idea and tried to do the same thing in Davenport. I eventually had a thick rolodex of people with ideas about housing, workers' rights, civil rights, and so forth. That is partly how we were able to do so many things at once. I imitated.

Perhaps it was Fr. Mottet's humility or his ability not to take himself too seriously that helped him avoid the not-invented-here syndrome that makes us so enamored with our own ideas and stifles innovation in many organizations. Whether he called his approach "stealing ideas" or "imitating," he was an idea connoisseur and collector, along with inventing his own.

When I went to my first National Committee meeting, we had hundreds of applications to read and prioritize. I knew that community organizing and legal aid lead to institutional change, so I suggested we prioritize those and then deal with the others. They bought it. I said, "Here's a way to organize this," and I set it up so institutional change projects would be funded.

Chapter 11

If You Want Peace Work for Justice

In 1978, I was surprised by a letter that informed me I was one of thirty people nominated to become National Director of the Campaign for Human Development for the U.S Bishops. I wrote them a thank you letter that said I was honored but too busy. I had so many things going on, and I couldn't imagine packing up and going to Washington, D.C. Since I had to prepare for a meeting of the National Committee, I called a staff member in the bishop's office to find out if the new director would be on board for the meeting. She told me the rumor that all the applicants were turned down. I jokingly said, "Oh, I'll sit right by my phone. I may get drafted." It was a big joke, but when I went to the meeting, they treated me like I was the new director, and I said, "Something's up here."

I was in summer school at Notre Dame when I got a call from the Auxiliary Bishop in El Paso, Texas. He asked me to come for an interview, so I knew things were getting serious. I learned that thirteen people applied, and they narrowed it down to three. Bishop Thomas Kelly, the Executive Director of the U.S. Conference of Catholic Bishops, turned down all three names and said, "Give me some more names." When I went to Texas, I said to the bishop, "I will accept a call from the Church to do this job, but I won't apply for it because it will seem like I'm seeking something for myself." Five and half months later, a second letter requested me to reconsider, and I accepted. The man who really wanted the job was the top Air Force chaplain who held the rank of general. He showed up in a chauffeured government car wearing all his medals and braids. Staff in the office turned to one another and said, "Are we serious?"

One of Fr. Mottet's top-ten life lessons is: "Don't seek reputation for yourself but answer a call from the church." He valued his reputation because he knew it helped him get things done, but his humility kept him from seeking public approval or honors. At the same time, he wasn't about to turn down God or the church.

When I left for Washington, D.C., to be head of the Campaign for Human Development, my friends in Davenport gave me a pair of hip boots to walk through all the bull crap in Washington, D.C. I didn't know if I could do the job. It was a big step up. I went to the Shrine of the Immaculate Conception where Dorothy Day prayed for direction, and I prayed the same prayer she prayed down in the basement chapel. She prayed that God would show her how to join her faith with social action and justice work.

When Dorothy Day returned to her apartment after praying, she found Peter Maurin waiting for her. He became her mentor, and they worked together until his death. Dorothy Day wrote about her prayer at the basilica in her autobiography, The Long Loneliness:

> I went to the national shrine at the Catholic University on the feast of the Immaculate Conception. There I offered up a special prayer, a prayer which came with tears and with anguish, that some way would open up for me to use what talents I possessed for my fellow workers, for the poor. (p. 166)

By 1978 when Fr. Mottet moved to Washington, D.C., he had already resolved Dorothy Day's dilemma by combining social action with charismatic renewal, but he understood that he would face new challenges. He needed to find ways to create institutional change on a national scale and keep his spiritual priorities at the same time.

We visited the Basilica of the National Shrine of the Immaculate Conception. As Protestants, we are awestruck by the beauty and scale of cathedrals and basilicas. We spent hours soaking up the atmosphere in different parts of the magnificent

When I drove into Washington, D.C., in 1978, I had my old Chevy. I carried a case of oil because I needed a quart of oil before I needed gas. I was forty-eight years old. A nun at Notre Dame told me I was sure to love Bishop Kelly because he was approachable and lived a simple life. He even walked to work. The day I arrived, the Executive Committee of the Bishop's Conference was meeting. Bishop Kelly called down to the office where I waited and said, "Our meeting is about over. I'd like you to come upstairs, and I'll introduce you to the bishops." I went up to the conference office where a secretary sat at her desk. She said, "You can't go in until Bishop Kelly calls for you." I thought Bishop Kelly already called me, but I guess he didn't tell that woman. I sat there waiting, and when the meeting was over, I watched fifty bishops walk out. They looked so tired and burdened. I saw what a heavy responsibility they carried.

I never expected to live or work in Washington, D.C., so it kind of freaked me out the first year. I drove down the street and looked up, and there were all the things I usually saw on TV, like the White House, all the memorials on the National Mall, the Pentagon, and the Capitol. My office was within walking distance of the White House.

During Jimmy Carter's presidency, there were a lot of Catholics on the staff, friendly people interested in social justice. They got my name because of the Campaign for Human Development, and I had five invitations to the White House that first year for meetings about social justice. One invitation was in my first week on the job. As I walked to the White House, an African American woman with a little child said, "Hi, Father." Then a bus went by, and the driver said, "Hi, Father," I knew somebody had been awfully good to African Americans in that town.

I had so many friends who worked at the White House. On one of my visits, everybody was waiting for President Carter to come down the stairs. A woman I knew tapped me on the shoulder and said, "He's going to come down the elevator. Come and stand over here." The elevator door opened, and there he was. I said, "I'm from Iowa, and we got you startled." He said, "You sure did." It pays to have friends in high places. The Carter administration was falling apart. He was too much of an outsider. It seemed like his wife was the only friend he had.

The Iowa caucuses are the first big event of the presidential primary season. Candidates for their party's nomination usually spend a lot of time in Iowa cities. Fr. Mottet liked to say that during the campaigns, you can have breakfast in Davenport with a presidential candidate any day of the week.

When Pope John Paul II was elected in 1978, it was like the weathervane went "whoosh." I was eating lunch at a regional meeting in Boston, and I hadn't heard about his election. When we went to pay our checks, the waitress said, "I heard you've got a Polish Pope." I laughed because I thought it was a Polish joke. "No," she said, "I'm serious. You've got a Polish Pope." He was later canonized as a saint, but he was rigid on some things. He didn't mess around. A Polish nun who worked for me, said, "I'm Polish, but when they elected a Polish Pope, I knew he was going to be stubborn."

A Mattress on the Floor

I seldom met anyone who was from Washington, D.C. They all came from someplace else to get ahead or make it big time. The cost of living was extremely high, and so was the crime rate. My car insurance doubled. I always lived in the toughest neighborhoods. My experience in Washington, D.C., was a love-hate relationship.

When I was sure I had the job, I told Bishop Kelly I wanted to live in an inner-city parish. Most staff lived in a rather plush place. I had changed my lifestyle five years earlier, and I didn't want to change back. My goal was to eventually start a Catholic Worker house. I was put at Holy Comforter, a Josephite parish on Capitol Hill. In 1954, Holy Comforter Parish had influenced the Brown vs Board of Education Supreme Court decision because they peacefully integrated their Catholic schools. I guess the Supreme Court thought, "If the Catholics can do it in Washington, D.C., we can do it."

Brown v. Board of Education of Topeka was a landmark Supreme Court decision. It established that racial segregation in public schools is unconstitutional.

The Josephites worked primarily among African Americans. Some Sundays, I was the only white face in the church. Gospel music had become popular, and they had a gospel choir. When people called the rectory, they didn't ask what time Mass was. They asked, "What time is the gospel choir?" There was standing room only. During the sixties, it had become somewhat fashionable to be Catholic because of the Kennedys, and that reduced anti-Catholicism.

After my first week in D.C., I met Father Dick McSorley, a Jesuit priest from Georgetown University, and I told him I wanted to start a Catholic Worker house. He lived in the central city with the homeless and slept on a mattress on the floor. During World War II, he was a Jesuit in the Philippines, and he was arrested as a Japanese prisoner of war. Later, he taught at Georgetown University.

The Japanese government violated the Geneva Conventions with its horrific treatment of World War II prisoners. They were starved, beaten, and subjected to forced labor in mines and war-related factories.

Father McSorley knew a pastor at Luther Place Memorial Church, and he got them to donate a house to us. It was a big church with a statue of Martin Luther and a good ministry to prostitutes. We started a Catholic Worker house at 14 th and M, which was the busiest corner in Washington, D.C., for prostitution. We had anywhere from three to twenty prostitutes in front of our building twenty -four hours a day. Just a couple of blocks away, large crowds milled around the intersection dealing drugs. Sometimes we had i nteresting conversations with ladies on the street. I learned a lot about their lifestyle. The neighborhood was safer because there was always traffic going around the block looking over the merchandise.

One Saturday, I went to the grocery store in civilian clothes. On the way, a red-headed woman asked, "Do you want a date?" That was the legal question. I said, "Yeah, I'll take you for a cup of coffee." When I unlocked the door, she saw a "Free Medical Clinic" sign and asked if I was a doctor. When I told her I was a priest, she said, "Oh, my goodness."

Our Catholic Worker house took in women to prepare them for a job and their own apartment, and half a dozen women were in the next room. We sat down in the kitchen and had a cup of coffee. She told me she had spent three years in a Catholic school in Florida. Her mother worked the street and was up in the hotel. She sent the clients up to her mom. After the coffee, she said, "I gotta go back to work." She asked me if I'd say a prayer over her, which I did. She gave me a little peck on the cheek, and away she went. The next day, I came home from work all dressed up like a priest. From the corner, she yelled loud enough for everyone to hear, "Hi Father," and waved her hands like I was her customer. She thought I was her best friend, but it was a bit embarrassing.

We had no air conditioning, of course, so I put a towel around my pillow when I went to bed. I kept a dry one nearby so I could change a wet towel for a dry towel in the middle of the night. On weekends, it was so miserably hot that I took a book to the Smithsonian Museum to spend two hours walking around some section of the museum. That was about all I could stand. Then I went to the dining room and read my book to stay cool on Sunday afternoon. I had a bicycle to ride, especially on weekends when there was very little traffic. It was fun to ride around the Capitol, the Pentagon, the Supreme Court, and the White House.

I had so many unforgettable experiences. As I walked in the rain from work to the Catholic Worker house, a woman was talking to a guy through a car window. She stood up when I walked by and said,

"Damn freaks. I can't stand damn freaks!" I asked if she was having a bad day. "Yeah," she said, "bad day." She asked if I was married. I had my coat up, so she didn't see my collar. When I told her I was a priest, she said, "Oh my God, where can I get my baby baptized?" I directed her to the parish up the street, and she went on her way. Another woman on the opposite side of the street called me to come over and give her a blessing, so I prayed with her. She said she sure needed it.

During my first year in Washington, D.C., the farmers came to protest agriculture policies. They drove hundreds of tractors in from all directions. The tractors snarled traffic, and commuters couldn't get to work. Everybody was mad at them. They parked their tractors in front of the Capitol and went in to talk to the Secretary of Agriculture. The Chief of Police, who was a city slicker, thought he would outsmart those farmers, so he called the city garage and said, "We're going to corral these farmers." He told them to bring in every truck or tractor, anything they could get the motor started, and park them bumper-to-bumper. When the farmers came out from their meeting, it was hard for them to move their tractors.

That night in February of 1979, a seventeen-inch snowstorm hit. Doctors and nurses couldn't get to the hospitals because two inches of snow shuts down Washington, D.C. They don't have the equipment. Nobody knows how to drive in it. You can imagine what seventeen inches did to them. The farmers drove through the snow on their tractors to haul in doctors, nurses, and other emergency people and help clear snow from the streets leading to hospitals. In twenty-four hours, they went from being the enemy to being the great heroes.

No traffic moved on Capitol Hill where I lived, but I drove in from Iowa with snow tires. I went out, jumped in my old Chevy, and drove down the alley. A pastor stood there in disbelief and asked, "Where on earth can I get some of those snow tires?"

Don't Step on Land Mines

When I became Executive Director of the Campaign for Human Development in 1968, it didn't take long to find out how controversial we were. Fortunately, I had Tim Collins as my right-hand man, and he had been there from the beginning, so he knew what was going on. I always hire competent people and say jokingly, "Your job now is to make me look good." As I arrived at a bishop's meeting, I heard Tim say, "Hurry up! They're already attacking us." Someone was always trying to get a hand on the money. When there was a controversy at the bishops' meeting, I always listened at the back. We work with our committees. It's church politics.

The Archbishop of New Orleans, who was a paratrooper during World War II and kind of a tough guy, wanted to use the annual collection for inner-city schools where he felt it was most needed. The Campaign for Human Development wanted that money to fund institutional change projects. The National Committee had set brilliant standards to make sure the Campaign for Human Development funded projects that originated with people in need and empowered the poor. During a break, I talked with the paratrooper archbishop, and we eventually won.

Fr. Mottet understood the importance of inner-city schools, but the archbishop's recommendation was top-down. Fr. Mottet believed in bottom-up. He wanted to fund projects that started with the self-interests of the poor and empowered them to make change. He didn't make the mistake he regretted from City Council meetings in Davenport. He reached out to his opponent to build a relationship. Their conversation during the break was an attempt to understand the archbishop's interests and passions. By then, this approach had become second nature, and it worked.

The Campaign for Human Development reported to the Conference of Catholic Bishops. It was an adjustment to work for three hundred bishops. During my seven years as National Director, I had a good relationship with the bishops for the most part. After I went back home to Davenport in 1985, Bishop O'Keefe had the twenty-fifth anniversary of his installation as bishop. Two buses pulled up in front of the cathedral, and sixty-two bishops got off. I knew sixty of them. I found the bishops wonderful to work for. Most of them are very pastoral. They are priests who kind of got kicked upstairs. They had a pastor's attitude of deep concern about their people. There were two or three hard heads with civil law degrees, but they were a small minority. It was a different breed of bishops in those days, mostly from working-class families. Their dads worked in factories, belonged to unions, and might have been union leaders or organizers, so they had a different mentality.

Two years before I went to Washington, D.C., the Bishop's Conference developed a *Call to Action*, which was their latest thinking on peace, justice, and gender equality. I contributed some of what we had done in Davenport. The *Call to Action* turned out to be very unpopular with the conservative bishops.

"The assembly declared the church must stand up to the chronic racism, sexism, militarism, and poverty in modern society. And to do so in a credible way the church must reevaluate its positions on issues like celibacy for priests, the male-only clergy, homosexuality, birth control, and the involvement of every level of the church in important decisions." [29]

I wanted my official stationery to include a statement I picked up in Latin America: "Work for social justice is a constitutive part of the gospel." The bishops decided I could only say, "We think it to be." I knew it was essential, but I had to be cautious because some bishops were more conservative than others, and they could stir up a fuss.

I took the two feet model of social action to Washington, D.C., and the staff said it was a wonderful way to explain what we fund and don't fund. The two feet went all over the country and appeared in textbooks. I wish I had patented it. St. Augustine said, "You cannot give in charity what you owe in justice." I have that on my card.

When I asked Fr. Mottet for his top life lessons, the first thing he said was, "Charity can't make up for what is lacking in justice."

It seemed like the Campaign for Human Development was designed for me. I got to empower people to work for justice and get at the causes of poverty. I traveled the whole country over that seven-year period. I think it was the best job in the United States. The organization wasn't even Catholic until I left. Then one "C" was added.

When Fr. Mottet was National Director, the Campaign for Human Development was often referred to as "the Catholic Campaign." After he returned to Davenport in 1985, its official name was changed to "Catholic Campaign for Human Development."

During my first year, I was leaving the office when a woman on our staff ran to tell me a famous artist wanted to do something special for the upcoming tenth anniversary of the Campaign for Human Development. She asked me to give her a line for the artwork. I said, "If you want peace, work for justice," and I caught the elevator. It was a famous quote from Pope Paul VI. The artwork was like graffiti, the kind you'd see on the walls in the ghetto. We reproduced it and got a lot of mileage out of it. We even had bumper stickers made.

One of my first assignments was to plan the celebration for our tenth anniversary. We signed up for Milwaukee, but we changed to Chicago when we heard the new Pope, John Paul II, was coming to Chicago. We wanted him to speak to us. The priest organizing the Pope's visit needed office space, so we gave him half of our office and moved half of our staff across the street. As a return favor, the Pope agreed to speak to our group in Chicago. Tim Collins and I helped prepare the notes for his speech. We wanted him to say the right things about the Campaign for Human Development.

October 4, 1979, was one of the red-letter days in my life. We got up at four in the morning and went to the corner in front of a church where Pope John Paul II would stop his motorcade and speak from his car. It was the most stringent protection I've ever seen in Chicago. They even removed manhole covers to put a camera down to look for explosives. The police ran us into the church before he came, shooed all the other people away, and then let us come out. We held our signs up for television. The Pope stood up in his convertible and gave his speech. He praised "the Catholic Campaign," but he covered himself by saying, "I am told." It was brash, but in our promotional material, we quoted Pope Paul VI saying things we wrote ourselves. We got all that on film and used it.

Fr. McSorley and I started our second Catholic Worker house in an all-Black neighborhood in 1979. First, we cleaned the house out and put everything out by the street for the city to pick up. Our neighbors thought we were bad for the neighborhood and turned us in, but once we tuck pointed the house and made other repairs, they stopped their complaints. We wondered what we could do to be accepted. Someone said, "Let's hang a picture of Martin Luther King, Jr. in the front window," but I started a garden out on the side, and everybody stopped to talk to me. They said "You can't plant anything there. The rats will eat it." I was really doing one-on-one interviews to get to know the people. Then I sent the young people door to door in the neighborhood, and they established some strong friendships.

Fr. Mottet didn't say whether rats ate his vegetables, but it was the relationships that interested him. For him, relationships and results were inextricably linked. His rolodex card trays kept getting more crowded. While we were in Washington, D.C., we searched for the location of the home where he lived on Capitol Hill. The area, which was previously a slum, is now gentrified. We found an address he talked about and took a selfie in front of the building.

Fr. McSorley was associated with the Community Center for Creative Non-Violence, which operated the Zacchaeus Free Medical Clinic and Zacchaeus Soup Kitchen. They wanted to get permission to pick up the cases of food restaurants put in the alley. They picked it up at night and shared it with homeless people. Fr. McSorley got someone to sponsor a bill to give the donors a tax break. To promote this bill, they served a sumptuous meal in the halls of Congress made from food picked up in alleys.

I Invented the Egg McReagan

The next place Fr. McSorley and I moved was across the street from the House of Prayer for All People, which was started by Daddy Grace. He died in 1960, but he started churches up and down the East Coast, big churches with huge crowds. He was so successful that he thought he was divine and never cut his hair or fingernails. Daddy Grace's church had a pretty good formula, a lot of music and ushers in uniforms. No one could be elected mayor of Washington, D.C., without getting Daddy Grace's endorsement. When he left the front of the church, African Americans in uniform ran along on each side of his car like they do for the President. The church provided jobs and built housing. His formula made African American people feel dignified, and they got their self-respect back.

Fr. Mottet could not have been more different from Daddy Grace, but he admired a successful formula. Both Daddy Grace and Fr. Mottet worked for jobs and housing and understood power. Fr. Mottet recognized the importance of dignity and self-respect, and he respected every person.

We bought another house where there wasn't even a front door, so the cats, dogs, and rats ran in and out. We paid less than market price and made a down payment. Then we wrote letters to the newspaper of the nearby Arlington Diocese in Virginia. We told them what we did and how we lived. I think it made them feel a little guilty, so we raised a lot of money that way. We also got a couple of foundation grants to pay for the house and tuck point it. The first thing we did was buy a door. Eventually, we raised so much money that the diocese asked us to stop writing.

We went dumpster diving in the neighborhood and put the usable stuff on a brick wall in front of the house. The neighbors came and picked it up. That is how I learned to eat avocados. If they started to get ripe, they were thrown in the dumpster.

I got mugged in that neighborhood. It was dark and cold when I walked home from the Feast of St Thomas Aquinas in late January of

1982. Three teenage men hid between cars and buildings and then jumped me. The guy in front had a pistol in my stomach. The guy behind said, "Shoot him, shoot him," and the third guy went through my pockets. After all my surgeries, I didn't need another hole through there. I knew I had to be quiet and calm, or they would get nervous and shoot me. They took my briefcase and everything I had. The most valuable thing I lost was a notebook where I kept track of all the Reagan cuts that hurt the poor. The policeman said, "They will take your money and throw your billfold in the mailbox down on the corner." They didn't want to be caught with the evidence. I was happy they were so considerate.

When Ronald Reagan became President in 1981, an entirely different clientele walked around in Washington, D.C. Rich people with expensive cars moved in. It was an enormous change. Even the little hotel on the corner from our office had the doorman put on a top hat. That was the beginning of the widening gap between the rich and the poor in this country. There are a lot of policies that keep people poor, and there are policies that allow people to become "stinkin' rich." I saw it right away. I didn't get a single invitation to the White House while Reagan was President. He looked upon us as the enemy because we worked with the poor. I couldn't listen to Reagan's talks. I read them, but I couldn't stand to watch him or listen to him live. He was so persuasive, but his policies were so offensive.

Reagan wanted the churches to handle all social welfare. My view was that half the American people belong to a church, and only half of those were in church on Sunday, so he expected one quarter of the American people to carry the burden of social welfare. You can't dump it off on churches, just twenty-five percent of the American population. That was my argument. People who make all the money using our system have a duty to pay taxes.

Reagan advocated the trickle-down theory, which Pope Francis has condemned. They cut taxes for the rich and then cut programs to help the poor. I believe in bubble up rather than trickle down.

Fr. Mottet's reason wasn't theoretical. He supported what worked. A 2020 study by researchers at the London School of Economics concluded that fifty years of tax cuts have only helped the rich. In the study, per capita gross domestic product and unemployment rates were unaffected by tax cuts. "In fact, if we look back into history, the period with the highest taxes on the rich — the postwar period — was also a period with high economic growth and low unemployment." [30]

During the Reagan era, the government gave away food, but I think food stamps were invented to help farmers, not poor people. The purpose was to get produce off the market. Poor people got that stuff and sold it on the street. We got it legally. Saturday morning was my day off, and I got up to prepare breakfast at the Catholic Worker house. I cut those surplus buns in half and toasted them. Then I topped them with eggs and strips of cheese. I said I invented the Egg McReagan.

I chose to live with the poor and be poor. People have asked me whether it is possible to be an effective organizer and change agent without doing that. Congressman Jim Leach is one example. He became a friend when we worked on full employment. I wrote to him: "We come from different backgrounds. However, I know from twenty years of work in the African American community that a dad's decent job makes all the difference in the world." He wrote back and cited the Roosevelts, Kennedys, and Rockefellers, who were from substantial wealth but also helped people.

There is more than one way to come at it. My dad would have canonized President Franklin Roosevelt. During the Depression, we all sat and listened to his fireside chats. He was the friend of the poor, but if he hadn't had polio, he probably couldn't have identified with them. His wife reached out to the African Americans. She went out and visited poor people and brought back their ideas.

Michael Harrington, a lay person who lived in a Catholic Worker house in New York, got Robert Kennedy's attention in 1962 with his classic book *The Other America.* Kennedy went down South in 1967 to visit sharecroppers and saw that terrible poverty. Then he went home and promoted the War on Poverty.

Robert Kennedy accomplished a lot with the help of his brother. While campaigning in West Virginia, John F. Kennedy was exposed for the first time to the kind of real poverty described by Michael Harrington. He won the hearts of people there by meeting and talking with them across the state. He defused the fact that he was a Catholic. He promised to help them, and he did with a worker training program, a pilot food stamp program, and highway construction.

There are other examples. Lyndon Johnson started the War on Poverty when he became president in 1963, but when I talked to people in government who helped develop it, they were disgusted because the "Green Amendments" gave mayors veto power over poor people's organizations. That took the wind out of the sails as far as empowering poor people.

"Declaring an 'unconditional war on poverty' in his January 1964 State of the Union Address, President Lyndon Johnson launched a legislative blitz intended to go beyond addressing the symptoms of poverty to 'cure it and, above all, prevent it' through major new national efforts in health insurance, education, job training, and safety net protections for the poor." [32] *The war on poverty was carried out through the Office of Economic Opportunity. Lasting results include: Head Start, Medicare, Medicaid, Pell grants for students, community health centers, and the Civil Rights Acts of 1964 and 1965. The war on poverty did not eliminate poverty but did reduce it. Unfortunately, the Aid to Dependent Children program helped destroy nuclear Black families.*

Since the Citizens United Supreme Court ruling in 2010 allowed corporations to put money into politics, we are turning into a plutocracy. We have the best government money can buy, but we can't tell who bought it. I admire former Congressman Jim Leach. He tried to undo Citizens United. I also admire him for what he did for some Franciscan nuns from Dubuque. Their brother worked in Latin America, and his life was in danger. Jim Leach went to the embassy and said to the ambassador, "If anything happens to that priest, I will be on the next plane to your country, and I'll make sure all military and financial aid from the United States is cut off."

The Supreme Court's Citizens United v. Federal Election Commission was "a controversial decision that reversed century-old campaign finance restrictions and enabled corporations and other outside groups to spend unlimited funds on elections." [31]

Sending Old Underwear to the Inner-city

When I went to Washington, D.C., I missed my days at the Carmelite monastery. As a replacement, I went to the library to do planning. They say if you want to plan, get out of the office. Later, Fr. Geno Baroni started a retreat house on Capitol Hill so people could go there to reflect, contemplate, and pray.

During the riot after King's assassination in 1968, a hundred cities were going up in smoke. During the riot in Washington, D.C., Fr. Geno Baroni, who was at an inner-city parish, went to the religious goods store and bought all the black shirts and roman collars he could find. He put them on young, recently ordained Catholic priests and said, "Get out there, and keep it non-violent." [32]

Geno knew that his Slavic relatives had the same economic problems as African Americans. He called them "the PIGS," Polish, Italian, Greeks, and Slavs, and he started the urban ethnic program to help those groups. Geno took five priests from the large cities where riots had occurred to Combermere, Ontario, for a week-long retreat with Catherine de Hueck, a Russian Baroness who escaped during the Russian Revolution and plunged into work with the poor in Canada and the United States. Geno Baroni, Dorothy Day, and Thomas Merton were her close friends. On the retreat, they dreamed up the idea for a collection in November to fund community organizations that empower poor people. That was the basic idea for the Campaign for Human Development.

Fr. Mottet mentioned Msgr. Geno Baroni often. An article titled "The Greatest Scandal of an Affluent Society" includes a sobering quote from Baroni:

This 'urban revolution' threatens the division of our society into two cultures; those who participate in the rich productivity of modern society—the affluent, educated, productive and suburbanized; and those who are largely denied the privileges and benefits of the American mainstream—the poor, uneducated and unproductive. If we prove incapable of closing the gap between these two groups, our civilization will surely fail... [35]

Our Catholic Worker house was just a few blocks from the parish where Geno Baroni lived and worked. He knew all the politicians and had a lot of important contacts. Geno had coffee and doughnuts with President Lyndon Johnson and helped him understand inner-city poverty. He talked to him about people sending old underwear to the inner-city as an example of the ineffectiveness of charity. Later, Jimmy Carter appointed Fr. Baroni to be Assistant Director of Housing and Urban Development.

I carry a card in my pocket all the time with words from Geno Baroni's last homily before he died of cancer:

I have learned by faith that in the final analysis of one's life, there is only one final healing, death. And we know that final healing will be just. From my own life review, could I share with you my own prayer: Lord, I pray, help me to know that our limited charity is not enough. Lord help me to know that our soup kitchens and second-hand clothes are not enough. Lord, help me to know that it is not enough for the church to be the ambulance service that goes about picking up the broken pieces of humanity for American society. Lord, help us all to know that God's judgment demands justice from us as a rich and powerful nation. Let us pray that the Holy Spirit will provide new gifts to meet new needs. Let us pray that there will be new voices of justice, new people who will hear the words of the Lord and stand

> up as Christians to say, "Yes, the Spirit of the Lord is upon
> me. He has sent me to bring glad tidings to the poor."

As Director of the Campaign for Human Development, I did my annual fall tour to fifty parishes to hold press conferences and announce grants. I used Geno's paraphrase from Isaiah 61: "He has sent me to bring good news to the poor, to proclaim liberty to captives, to the blind new sight, and to set the downtrodden free. To proclaim the Lord's year of favor." I have quoted that in so many places to emphasize that charity will not do it.

Through Fr. McSorley, I was invited to attend a reception in the backyard at Robert Kennedy's home several years after he was assassinated. When Iowa Representative Jim Leach came up to me, I said, "Jim, I want to thank you for your good work on Central America." He didn't know I would be in favor of anything he did, so he said, "Why don't you come to dinner tonight at my house?" I went and had cold chicken out of their refrigerator. Democrats respected Jim Leach for his intelligence and willingness to work across the aisle. You work where you can. That is an organizing principle. You work across the aisle like Ted Kennedy and John McCain worked together on immigration. You bury the hatchet, and you work. There are no permanent friends and no permanent enemies. Recently, our bishop was on the same platform at an immigration rally with people who believe in abortion and gay marriage. You're going to get shot down when you do that.

I ran into another Kennedy relative, Sargent Shriver, at a meeting where I was giving a talk, and he invited me to dinner at their house with his wife, who was Kennedy's sister. When we met, I said, "I'm Fr. Mottet from Davenport, Iowa. I'm a Shriver delegate." He said, "It's good to meet you. There weren't many of you." Shriver ran in 1972, and I went to hear him because he had spoken at the Catholic Interracial Council in Chicago. During his campaign stop, I said, "This guy is spouting Catholic social teaching," and I became a delegate for him. Sargent Shriver became a great friend. Sometimes I went to his office in the Watergate building to meet with him.

I met some great politicians who were very concerned about justice. In the summer, they sometimes sent their student interns to visit my office. I always took them to the Catholic Worker house to give them a bowl of soup and tell them about our work with the homeless. I wanted them to experience how poor people live. They often wrote afterwards: "The best part of my summer was going to the Catholic Worker house."

You need to meet people and understand their problems. Notre Dame has what they call "the urban plunge" where students go to the inner cities and get acclimated. They get to know the people there. I was at Notre Dame for a meeting a few years ago, and they were so proud of their two-million-dollar building for social activism. They talked about their urban plunge, and I said, "I'm from a little college out in Davenport, Iowa, named St. Ambrose, and they did this fifty or sixty years ago. I'm glad Notre Dame is catching up." It's called "immersion." It's how our home visits between Black and White people worked in Davenport. Sr. Concetta used to invite people to Project Renewal to sit around her kitchen table while she explained what was going on in the neighborhood. They met the kids and some of the adults. That immersed them in the situation, and then they could do something about it.

Connect the Self-Interest of the Poor with the Self-Interest of the Person in Power

The Campaign for Human Development had two functions. The first was education, teaching Catholics and others about poverty and the needs of people in relation to the gospel and the social teachings of the church. The second purpose was funding. We funded self-help groups.

It is very important to identify self-interests. Everyone has self-interest. Jesus' self-interest was to do his Father's will, and that led to his death. A lot of people, especially church people, think self-interest is selfishness, and that it's contrary to the gospel. It isn't. Poor people have the right to organize and to stand up on their own two feet and make demands. We empowered people by training leaders to be effective starting with the basics of community organizing like the one-on-one interview. Leadership training helps lay people to be leaders in their community, to be action-oriented and not victims.

We worked to change policies, laws, and decision-making processes. People all over the country told me, "I never thought I could talk to the mayor or the governor or the president of a company, but you gave me the training, and I can go in and talk to them." Training in community organizing empowered them to meet with those people and express their concerns. If it was an immigration issue, they met with a congressman and said, "There are this many thousand Hispanic people in your district. They are concerned about this, and they are prepared to vote." A congressman knows how to count the votes. They went in there with their ammunition.

A great deal of community organizing and development is about power. Fr. Mottet's tactics were designed to gain power, use power effectively, and not give power away unwisely. Saul Alinsky wrote in Reveille for Radicals: ". . . only through the achievement and constructive use of power can people better themselves. . . nothing can be lifted or moved except through power." (p. 29)

One of the examples I use a lot is Communities Organized for Public Service, which is one of the most effective groups. It started in San Antonio and then branched throughout Texas. The governor of Texas appointed Ross Perot, a conservative businessman, as chairman of the Education Committee. Communities Organized for Public Service wanted to even out the inequalities between schools where rich people lived and schools where poor people lived. Ross Perot had influence over the state's education fund, and he wanted to sell computers. They went into the meeting with him knowing that was Perot's self-interest, and they leveraged six million dollars for poor schools. It was a shock to the legislature. There were several lawsuits over that. The principle is: connect the self-interest of the poor with the self-interest of the person in power.

Fr. Mottet's story about Ross Perot is one he used a lot, but it is unverifiable. Perot did spearhead a drive to reform education in Texas, and he made his fortune in the computer business, but there is no record of a connection with Communities Organized for Public Service.

Another case was in Los Angeles. Based on personal interviews, organizers learned that poor people in East Los Angeles paid higher auto insurance rates than people in the high-income areas. The organizers went to Governor Jerry Brown to get him on their side, and they got legislation passed in California. The argument was that people in poor areas drive wrecks, but they don't have more wrecks, and there is no research to justify charging poor people more. They got this outlawed in California, and then took it to Congress and got a national law passed.

"California Proposition 103, enacted by voters in 1988, requires auto insurance prices to be based primarily on how a person drives – driving record, miles driven annually, and years of driving experience. . . insurance companies have for decades illegally subsidized discounts for drivers with white collar occupations and college degrees by forcing other drivers to pay more." [33]

Gale Cincotta is an example I use all the time. She was a widow in Chicago with five kids, and she was a hell-raiser. She tried to get a loan to fix up her house, but the bank wouldn't loan to her. If you can't fix up your house or your porch, the neighborhood runs down, the value of your house and others in the neighborhood goes down, and crime goes up. She worked through her organization to get a federal law passed to require banks to loan money to people in the neighborhood where they take the money. She organized from her kitchen table and affected national policy.

Chapter 12

We Were the General Motors of Community

Organizing

Sometimes people ripped me up one side and down the other. Bishop Kelly called me shortly after I arrived and said, "You don't have to do this, but I would like you to have an interview with a reporter from St. Paul, Minnesota." It was a German newspaper called *The Wanderer,* which was against Vatican II, so they were against the Campaign for Human Development from the very beginning. I agreed to the interview, and I prayed hard. Jesus said, "Don't worry about what you have to say beforehand. I will give you the words." I said, "Lord, you promised this. Now give me the words." The reporter asked what we were doing and why. I explained that we were implementing Vatican II, papal statements, bishop's statements, and the gospel. Someone I knew and respected read the interview and said I made that guy look stupid, but I was always careful about what I said because I was afraid of hurting our program or hurting the poor.

One time, a newspaper reporter somewhere in the South called me to ask what I think about all the money spent on church buildings. I told him a church is the home of poor people as well as rich people. Before people could read or write, stained glass windows, paintings, and the Stations of the Cross taught people. The Catholic Church has always been a promoter of the arts. People couldn't take a trip to the Holy Land or visit fine museums, but they could meditate on the passion of Christ in their church. We try to make the altar beautiful for the body of Christ, but the body of Christ is out there on the street. Jesus said, "Whatever you do for the least, you do to me." *(Matthew 25:40)* We can do both, have beautiful churches and take care of the poor. We can have both beauty and justice. I don't know if he printed that.

I had to bite my lip so many times. I remember when I was signed up to speak at the Washington Press Club at the beginning of the Reagan administration in 1981. The Press Club seemed like the big time, but I had to avoid their traps. When they asked political questions, I mentioned things Democrats voted for and said I disagreed with them too. I had to be so careful because I didn't want to hurt the program and get the bishops mad.

I don't like firing people, but I knew I had to fire a guy who got too big for his pants and tried to run the place. He often went over my head. My predecessor told me he regretted not firing that guy. When I went to Bishop Kelly, he said, "You've been up here more times than your predecessor was in five years." He gave me good advice. The man I needed to fire was Hispanic, and the bishops were coming for their annual meeting. He didn't want this to blow up while they were in town, so he told me to wait until they got home. I followed his advice and waited to replace the man with another Hispanic. It was a shock to the rest of the staff, but I reassured them that everybody else was safe.

No Permanent Friends and No Permanent Enemies

From the beginning, there were attempts to kill the Campaign for Human Development led by people who thought the poor should not be empowered. They didn't think we should fund African American or Mexican American groups. Now their thing is abortion. We always had to be careful. If we funded a group that rode to work on the same bus as abortion advocates, those people would take after us.

A Reagan staff member from Texas attacked us all the time. He came to visit Bishop Kelly because he was sure we were destroying both church and state. He talked about all the riffraff and radicals we funded. I said to him, "You wouldn't have been very happy with Jesus. They complained about him because he associated with sinners and ate with them." He went ballistic. When the Communities Organized for Public Service organization in San Antonio met with him, they videotaped the meeting. He tried to get them to sit with him to show that he wasn't against them and that he was a friend of the poor. They refused. They used the videotape to train their leaders about how people will try to co-opt you and negate your message.

Jesus made people so angry when he spoke in the synagogue in Nazareth that people wanted to throw him over the cliff. In one of my sermons on Luke four, I explain that they tried to throw him out of town shortly after he said, "The Lord has sent me to bring good news to the poor, liberty to the captives, and freedom to those in prison." *(paraphrase of Luke 4:18)* We should expect this reaction. When I was involved in civil rights work, I said to my relatives, "Don't be surprised if I get thrown out of town."

We had to fight the battle between charity and justice all the time. The important thing is empowering the poor and working for institutional change to get at the causes of poverty. It is not important who we associate with to do that. The bishops face this all the time. Critics say, "You mean the bishops worked with that guy?" They were working on housing, which was an area where they agreed.

Along with institutional change, the important thing to understand is the difference between public relationships and private relationships. In public relationships, there are no permanent friends and no permanent enemies. That is the key distinction. You work together where you can. There is even more criticism now than when I was at the Campaign for Human Development. Politics is more radical, and some people think helping poor people is radical politics. Why can doctors, lawyers, and bankers organize, but poor people can't?

We worked with a variety of other groups. We agreed on housing, but we disagreed on abortion and gay marriage. I am still opposed to both euthanasia and the death penalty. A group like Planned Parenthood would not have been able to get a grant from us. Some Catholic groups put cards that criticized the Campaign for Human Development in the parishes to discourage people from donating to us. It's hard to increase the dollar amount of donations with that kind of opposition.

We tried to overcome guilt by association. In the aftermath of Roe vs Wade and the peace movement, opponents accused us of both communism and watering down the gospel. There was enormous tension. We invited bishops and theologians to help us think through those issues and review our printed material. We also convened some of our buddies from the various organizing networks and asked them to help us strategize. We needed to influence the opposition and make a leap of progress in certain places. One key piece of advice was that we needed committed people on the ground doing the work, people who could influence their bishop.

A community organizer from the Industrial Areas Foundation helped us think this through strategically and come up with a way to advance our mission in parishes.[34] Since we couldn't be everywhere, we selected parishes where we could make inroads with the social action message. We named it "the target program." We knew it was a waste of resources to work with some communities, so we worked with parishes where we could make an impact. The target program had a fundraising piece, but it was also educational. You must find your potential allies. Some of your best allies turn out to be the ones who were most opposed. Once they see the results, they get an "ah-ha." You have no permanent friends and no permanent enemies.

One of the groups that was killed by the money classes was the Association of Community Organizations for Reform Now. I knew the founder. Like Mother Teresa, they went to the poorest of the poor, who are frequently African Americans and Mexican Americans, and registered them to vote. They registered millions of people who had been left out in order to help them take some control of their lives. They made a lot of mistakes, but they were doing what the church should have been doing. Fox News went after them. The Campaign for Human Development was the first to defund them because they broke the rules and made stupid mistakes, but that was after I was back in Davenport. The death of the Association of Community Organizations for Reform Now, usually called "ACORN," was a great tragedy because it silenced the voice of the poor. The Nuns on the Bus make up for some of that by registering voters and getting people to vote.[35]

Leveraging Money

The Campaign for Human Development had rules about who could receive grants. Proposals had to be for institutional change and consistent with Catholic social justice teaching. The organization's board had to be at least fifty-one percent poor people, not counting priests or nuns who were voluntarily poor. That caused organizations to actively recruit poor people. If a proposal seemed like a way to solve a problem, we let them set up an advisory board of poor people until they could get their board.

We funded a lot of successful housing programs that were copied all over the United States. Our Annual Report always highlighted our best projects. We talked about those successes because they inspired people and leveraged money. Anyone could read the Annual Report and think: "Well, they funded this thing. Can we do that?" An organization in San Diego had priests play basketball against the police as a fundraiser. The bishop sat on the bench of the priests, and the chief of police sat on the other bench. It was a great thing, and that organization won the approval of the bishop.

One of our early grants was to a group in Connecticut that worked in a chicken processing factory. The workers wanted to buy the company, but they didn't have good management. They sold chickens for less than they paid for them, so they went down the tubes in a matter of months. Later we funded a group in Boston that was founded to provide good management for poverty projects, especially worker owned businesses.

We funded Cesar Chavez' work even though part of it was charity. Chavez knew that he couldn't form a union without having service centers for poor migrant workers, so we funded service centers that led to other things. In Yakima, Washington, which is great fruit country with a lot of migrant workers, he needed a radio station. He put antennas on top of mountains so the signal would get down to the fields, and workers could listen. We funded that radio station, and later it became a community college. Someone asked how things I start so often turn into something bigger and better. That's not me. It's the people. We trust people and empower them.

Geno Baroni's big thing was leveraging money. He focused on Brooklyn where urban renewal was more like urban removal, basically bulldozing neighborhoods.[36] Gino, Ed Chambers, and a building contractor started to rebuild rundown neighborhoods. They raised money wherever they could. The Bishop of Brooklyn, who we called "Mugsy," had a cemetery fund that sat in the bank and grew. They managed to get ten million dollars from that fund, and they used it to leverage money for housing. They went to other churches and said, "The Bishop of Brooklyn just gave ten million. What are the Baptists going to give? What are the Lutherans going to give? What are the Episcopalians going to give?" That housing project was imitated all over the country and became national legislation. People read about it and thought, "Oh, heck we can do that." I did the same thing. I stole ideas.

Fr. Mottet wasn't just an idea stealer and imitator. He wanted projects to be copied. A successful project was like seed money. It could lead to other successful projects, improved federal legislation, and more world change.

We had a lot of money going out in grants, so I had to make sure it came in too. Notre Dame was famous for raising millions. Their professional fund raisers came to advise us and said, "Small contributions are important, and you've got to work with people." A Notre Dame donor gave five hundred dollars and then five thousand. They kept working with him, and he finally gave five million. We listened to those people and tried to do a better job with our promotions.

During my years at the Campaign for Human Development, our budget went from about six million dollars to eight or nine million. We were evaluated by a national company that reviews charitable organizations, and over ninety percent of our money went to the groups we funded, not to advertising and office space or things like that. We were the General Motors of community organizing. I met with Archbishop Roche when he was President of the Conference of U.S. Bishops and complained that we had trouble keeping up with inflation. He was very supportive, but he said, "Nobody keeps up with inflation."

At that time, corporations would not fund community organizing. It was considered too radical, but when poor people are shut out and dissatisfied, it can lead to a revolt. Later, groups like the Ford Foundation started putting millions of dollars into organizations that empowered poor people with a sense of dignity and control of their neighborhoods and their lives.

In my second year in Washington, D.C., I made my first trip to Europe to visit Mondragon, the famous worker owned co-op in the Basque region of Spain. I hoped I could transplant that idea to Hispanic communities in the United States. The trip was part of my work, but I paid my own way and took our program officer for the west coast, who spoke Spanish. It was a great trip. Mondragon is up in the mountains on the border of France. The Basques lost their civil war, and they hate the Spaniards. They even speak a different language. The road signs had names of towns in both Spanish and Basque, but the Basques spray painted over the Spanish. The day we left; they blew up a bank.

It was hard to find the place. We drove around in the mountains in a little rental car and asked, "Where's Mondragon?" "Mondragon, never heard of it. Oh, you mean MondragON. It's right over there," they said. We had the accent on the wrong syllable. I remember the nice meals we had there. They are surrounded by oceans, so they ate a lot of fish dishes. Mondragon had become so famous that they had a young woman who did nothing but handle visitors.

A priest and five young men, who were part of a Young Christian workers group, started Mondragon by producing kerosene lanterns. In little towns in that area, the most modern and attractive building was the co-op. They started their own banking system to handle their money and schools to train their workers. They became the number two producer of household appliances in Spain. It was quite a revolution.

In the Mondragon co-ops, management could not make more than three times as much as the line workers. Later, they had to raise that to recruit financial managers for the banking system, but it was still way less than in the United States where it's four hundred or five hundred times as much. We are off the charts. I thought the Campaign for Human Development could make a big difference if we funded a lot of worker-owned co-ops.

According to the Mondragon Corporation website, Mondragon currently consists of ninety-six separate, self-governing cooperatives, more than eighty-one thousand people, and fourteen research and development centers. It is the leading business group in the Basque area and the tenth in Spain with sales in more than one hundred fifty countries.

Unfortunately, that business model was not far along in this country. The Campaign for Human Development came close to funding a worker owned co-op. We met with an organization of fishermen that wanted to catch fish, ship them all over the U.S., and open restaurants. It was going to be worker owned. They had a plan to leverage money and empower people, and they were working for institutional change. I was scheduled to meet with the Cardinal in their area to get his support, but during the night he had a heart attack, and we couldn't move forward.

The Seamless Garment

Meetings of the Conference of U.S. Bishops were opened to the press after Vatican II, but they were so boring reporters fell asleep. That changed in 1983 when the bishops started discussing the peace issue and nuclear war. TV cameras from all over the world were there. Every time there was a break, reporters went out into the hall with their crew and buttonholed a bishop. Representatives from Japan were there thirty-five years after their country suffered the nuclear bomb. Suddenly, the church came alive because the debate was exciting. Hearings were held, and drafts of the bishops' statements were discussed at universities. All the bishops discussed the draft with their staffs. Archbishop Bernardin from Chicago was chairman of that committee.

The Pastoral Letter on War and Peace included strong statements about nuclear arms proliferation:

> It is never permitted to direct nuclear or conventional weapons to 'the indiscriminate destruction of whole cities or vast areas with their populations . . . The intentional killing of innocent civilians or non-combatants is always wrong . . . The arms race is one of the greatest curses on the human race; it is to be condemned as a danger, an act of aggression against the poor, and a folly which does not provide the security it promises. [37]

At the Catholic Worker house, we had brother and sister siblings, whose dad worked in nuclear energy and created parts for the nuclear bomb. The family had a newborn daughter who was very sick. The dad promised to work for peace if his daughter lived. When she lived, he drove his Volkswagen bus and parked out front everywhere John Paul II showed up. It had a big sign on the side: "Condemn Nuclear Weapons." When the Pastoral Letter on War and Peace by the

National Conference of Catholic Bishops came out in 1983, it finally happened. It pays to advertise.

Archbishop Bernadin came up with the concept of "consistent ethic of life," the idea that life is sacred from womb to tomb. It was a stroke of genius. The brains behind Bernardin's concept was my friend, Fr. Bryan Hehir, who taught at Harvard. When Bernardin spoke, we all looked over to see if Bryan Hehir was moving his lips. Bernardin tied together the violence of abortion and the violence of war and injustice. Some conservatives opposed this idea because it took away their single issue, opposition to abortion. We've been beaten over the head with this single issue.

Bernardin, then a Cardinal, used the metaphor of the seamless garment, Jesus' seamless robe that wasn't torn by his executioners, to link opposition to abortion with opposition to nuclear weapons, capital punishment, and other life issues. Cardinal Bernardin faced a lot of opposition. People carried "Talk Is Cheap" protest signs.

It's hard to explain how the right to life issue came to be separate from social justice. The first right a person has is the right to life, but what about the mother who is struggling on food stamps and has a job with low pay? She will feel pressure, especially if she is an African American woman. The single-issue people elect someone who agrees with them on abortion but is against everything else the Catholic Church stands for.

There was a big brouhaha because The American Life League, which focuses on the single issue of abortion, considered the Campaign for Human Development guilty by association when we worked on issues like fair housing with organizations that supported abortion and gay marriage. We only cooperated with them on issues about which we agreed.

Pro-life became a litmus test for church teachings and actions. Fr. Mottet was opposed to abortion, but he objected to prioritizing the abortion issue above all other justice issues.

People who make the guilt-by-association argument don't understand or refuse to understand the difference between public relationships and private relationships. Private relationships are family and close friends. You stick with them no matter what. Public relationships are different. You work together on issues where you have agreement. Cardinal Krol, who was President of the Bishops Conference before I got there, said, "We'll follow the same rules as the Vatican." The Vatican funds the United Nations to do projects like the United Nations Children's Fund, but the Vatican doesn't agree with the United Nations on other issues. In the same way, the Campaign for Human Development funded groups that agreed with us on specific issues.

When organizing first started, just one neighborhood was involved. Then it expanded to part of a city and, eventually, a whole city. It became state-wide, and then it became national. It got complicated because we had coalitions to deal with.

You Only Get One or Two Minutes

Each year from 1978 to 1985, I left Washington, D.C., after Labor Day and travelled the country to announce grants and promote groups that worked for justice. If I didn't go out and meet the people, we would just be a national office that nobody knew. People needed to see how their money was being used locally. I went to about fifty dioceses a year. I always picked up The New York Times in the airport before I held a press conference. I began with a statement relevant to the news. Reporters often asked, "Where'd you get that?" I got it from *The New York Times* that morning. The other papers picked it up a day or two later. I also read *The Washington Post* and used it for groups in that area, and I kept up with the *Des Moines Register* and the *Quad-City Times*.

I went all over this country preaching that people had the right to self-determination, the right to express their voice, and the right to justice. I said ordinary people could be trained to organize their communities. I was preaching the gospel, but people often said they had never heard that before. Travelling the country was a great opportunity to teach, and I loved it. It gave me a national pulpit. People told me they heard my voice on the radio when they were driving at midnight. I walked into the best job in the whole country.

Back in Young Christian Students days, I learned from Matt Ahmann that you only get one or two minutes on radio or TV, and you must have your ideas down so you can shoot them like bullets in a few seconds. I couldn't read a speech or give someone else's speech, so I spoke from outlines. If there was an exact quote I wanted to use, I wrote it out. I always put all the information I needed on a card when I went into an office or a diocese. I won some people over, and those who disagreed shook their heads like crazy.

I tried to get to all the seminaries that prepared diocesan priests because I remembered how much outside speakers influenced me. I quoted scriptures, papal encyclicals, Vatican II, and the U.S. Bishops. They argued just by the looks on their faces. A few of them challenged me openly. At St. Mary's in Baltimore, I said that some people call this communism. A guy got up and said, "Well, it sounds like communism to me." I said, "Communism means the state owns all productive property. Does that happen in the United States? Is that what we're trying to do? No. We are trying to empower poor people, so they are heard." After all, Pope Francis has been called a communist.

I ran into a lot of trouble when I spoke at seminaries, so I had to be very careful. When they asked questions like, "What kind of justice?" to get into classifications, I said, "Just ask your seminary professors. They will be able to tell you." Conservative seminaries were opposed to the bishop's pastorals on nuclear war and the economy. At a conservative seminary in Portland, I said, "I want to tell you about my background. I grew up in poverty, and I was facing death a few years ago." That kind of opened their minds, but one guy disagreed with everything I said. When he got up and walked out, he hit the crash bar on the door real hard, and I busted out laughing. You know you've arrived when you get people to do that.

A group from Russia visited us at the Catholic Worker house, but they were still "commies." I saw how much that changed when I was back in Washington, D.C., for a visit in 1987, and Gorbachev came. He was like a gift from God, like King Cyrus in the Old Testament. He stopped his caravan in the big intersection between Independence Avenue and K Street and said, "I want to meet the people." He got out and plunged into the crowd, and they chanted, "Gorbie, Gorbie, Gorbie."

In the sixth century BCE, Cyrus the Great, king of Persia, established the largest empire known until his time. In the Bible, he is famous for freeing the Jewish captives in Babylon and allowing them to return to their homeland and rebuild the temple in Jerusalem. (Ezra 1: 1-4)

When I was in Los Angeles, I stayed overnight at an inner-city parish that had a soup kitchen. The cardinal lived there in the rectory, and the police department had an officer on the corner to protect him. When I went to morning Mass in the chapel, I looked back and saw all the winos with the cardinal right in the middle.

One of my staff members was with me when I spoke to a group of priests in Portland, Oregon. After I taught from scripture, he said, "Man, I didn't know you could talk like that." Since I tried to bring in current situations, I'm sure people thought I was making political speeches, especially during the Reagan administration, but they were theological speeches, social justice speeches.

The Campaign for Human Development funded groups that worked on immigration reform, housing, and employment. We wanted to change laws, policies, and decision-making processes. It's easy to say, but I'm still working on it. I like to tell a story about Pope John XXIII, who had a great sense of humor. Once they asked him how many people work in the Vatican. "Oh," he said, "about half of them," and, "What do we do, Holy Father, if the Lord returns?" "Look busy," he said. I'm sure that when the Lord returns, we will still be working for justice. It's like your car. You have to tinker with it and repair it all the time because it wears out.

I thought faith-based organizing was the most effective, but applicants for grants didn't need to have a connection to the Catholic Church. Muslims, Jews, or people of no religion could apply.

A lot of young community organizers were Jewish. One of them wanted to start a Jewish organization based on the Campaign for Human Development that would be called "The Jewish Fund." Jewish people understood the justice issues, which are strong in the prophetic scriptures. They were involved in our interfaith civil rights meetings. They had interests in common with us. We received a lot of criticism for funding groups that weren't Catholic. Conservative Catholics tend to want all funding to go to a Catholic charity.

When I went home to Davenport after seven years in Washington, D.C., I was glad to be away from the hustle-bustle and not be on airplanes all the time, but I missed the tremendous amount of information I always had while I was there. I usually knew someone who worked in the Capitol or had a friend who did. The Campaign for Human Development had reliable information coming from all over the country since we worked with the national bishops and were connected to Rome. It was like a great switchboard for the church and for the world.

I never dreamed of being pastor of Sacred Heart Cathedral, but several of my staff members got wind of it when they went to a meeting in Chicago. When they came back, they said, "We met a wonderful priest, Msgr. Menke. He's pastor of the cathedral in Davenport, and he said you're going to replace him." I was so surprised. When Bishop O'Keefe came for his meeting in November, we had lunch together. He said, "Stay as long as you want, but if you want to come home, I'll write a letter." After being in Washington, D.C., for seven years, I thought I had used up all my ideas and was just minding the store. If I stayed, it was just a career, so I told him I was ready to come home. I was fifty-five, and I thought that was ancient. Then he said, "I'd like you to be pastor of the cathedral."

Fr. Mottet's right-hand man, Tim Collins, probably knew the full story of those seven years in Washington, D.C. better than anyone else. Fr. Mottet credited Tim with knowing "where all the bodies were buried," which meant he knew what had gone wrong in the past and what could lead to trouble. Tim kept the operation running smoothly while Father was out front as the national spokesman.

We thought he might tell us about struggles or outstanding projects, but when we interviewed him, he focused more on purpose, character, and values than on achievements, wins, and losses.

> I worked for the Bishop's Conference with the Campaign for Human Development from the beginning. Over the eight years I was on the staff before Marv came on the scene, I was a sponge of sorts, and I picked things up. I knew the bishops, and I knew who our friends were and who was going to be a problem. I remember the search for an Executive Director. The new director would be walking into some messy situations. I knew Marv from his membership on the National Committee. The General Secretary called me and said, "Who's this guy Mottet?" I said "Get him. He's the best."

> He had credibility from his personal story and from his life's work in the civil rights arena. I could not think of a better person to seriously consider for that job. He is smart as a fox. When Marv started the job, it became clear to me right away that he was very organized in his thinking and very strategic. The other thing that struck me early on was the friendship and the work relationship that developed.

> I don't think he fully understands the depth of his role over the last fifty years. He is so humble and so modest. He lent a lot of credibility from his years in the trenches of civil rights and social action. People believed in him. We were

together for dinner a couple of Novembers ago when he came east for a meeting. Our conversation was all "we." Remember when we did this? Remember when we did that? He talked about how they underestimated us, but "we" was the relevant pronoun.

In addition to Marv's Campaign for Human Development responsibilities, he and Fr. Dick McSorley started Catholic Worker houses. He was committed to it, but you have the social work side of it twenty-four-seven. It doesn't end when you get home from your job at the end of the day. Eventually, he and Fr. McSorley handed that off to two other people. He knows how to start things and then let others lead them. It is true empowerment.

He was the public face of the campaign. When he visited projects we funded, he spoke from his own story about what we were doing. We made a conscious effort to tell the powerful human stories of lives change. He brought the invisibility of the poor to people's attention.

His style is very collaborative. I grew enormously in my affection for him. His sense of fair play helped him know what needed to be done for poor people to help unstack the deck. He wanted the goals and objectives of the Campaign for Human Development to take root in people's lives. On election day, he wanted them to pull the levers in a way that would help the poor.

Marv had a glorious sense of detachment, probably because he went through that life threatening illness in the late sixties. He was the last person in the world who would get attached to a nice car or a nice suit of clothes. There was no self-interest, nothing in it for him. It was totally altruistic and rooted in his sense of Christianity and who he is, not just as a priest, but as a human being.

In his seven years as National Director, we lived through the good and bad together. There was hostility from enemies who thought the organization was political. They thought we were the democratic party of prayer and that kind of thing.

I think he was sad to leave for home, but he knew it was time. He stayed longer than he ever expected. His story is important because he is a model of how to help the poor, not from the top down, but from the bottom up. He didn't superimpose a model from the top to make changes or arrive at solutions. The grassroots approach truly embodies the whole notion of empowerment, which is a prime ingredient in Catholic social teaching and the gospel message. It was stunning.

For seven years, Fr. Mottet had lived out his trademark two feet of social justice model. "If you want peace, work for justice" became his personal slogan. All that time, his work was guided by the principles of institutional change and the distinction between public and private relationships. How would he transfer those ideas to pastoral ministry back in Davenport?

Chapter 13

The Luckiest Thing that Ever Happened to Me

When I came back to Davenport in 1985 to replace Msgr. Menke, Sacred Heart was a dying parish. It had been going downhill for thirty years along with the neighborhood. It was a disaster. We were so close to bankruptcy that I sold furniture out of the rectory to pay bills for the school.

The Sacred Heart neighborhood was seventy percent rental housing. Several corner groceries run by Italians had closed. A lot of houses were abandoned, which had a terrible effect on the neighborhood. One of the famous ones was right across the street from the cathedral. The FBI contacted me about using our steeple for a lookout because they were watching people at that house. I took them up there, and they said it was perfect, but they made an arrest before they ever used the steeple.

A woman with mental problems often called the police and said she saw smoke coming from the steeple at Sacred Heart. She also called about St. Paul's parish. That Pastor knew who she was and turned her in. Firemen with heavy coats and all that heavy gear climbed the steeple in August heat because of her phone calls.

There were several "hoods" in Davenport, and the Sacred Heart neighborhood was one of them. People sold drugs across the street from our rectory. The police parked their car in our parking lot so they could watch. When a woman who tried to buy drugs thought they charged too much, she had her friends beat out the windshield. Another woman called me late at night and said she needed twenty dollars, the price for a shot of drugs, for medicine for her kids. I said, "Your kids always play out in the street. If you want to take care of them, protect them from the street traffic? I know what you're doing for your twenty-dollar drug hit."

My experience in Washington, D.C., helped a lot. I wasn't afraid. I welcomed being appointed to Sacred Heart parish where I could use my social action and housing background. People at a clergy meeting complained about a guy who went around begging for drug money. He knocked on the chapel door when the lights were on and came in. He could cry like a baby. One of his lines was, "My mother died over in Rock Island, and she left me a house." I said, "If she left you a house, why are you living in the homeless shelter?" You learn all those tricks. The doorbell rang once, and a guy said, "Some people are chasing me, and I need you to take me across the river to my family home. I'll lose my life if you don't take me." It was another shakedown.

Before I got to Sacred Heart, Msgr. Menke converted the convent to transitional housing for women leaving hospital or mental health facilities. It was full all the time. The convent was originally for nuns who came from Chicago to teach at Sacred Heart School. One of them wrote back to Chicago: "The boys out in these parts are just as tough as the boys in Chicago." When I was first ordained, I used to visit the convent to hear confessions. It was the most uncomfortable house I had ever seen. The floors were hard, and the chairs were hard. Nothing was soft. I'm sure it was deliberate for doing penitence.

Msgr. Menke was the best thing that had happened for inner-city Davenport in a long time. He was President of St. Ambrose before he became pastor of the cathedral. He said, "I can't believe I was on this campus for twenty-five years and didn't know the problems that existed two blocks away." He had already started several social action initiatives, but he didn't have an organizing background. I brought that. I had been a priest for almost thirty years, but I had never been a pastor.

After I got home in August of 1985, Msgr. Menke stayed on for three months while I got oriented. I hoped to take time for a retreat with the Trappists, but he said, "I'll take care of the parish and the school. I want you to get out into the neighborhood right away and get to know it." He was trying to open the parish out into the community, which was exactly what I wanted, but he wasn't sure how. After he tried unsuccessfully to get other pastors in the neighborhood involved, he went ahead himself. He started the biggest clothing center and the biggest food pantry in the Quad Cities. Our parishioners worked in those centers.

Menke's centers got so big that he had to move them out of the cathedral to the Kahl Building where he rented two or three rooms. When he went to V.O. Figge, President of Davenport Bank and Trust, to pay the rent, V.O. said, "You're not paying this by yourself, are you?" "Well, who else would?" Menke said, so V.O. donated the space for rooms. I'm sure Msgr. Menke spent a lot of his own money on other projects.

When I went to the cathedral, Msgr. Menke was giving out money like it fell from the trees. I asked him why he did all that, and he said, "I don't want to turn Christ away." People in need got off Interstate 80 and asked what church to go to for help. Word spread that we gave vouchers for gas. Pretty soon there was a long line at the rectory, more than we could handle, and we had to stop. Two or three women often waited for help in the sacristy after Mass. There wasn't time to be courteous, much less help them.

Fr. Tom Stratman and I started a program in an old hotel downtown that did information referral. It was a central place where donors could send money and people could go for help. They knew what all the agencies did and could send people to the best place for help. We got other churches to join, and it spread all over the Quad Cities. Churches United eventually took it over.

One day I went to the referral office and found a man crying. He said, "I've been all over this town being turned away, and that woman in there treated me with such kindness. She wrote out this voucher and told me where to go for help." I think those are important stories to tell. The luckiest thing that ever happened to me was when I went to Sacred Heart parish.

During my first year at Sacred Heart, I was trained in Project Rachel,[38] which helps people in the aftermath of an abortion. The purpose is to bring that person to peace and healing. It's amazing what happens. A couple came to Sacred Heart and wanted to put a granite stone in our garden where people could pray for all aborted babies. I didn't ask about their background, but I was sure they had an abortion. There is a private toll-free number at St. Vincent's where the mother or someone else can contact a priest.

Two women around age sixty-five worked in the office, and they weren't fond of each other. They needed to learn how to use a computer. One of them said, "I won't do it." I never like to fire people, so I persuaded Betty Anderson to come back to work for me. I wanted Betty to fire them. She had retired at the Social Action Department because her asthma made it too hard to get up the stairs at the old building, and she was sick for a while. I called her and said, "I don't suppose you would want to come back to work." She said, "You're kidding, of course," but she let me hire her. It was supposed to be a short-term thing to get the computers started, but she ended up doing all the human resources work, except when it came to nuns. Betty managed to fire the two women nicely. She made a big day of it and said it was their retirement. She arranged a recognition in church that Sunday with beautiful big flower baskets. It went off smoothly. They were still mad, but at least they got a lot of sympathy and goodwill from the congregation. Betty always remembered those things even though she didn't care whether she got any thanks.

The Biggest Surprise of My Life

Msgr. Menke told me about a guy named John, who knocked on the door from time to time. The secretary could hear his gruff voice through the wall. He said, "These damned lawyers and damned bankers. All they want to do is steal your money. I think I'll give it to the church." Msgr. Menke got occasional twenty-five-thousand-dollar checks from John and his family, but the church got closer and closer to bankruptcy. I found those cancelled checks when I came to the cathedral. That's how Menke stayed above water. He lobbied Bishop O'Keefe to get me appointed to Sacred Heart because he knew I would keep those inner-city programs going.

John Corsiglia and his siblings lived on Sixth Street four blocks south of the cathedral. They weren't very well known. The two brothers and one sister never married. The Corsiglia brothers ran a candy store and a bar in Rock Island. Since Iowa was dry, cars were parked for blocks in all directions from their store to pick up booze for Christmas and Easter. They were a hardworking Italian family who also got into rental properties and did all their own work.

Msgr. Menke said, "If you can just hang on for a while, there are a couple of old bachelors down the street, and they are going to leave us a million dollars." A month later, I got a call to come because one of the brothers had died. I walked into a moth-eaten house on the corner of Sixth and Le Claire in an African American neighborhood. A policeman was there. John died in his sleep with a hammer under his bed to defend himself in case of a break-in. The other brother, who was kind of feeble-minded, was taken to a nursing home where I visited him and got to know him.

When that brother died a short time later, the estate was settled. The news broke very quickly. Msgr. Menke thought it would be a million, but it was over three million. The Corsiglias just rode the stock market up, but John looked like a beggar when he came to the office door. When the Corsiglias came to church, they sat in the back seat. After that I had a rule: "Don't turn away beggars, and don't criticize people for sitting in the back seat."

A friend of mine, who worked in the trust department at the bank, took care of the Corsiglias. He called me when the younger brother died and told me their whole story. One time, John hired a cab to take him home. He thought the guy charged him too much and refused to pay. The driver took John to the police station where the policeman called the bank and talked to my friend. The banker said, "Tell that cab driver to take him anywhere he wants, and I'll pay him. He can buy that cab company several times over."

They were multi-millionaires, but there were mice everywhere in their home. There was a quart of ice cream, a container of milk, and some sliced lunch meat in the refrigerator. My friend once heard John arguing with his brother about whether they could afford Meals on Wheels. People who knew them when they were younger said they bought nice suits and drove reasonable cars, but not fancy ones. While other people went to Florida and spent all their money, they stayed home and just let it grow. None of them married. The two brothers wouldn't let their sister marry because they heard some guy was after the money. Their parents had come from Italy with nothing. I had their citizenship papers framed and hung on the wall of the cathedral with pictures of the family. Everybody wanted to know the story of the three million dollars. Sister Concetta was Italian, so I gave her the credit. Sacred Heart Cathedral is still in existence because of the generosity of that family. It was the biggest surprise of my life.

Before I got word of the three million dollars, we were so broke that I had practiced my chapter eleven bankruptcy speech. Word spread like wildfire. One of our parishioners heard it on the street in Chicago. We kept quiet for a week or two and then announced it to the whole parish.

My first reaction was: "How do you spend that much money?" I knew we needed a new pick-up truck because our old one was always breaking down. The main thing was the six rundown buildings we had to restore. Even with that much money, it was a struggle to keep that place going and stay on top of the neighborhood at the same time. There was a school to keep alive and a lot left to be done. I knew it was the right thing to give the teachers a raise, and we had to put in air conditioning. Our first project was to tuck point the buildings and put on new roofs to keep them dry and safe.

Fortunately, V.O. Figge loved the cathedral. His daughters were married there. He used money from the estate of his wife, Elizabeth Kahl Figge, to help paint and decorate the church. I was just getting to know her when she died. Since her maiden name was Kahl, she used to say, "My name is Figge, but I used to be a Kahl girl."

The first thing I asked him to do was fix up the chapel, but he was interested in art and was an art collector. V.O. remembered a picture from his daughter's wedding, and he agreed to have it repaired. Sometimes he sat there all day to make sure the painter got things just right. Next, he agreed to repair a famous painting of Saint Margaret of Scotland, which had been incorrectly repaired twice. It was ripped like it had fallen over a pew. St. Margaret became Queen of Scotland by marriage, but she had a scoundrel of a husband. He built her a chapel because she prayed all the time. She reformed the church and started monasteries, but her main thing was helping the poor. In the painting, she is giving food to the poor. That was charity, not justice.

V.O. agreed to send it to a museum in Ohio. Trucks from the museum arrived at night to take the painting out, and they charged fifty thousand dollars because I made the mistake of telling them we received fifty thousand dollars to fix up the chapel. They immersed the painting in liquids to clean it, removed the old stitching, and repaired it correctly. The painting still hangs in the right front side of the church. The cathedral was originally St. Margaret's Church, and our school was named St. Margaret's. Two classrooms were used to create St. Ambrose College, which was a college seminary at that time. We have a plaque at the back of the church stating that the redecoration of the Cathedral is to the credit of V.O. Figge.

You Can't Save the Parish Unless You Save the Neighborhood

I knew we had to go out into the neighborhood because it was in such bad shape. We started right away with a holy hour at the church. We got volunteers and sent them out into the neighborhood to knock on doors and ask, "What do you want for this neighborhood?" Our volunteers were a little frightened, so we prayed for their protection. They wrote those answers down, and we announced a meeting at the cathedral. The neighbors wanted the same things we did.

Knowledge has force in organizing. If you give information when it's not appropriate, you give away power. You first develop power by knowing the people and their self-interests. If it's top down, it won't work. If you want to empower poor people, you start with individual meetings to learn about their interests, concerns, and passions. Then you hold a group meeting and put those concerns on a chalkboard. You can only work on a maximum of four, so you prioritize them and work on one or two at a time. It is always bottom up.

Fr. Mottet's insistence that development must be bottom up, not top down, was his practical way to engage people and make progress. Cooks Point was a bottom-up initiative that started with barrio residents in need. Fr. Mottet sent conscientious objectors out across the Davenport Diocese to identify needs and listen to people who were suffering injustice. The Campaign for Human Development empowered organizations to make needed changes they identified and developed themselves.

Before the meeting, I met with three of the biggest African American men I could find. They were former football players, and one was an NBA player. I had breakfast with them and said, "You know, if you guys would help me, I think we could turn this neighborhood around."

When we held the group meeting at the cathedral, we called all the parts of the neighborhood together with the Mayor and City Council.

We had the city officials in front, and the sanctuary was divided into four sections representing four sections of the neighborhood.

We asked each section to send someone to the microphone to tell the Mayor and City Council about the worst problem in that neighborhood. After all four sections did that, I said to the Mayor and City Council, "Now we're going to show you these problems. We're going to have a procession." We had a little Black kid, who was part of the Cribbs family, hold the cross. Since that was a bit dangerous, the Cribbs family followed along in their SUV.

Since those big guys were with us, we marched right through the gang area. There were at least a hundred people marching. We were a religious procession. The gang members flashed hand signals, but I didn't understand them. When we got two blocks south of the cathedral, the mayor said, "We don't want to start a fight." I said, "We're not going to start a fight. We're just going to show you the four places they picked."

The first house we showed them was a rental house with the basement full of bicycle parts because those people stole bicycles. I admired that family in some ways because they understood capitalism and they earned their own way. They were an infamous family who came to Davenport on a bus after the city council in Missouri paid for one-way tickets. An African American church hired a Black minister who intended to work with the family and convert them. I don't know how that ended, but one of the children was killed on Locust Street near the Cathedral. She was on a bike. Some kids who were speeding hit her and pinned her body under the car. The police used jacks to raise the car and pull her body out. That is the kind of fate these people faced.

A Black policeman, who was a handsome dude, went to talk with a drug-dealing family, and because he was African American, they showed him where all the drugs were hidden. When I saw him at Mass, I used to say, "How's the hood?" My friend Fran Riley from KWQC News used to call me and say, "Any news? What's going on in the neighborhood?" When he had a slow news day, he came over and we walked around.

The neighborhood felt like the dry bones in Ezekiel 37: "Dry bones, see, I will bring my Spirit upon you."[39] I knew it would take the Holy Spirit to renew the neighborhood. Davenport was so depressed. It seemed like everything south of Locust Street had died. One of the jokes going around was: "There's two things that you can't get rid of. One is AIDS, and the other is a house in Davenport."

With so many problems in the parish, people were surprised that I organized Quad Cities Interfaith within my first year back in Davenport. When you have your back to the wall, you do whatever it takes.

I had tried unsuccessfully to start Quad Cities Interfaith before I went to Washington, D.C. The first president was a rabbi, a close friend of mine. A Rock Island businessman helped me borrow ten thousand dollars for start-up costs from Patricia Hewitt, the wife of Deere and Company's president. We didn't have a trained organizer, and I didn't know how to organize in those days. I made mistakes. I can't remember all the details, but it never flew. We couldn't get the other churches involved. Eventually Geno Baroni gave me the money to pay Mrs. Hewitt back.

It was different when I came back in 1985. I found some Protestant ministers who were already meeting because factories had closed, twenty-three thousand jobs were lost, and they were losing members. They usually don't talk to Catholics, but they were losing money, and that made it easier to talk about this stuff. What they were trying to do was all charity. Those ministers had almost talked this to death for two years. There was too much focus on charity and not enough on justice. Food baskets only help people for two or three days.

I brought in a skilled organizer from the Gamaliel Foundation in Chicago. In a couple of meetings, he walked us through the fog. What he accomplished was so amazing the group agreed to pay him five hundred dollars. At first, it was mostly the First Christian Church of Rock Island, the Second Baptist Church of Rock Island, and Church of Peace, where we had a lot of our meetings. When it started to work, they called me "the wise man from the east." You can still see some of those people at Quad Cities Interfaith meetings today, but most of them are retired, and others are deceased. I'm not long behind them.

The Gamaliel Foundation, which does great work all over the country, is named after Gamaliel, a great Jewish teacher, quoted in Acts 5: "If this plan is of man, it will fail, but if it is of God, you will not be able to overthrow them. You might even be found opposing God." In 1986, Greg Galluzzo became Executive Director of Gamaliel, and we hit it off right away. Greg used to visit me every week and stay overnight at the rectory. I think he mentored Barack Obama in Chicago. I always wondered if Barack Obama worked for one the groups we funded when he was a community organizer. One time I saw him get off a plane, and he said, "Good to see you again". I think he was faking.

My experience at the Campaign for Human Development convinced me that faith-based organizing was the most effective whether people were Jews, Muslims, or other faiths. The Catholic Interracial Council was a good example of faith-based organizing.

Fr. Mottet recommended Gregory Pierce's book, Activism that Makes Sense, *for the best understanding of faith-based organizing. According to Pierce:*

> Community organization is an attempt to combine existing civic, religious, business, union, service, and volunteer organizations in a particular area into a new vehicle that can negotiate with other power institutions for the self-interest of its members . . . Many people accept that they need to actively engage in the problems of the world, but since they don't know how to do that successfully, they don't make a dent in the problem, and they become burned out or disillusioned. The problems are too big to be solved by individuals. For religious congregations, community

organizing is an uncomfortable necessity that forces them
to deal with self-interest, power, alliances, controversy, and
leadership. (p. 45)

Interfaith cooperation wasn't a new idea. It started because of World
War II. Priests and ministers who opposed Nazism were in prison
together, and the ecumenical movement grew out of that. In the
United States, the labor movement brought Catholic and Protestant
ministers together. Saul Alinsky's Industrial Areas Foundation in
Chicago was one result. Alinsky became a friend of the Archbishop
of Chicago and started out using Catholic money. Then he got money
from a big Jewish department store in Chicago.

Eventually Quad Cities Interfaith included about thirty churches. It's
hard to get clergy, especially Catholic clergy, involved in the
community because they don't think about public relationships.
Seminaries tend to reduce everything to private relationships. First
you have a relationship with Jesus and then all your parishioners.

One of our problems was that the city fathers of Davenport thought
federal money was poison. We could have done so much more. I
disagree with Dorothy Day on that issue. She wouldn't take
government money, but I'll take it when we can get it because it is for
the common good.

When the gambling boat issue came up in Davenport, I voted against
it. I think it does more harm than good. Some Protestant ministers
condemn the use of funds from gambling establishments, but I'm in
the social service business. I'll take all those millions of dollars and
run to the bank. When you serve the Lord, you use the tools you can,
even though they're not perfect. Jesus helped the poor. Maybe those
loaves and fishes came from a gentile, but he multiplied them. I
visited a famous pagan shrine that Jesus went to in Caesarea Philippi.
There is a rock background with pagan altars built into the rock, and
that is where Jesus said, "Thou art Peter, and on this rock, I will build
my church."

When we started Quad Cities Interfaith, the St. Vincent's fund, which had supported the St. Vincent's orphanage, was sizeable. At a staff meeting one time, I was pressing Bishop O'Keefe to approve twenty thousand dollars for a joint program between Iowa and Nebraska. He said, "Mottet, you've always got your hand in the coffer." I said, "Not for me, Bishop. It's for the poor." He approved my request, and it passed the Board. A priest friend, who was at the rich parish in Bettendorf, said, "Wow, I wish I could find money like that." I said, "Well, you just gotta know where to look."

I was offered several free houses, but I had to turn them down because I didn't have the money to start Interfaith Housing until 1993. The first money we got was after several big storms and floods. The U.S. Catholic Bishops started a nationwide collection to help churches in devastated areas. Several million dollars were in this fund. I worked with Dan Ebener, who headed the Social Action Department then, to get one of those grants. It was at least a quarter of a million dollars, and it had to be invested in housing. That was big money to us, but it didn't last long. We used that to start Interfaith Housing. We bought inner-city houses, fixed them up, and put families in them. We started in our neighborhood, but we worked wherever we could buy a house at reasonable cost.

One of the people who knew Fr. Mottet best was Dr. Dan Ebener, who worked closely with him for twenty years and continued to be a close friend. When we asked Dan to describe Fr. Mottet's influence, he said:

Marv came back to Davenport shortly before I did. I don't think I would have gotten the position of Social Action Director without his good word in the interview committee. At that point, he became my pastor, my mentor, my ally, my friend, and much more. We deepened our relationship during the twenty years I worked at Social Action. He lives out the values of the gospel of Jesus Christ more than anyone I know. He does what he says and says what he does. He has been a rock, as solid as can be.

Our first project was Quad Cities Interfaith. Initially, Marv asked me to serve on the board, but we realized that a better role for me was as an ally because I was the Diocese Director of the Campaign for Human Development. We worked together to recruit churches into Quad Cities Interfaith and develop leaders. We went together to training in Chicago and brought training to the Quad Cities. It was eye-opening. Marv was the person responsible for connecting Quad Cities Interfaith to Gamaliel Foundation, and without that, we would never have gotten off the ground.

There had been false starts with Quad Cities Interfaith, and church leaders were about ready to cash it in when Marv told them about Gamaliel and brought in organizers. Marv convinced me of the need to send people to be trained, and we set aside funds for that. They became leaders in their churches, not just in Quad Cities Interfaith. "Self-interest" was a big word for Marv. It was in the self-interest of pastors to send people for training because they got real leaders.

My profession now is training young leaders. It was Marv who helped me see that the change I wanted to bring about in the world was too big for one person to lead. The focus needed to shift from leading the change to developing leaders who will lead the change. I shifted from trying to be the charismatic leader, who everyone dances behind, to the person behind the scenes who develops other people. This not only changed the direction of my life in the nineteen eighties, but it has come full circle to direct what I do and what I teach. When I teach leadership at St. Ambrose or anywhere in the world, I continue to use some of the same exercises we learned in that Gamaliel training.

Marv always found time to garden and take care of himself. Gardening was a way to get people into a neutral environment to talk. The gardens he started at St. Vincent were influential in starting community gardens where people had a little plot of land to grow their vegetables if they didn't have room in their own yards.

In his later years, he became mostly the idea person and let others be out front. It is not an exaggeration to say that for years I got between two and five calls a week from Fr. Mottet, and one of those calls would be about some new idea he had. It would take an army of implementers for all the ideas he had. We had to vet the ideas to do the ones that were possible. He made connections that others couldn't see and had the ability to build consensus.

We worked with the Davenport Police Department to control crime. Abandoned houses and a high percentage of rental property run down the neighborhood. Landlords don't put money into rental houses. When we fixed up a house, the neighbors would say, "Where can we get some paint? What can we do to make our house better?" It was contagious. I bought a used tiller to help people start gardens. People came back after several years and said, "Boy, the neighborhood looks better." Crime went down considerably. We were on a roll.

It is easy to get houses because people want the tax write-off. Interfaith Housing fixed up four houses a year. This created jobs and improved the neighborhood, but it was a constant battle. We lost money on every house we fixed up. Our competition was the slumlords trying to turn over a fast buck.

I found one of my former students, who had a knack for fixing up old houses, and we hired him as Director at Interfaith Housing. We had such a reputation for honesty and good work that the city asked Interfaith Housing to take over a failing program. We could only find one developer who would work south of Locust Street. We bought an octagon house down on Sixth Street. The reason it was an octagon was that Italians thought the devil hid in corners. We bought it and fixed it up, and then we found a buyer. After that, we bought a beautiful house where there had been a fire. When we sold the house, we had money to invest in the next one. Interfaith Housing is still going on. I gave up my job as president a couple of years ago, but we get together for lunch about once a year.

Fr. Mottet's two major community organizing initiatives in Davenport both had the word "interfaith" in their titles. His commitment to interfaith work was a practical recognition of the broad-based effort the revitalization of Davenport would require. Beyond that, it was another example of his distinction between public and private relationships. He helped churches, individuals, and organizations recognize that they didn't have to agree about everything to work together on issues of common self-interest.

At one point, we were going down the tube. I'll tell you who really helped us. It was the Quad City Bank and Trust. I called in all my chips. One of my former students was head of the bank. We went to him, and he loaned us the money we needed. I said, "You saved us from going under." He said, "That's what banks are supposed to do."

A professional fundraiser gave me good advice. He said, "You have to know who is in a giving mood and what they will give to." I heard about a donor who gave to housing, so I went to see him and his wife. I think she had most of the money. I knew their son, a photographer for the *Quad-City Times*. He took a well-known photo of a little African American child looking up the steps at a policeman at the door. That photo was framed on their living room wall. It was a classic. We talked about that picture for a while, and I said, "I would like to have a copy someday." We needed twenty-five thousand dollars to keep Interfaith Housing afloat. I had it in fifteen minutes. When I walked out, I said, "Darn, I should have asked her for fifty." The people at Interfaith Housing breathed a sigh of relief, and I was the hero for a day or two.

It is important to know a person's interest and passion in fundraising, just like in organizing. I went to the Vice President of a bank to ask him to support our school, but he didn't believe in Catholic education. I needed to buy a house across the street from the cathedral, so I went to talk with that banker again, but about the house. This time he agreed. By then, I knew his interest. He lived in the parish and cared about property. You go where you can. Fundraising is about building relationships. After an interview, I put the person's name at the top of a card and wrote notes. Later I studied the cards. To build a relationship, you reveal enough of yourself to make someone comfortable, but the goal is to get information about them.

I wanted to buy a decaying house on Tenth Street across from the front of the cathedral. I asked someone to buy the house, and he said he would if I could get a good deal. I went back to the owner and got a lower price, and that man bought the house. I don't want to beat a dead horse, but the number one mistake is not asking. The number two mistake is not knowing the person's passion.

Fr. Mottet was a remarkably successful fundraiser. One of his top-ten lessons is: "Be fearless in asking for favors." This lesson is closely linked with two others: "Everything important I have achieved came from relationships," and "You have to know people's interest and passion to get them involved."

While I was still in Washington, D.C., I was elected Chairman of the Board of the Gamaliel Foundation. I think it was a political move because they wanted Campaign for Human Development grant money, but I was Chairman after I came back to Davenport until I had to go on dialysis in 1997. Quad Cities Interfaith was the first branch of Gamaliel Foundation outside of Chicago. My involvement with Gamaliel really helped refine my ideas about organizing.

Organizations that oppose Gamaliel claim that it was founded by Saul Alinsky, but this is unsubstantiated. It is more likely that Gamaliel is connected to Fr. Mottet's friend Jack Egan and the Contract Buyers League. Gamaliel works in three areas: building strong local organizations, developing powerful leaders through training, and running nonpartisan advocacy and civic engagement campaigns. Gamaliel, with its forty-four affiliates in seventeen states, the United Kingdom, and South Africa, is an example of broad-based organizing which spans varied communities with many interests in a city or region. Gamaliel works to create networks of public relationships they can rely on in the political or social spheres. "This approach requires slow, quiet work that rarely, if ever, trends on social media." [41]

Gamaliel training includes topics that became second nature to Fr. Mottet: the one-on-one relational meeting, the world as it is versus the world as it should be, power, and self-interest. Gamaliel has been accused of using deceptive strategies to pursue its liberal ideology. Within the Catholic Church, it is accused of supporting issues that are at odds with official doctrine.

Loxi Hopkins, a Methodist woman, became the best organizer and leader I ever brought into Quad Cities Interfaith. Sacred Heart Cathedral had an annual collection after Mass for a respect-for-life program. Loxi Hopkins, one of the volunteers for that program, stood out in front of the cathedral to collect money. When I talked with her, Loxi said, "What am I doing over here collecting money for this when my church over there believes in abortion?" I said, "We can fix that. Come next Wednesday night at seven o'clock." She showed up and brought her husband because they had agreed to always do things together. He did not intend to become a Catholic, but he was hooked, and the whole family came into the church.

When we ran out of money to pay an organizer, Loxi took over for a year, but she said, "I never want to do it again." She tried to organize three churches just north of Sacred Heart. We hoped those churches would come into Quad Cities Interfaith as a group. They never did, but they now have a community garden, and they do things together. That wasn't what we intended, but it was a great move for those churches and the neighborhood. Loxi is an outstanding leader, and she is still going strong.

Around 1989, we began Healing Masses at Sacred Heart. We were still working to repair the church and the school. It was interesting how we got the sound system fixed. We had started a prayer group among the Hispanics at St. Mary's. A man who ran an Enterprise car rental company came to the prayer meeting with his father, who was involved in charismatic renewal in Kansas City. I knew the son made a lot of money because he wore an expensive overcoat. The father came to me for prayer. I always ask people what they want to pray for. He said, "I want you to pray for my ministry. I pray for healing in Kansas City, Missouri." Sometime later, a healing Mass was scheduled at Sacred Heart, but a snowstorm cancelled everything. People asked if we would cancel the Mass, but I said, "No, if two people show up, we'll pray for them."

About a dozen people came. One of them was the son of that man. We talked before Mass, and he said, "We ought to be able to improve this sound system." I told him we had already spent a lot of money on it. He handed me a pew envelope when he left. I opened it in the morning, and there was a check for ten thousand smack-a-roos. Later, he checked on the actual cost of the sound system and gave another seven thousand dollars without even being asked. I knew for sure that was the Lord.

The Elephant Was Being Unloaded

Around Sacred Heart, you always know what day of the week it is because everything revolves around Sunday. You're following a schedule. After I retired and was living at St. Vincent's, it was hard to tell what day it was. Bishop Franklin, who was my classmate, came in one day and said, "What's today?" I answered, "Well, today is Thursday. And what's on the schedule? Nothing."

The best time of the week for me was when I prepared the Sunday homily. I watched television or listened to the radio to see what was going on. I read the newspaper and put that together with what people were experiencing. It was my most enjoyable time because it was a time of prayer and reflection. I always listened to other preachers. One idea from another preacher can improve your homily. I started on Sunday night and read the scriptures and kept notes every morning for the whole week. By the end of the week, my homily was ready to go. Sometimes I read whole gospels or other books of the Bible.

We had a lot of Masses at the Cathedral. I started homilies with a story or joke. If you try to cover too much material, it doesn't work, so I could always cut one point. I tried to know the people, but they went by so fast while I stood at the door as they came in and went out.

I used the one-on-one interview in many situations, even my Tuesday and Thursday hospital visits. It was an opportunity, not a chore. Those people weren't going anywhere. They were glad I was there, and they usually wanted to talk about their lives. After they came home, I looked out from the pulpit at Sunday Mass, and I knew them. Besides the hospital, weddings and funerals are where I really got to know people. You can spend time with them then.

We had an outdoor parish festival every year at the eleven o'clock Mass. I hated outdoor Masses because of the wind, flies, and bugs. The festival was on the Feast on the Holy Trinity, which is one of the hardest homilies. I was trying to remove all the mystery of the Holy Trinity, but the festival committee had rented an elephant for the day. While I gave my homily, everyone was watching the elephant being unloaded. When the elephant got off the trailer, he let out a huge bellow. I said: "If anybody had told me at the seminary this would happen, I would have said they were crazy." They didn't learn much about the Blessed Trinity, but they got their pictures taken with an elephant, and somewhere there is a picture of me on the elephant.

A young Greek Orthodox woman named Patty came to church, and we became very close friends. She's a bubbly person. She came to daily Mass, and she often cried because she couldn't get pregnant, so I commiserated with her. I invited her to go with me to Washington, D.C., to a program on evangelization. While we were there, I took her to the Shrine of the Immaculate Conception where Dorothy Day prayed and where I prayed when I first went to Washington, D.C. She didn't get pregnant, but the first girl she adopted was conceived on that day. She named her Hannah after the Old Testament woman who could not conceive. The prophet thought Hannah was drunk because she sobbed so much when she prayed in the temple. Patty identified with Hannah because she felt left out, and she carried a heavy cross.

When the call came from the hospital that it was time to pick up the baby, Patty's husband was out of town on business, so she called me and asked me to go with her. When we got there, we saw that little baby in a stocking cap and mittens because it was winter. The adoption required them to stay in Illinois for ten days, so they stayed with the Toneys, who had moved to Illinois by then. Charles and Ann became extremely attached to Hannah.

Patty's daughters, Hannah and Clara, were baptized at the Carmelite monastery. The Carmelites, who prayed for my cancer healing, had also prayed for Patty. In the Greek Orthodox Church, you don't just put oil on the forehead. You oil the whole body. In wrestling matches in ancient times wrestlers covered their bodies with oil so they couldn't hang on to each other. The idea is that Satan can't get ahold of you if you are covered with oil. The grandmothers oiled them, and I did the baptism. The Orthodox baptize babies by dipping them in water. You put your hands under their arms and dip them, but not their head. I about drowned a couple of babies that way.

Chapter 14

Never Choose an Issue that Will Divide

One day, I talked with a young boy named Tony, who was a fifth or sixth grader. He was a good altar server, who happened to be African American. I asked Tony if he had ever thought about being a priest. He said, "Uh, no," and I asked why not. He said, "It's boring." I told him he should follow me around for a couple of days if he thinks it's boring. He said, "Yeah, my mother says she'd like to have me follow you around for a while, too." Tony wound up in jail even though his dad was a police detective. He had wonderful parents, and I think he got straightened around, but the important thing in vocations is to raise the question. When you ask, people raise their horizons, and you cause them to think. I will never forget that day when I was laughing at a cartoon and Fr. Broderick asked me the question I thought about for seven years.

After that, I went across the parking lot to the school and told the junior high grades about my "boring" life as a priest. I told them about the civil rights movement and meeting people like Martin Luther King, Jr., John Howard Griffin, and Sargent Shriver. I told them how we started the Pacem in Terris Award, and I met Mother Teresa and Cesar Chavez. I told them about going to Washington, D.C., and having five invitations to the White House in one year. I made sure they didn't think my life was boring.

A Pastor Cannot Be a Rigorist

People struggle with what you could call "the Catholic issues." God has chosen to use humanity, so the Catholic Church is very incarnational. We use oil, water, and bread as sacraments. Jesus said, "The Father sent me, so I send you." One of the jokes about Catholic liturgy is our "smells and bells." We use the senses more and have more artwork in our churches than Protestants do. In the early church when people couldn't read or write, they needed stained glass windows to tell stories. People could sit there for hours looking at the windows or stations of the cross and see the stories of faith. The statues helped them to think about the saints. Saints are our family heroes. I think saints are better role models for young people than rock 'n' roll singers, athletes, or people on drugs who lead wild lives. For centuries we named children after their patron saint. The saints had their failings, but they lived their faith.

We used to say that some Lutherans are more Catholic than the Catholics. A prominent musician at Augustana College had cancer at the same time I did. He came to me many times to ask me to pray for him. One time he asked me to pray over him for the baptism of the Holy Spirit, and I did. He and his wife were devout Lutherans. When I came back to Davenport, they came to Sacred Heart. They sat toward the back of church. One time an usher asked, "Who is that devout couple over there? They are so prayerful."

Many Protestants are wonderful saintly people. I had a close friend in ordination class who was a Missouri Synod Lutheran convert. Lutherans used to have confession when they came to Sacred Heart, but they had to change because people complained that they seemed too much like Catholics. I sometimes call the Reformation "the revolution." Coming up to the five-hundredth anniversary, the Lutherans and the Vatican have made a deal that we won't say nasty things about each other because we have more in common than what separates us.

A man from a Protestant church visited me because he knew we had charismatic prayer groups and organized prayer breakfasts. He took me to a meeting with evangelical ministers. After I sat there for a while, I finally said, "We need to talk to each other because we can learn a lot from each other." No one said a word. Apparently, they didn't think they could learn from Catholics.

I talked with a Lutheran woman who was married to a Catholic man and came to Mass with him every Sunday. She said, "I grew up in Chicago. The Catholics were so mean to Protestants, and they persecuted us." I said, "We should get together because we have something in common. I grew up in Ottumwa, Iowa, where it was just the opposite."

If you are a pastor, you cannot be a rigorist. For example, when Father Tom and I worked on marriage cases with people of two different faiths, I just looked for movement in the right direction. Were they moving closer to Christ and conversion to Catholicism? If they were, I didn't interfere with them even though, from a legalistic perspective, they were breaking the law. Father Tom and I felt we had to be open, receptive, and compassionate. You can't be legalistic if you're a pastor. I think Pope Francis would agree.

Someone asked me to describe the essence of being a priest. In the Mass and in the sacraments, you are there *in persona Christi*, in the place of Christ. In the confessional, you listen. Is the person truly sorry? Are they being honest in their confession? Is there repentance? Then you say, "In the name of the church, in the name of Christ, I absolve you from your sins." It is Christ who forgives the sins. People meet Christ in the sacraments, so the priest is there as an instrument of Christ. If a priest doesn't act like Christ, it's a bad sign.

He Shot Him Full of Lead

We had a guest room at the rectory. I wasn't afraid of taking people in. We did that all the time at the Catholic Worker house. A seminarian, who stayed at the Catholic Worker in Davenport, wrote a letter about a valuable lesson he learned. The doorbell rang one night when he was at a rectory. Everyone else was afraid of the person at the door, but he knew he could deal with him. He had learned not to be afraid of people. My predecessor let two migrant men live in the basement of the rectory, and I wanted to continue that.

Msgr. Menke also invited a man named Richard to stay at the rectory. Richard had a terrible speech defect. His dad was a well-known doctor. Richard's parents sent him everywhere for help. When he got into an argument with his dad, he couldn't speak, so he decided to go to the Trappists, where they don't speak. After a while, he left the Trappists and came back to Davenport. His mother left him a little money when she died, so he had a room at a hotel, but his money was running out. Msgr. Menke said, "Richard, why don't you just put your money in the bank and let it increase, and you come live with us." Richard lived at the rectory, and everybody knew him. He prayed all the time. If I went to the church at night and discovered someone on the floor, it was Richard praying. When he rested, he prayed the rosary in his bed. Fr. Tom and I used to say, "In heaven, we will be waiting on Richard."

I learned Richard's story from a family who lived across the street. Richard's father was mowing the grass one Sunday, and Richard said, "You shouldn't be working on Sunday." That made the dad mad, and he said something to Richard. Richard had a temper. His dad laid down to take a nap, and Richard went in and shot him full of lead. He spent twenty years in Fort Madison for that. The men there respected Richard. A psychiatrist at the prison said, "People thought Richard was mentally defective because he couldn't talk, but he is borderline genius." He was a champion chess player. He wrote a book in longhand about chess. It started out: "This is for you, Lord. It is my gift to you." He hired a woman to type it up.

Fort Madison is the Iowa State Penitentiary in Lee County, Iowa. It is a maximum-security facility with a capacity for 760 prisoners.

Richard cleaned the cathedral, and he was a gardener. He took care of the flowers, and I took care of the vegetables. Every time Msgr. Menke left for a retreat or trip, Richard dug a little further out into the yard and planted hostas. One time he entered a flower show with flowers from some else's garden, and he won the prize. They found out and told him he couldn't enter the show again. We teased him about that, but you had to know when to let up. He could only take so much pressure. We always thought he was a living saint.

Eventually, Richard fell a couple of times and had to go to a nursing home. When he was dying, they moved him to a hospice. Fr. Tom and I went over, and he was just hanging on to life. When we walked in, I anointed him, and Fr. Tom talked to him. His breathing was heavy. The nurse said he had been breathing like that all day. Once we were there, he took his last breath. The nurse said, "He just waited until you got here. I've seen that many times. They wait for someone, then they take their last breath."

Come and See--Go and Tell

It was wonderful to pack the cathedral. The Catholic Interracial Council packed it years earlier when we had the Brotherhood Mass. Afternoon Mass was rare then, but we got permission. Because of a big snowstorm, people couldn't get to morning Mass, so we were able to pack the Cathedral in the afternoon. We just lucked out, so we kept having the Brotherhood Mass every year.

We packed the place again after I was pastor when we opened the cathedral for a repentance service in response to an antisemitic incident. The Lutheran Pastor got the people behind him, and they walked over because there wasn't enough parking. The program was about to start when John walked in with hundreds of people. I said, "Well John, you're going to be made a monsignor."

Another big change was when the Vietnamese congregation moved to Sacred Heart. They had been at the St. Ambrose chapel for twenty years, but they outgrew the place and wanted to get their own church.

They looked at two failing parishes in Davenport, but they wanted more space. When I heard about it, I had an idea: We have the room at Sacred Heart. Why don't we just invite them here? They couldn't financially support taking over another parish. I seized the day. *Carpe diem.* They doubled our attendance at the Easter Vigil, which is the most important feast of the year.

We had several meetings between their parish council and ours to consider everything. They told us their concerns, and we responded to them. We were impressed by their faith. They had experienced three hundred years of persecution and martyrdom in Vietnam. There were at least a hundred families. They had a big procession from St. Ambrose with music and a police escort. Immigrants are often afraid of police and don't report crimes, so the Davenport Police Department had a person who spoke Vietnamese to act as a go-between.

We met the Vietnamese congregation in front of the church. They had their costumes and music and a statue of Our Lady of La Vang. It was a big celebration with firecrackers strung all over. We bought a house for their priest, and they had their own Mass. I remember the first time I attended a Vietnamese Mass in Washington, D.C. I thought they were singing, but someone said, "That's not singing. That's their language. It's musical." The same word can mean different things depending on the pitch. It must be difficult to understand. I never could learn more than a couple of words in Vietnamese. They were such wonderful people and very devout. They lived their faith. The big thing in the Vietnamese community is Our Lady of La Vang, which is like Our Lady of Guadalupe to Mexicans.

According to the Roman Catholic Saints website,

> In 1978, a small group of Catholics from the jungle village of La Vang in Viet Nam, escaped persecution by hiding in a thick jungle area where they suffered intense privation, danger, and illness in order to practice their Catholic faith. While they were praying the rosary at dusk, the Virgin

Mother and her Child appeared in a glow of light. Mary told them she was aware of their hardships. She told them to gather certain leaves to make a tea that would make them healthy and said, 'From this day on, prayers said on this spot will be heard and answered'."

We taught them things like how to dress their kids to keep warm in the winter. One of our families rented a big house on Kirkwood Boulevard just north of the cathedral for a large family. Every room upstairs was one of their children's rooms. When they got married, they still stayed there. Most of them were employed at the packing house in Illinois, and they were hard working. They shared cars and rides. Banks loved to see the Vietnamese come in because they knew they would be responsible and pay back their loans. Many of them started restaurants and nail shops. They expanded their businesses and hired people. Immigrants help our economy. Not only do they provide the labor, but they start businesses like ethnic restaurants. They revived Columbus Junction, Iowa, which was a dying town.

Sacred Heart parish was inner-city, and not many people wanted it, but I gloried in it and worked hard. It would be discouraging if everyone ran away, but people came, and the crowd increased. We were the most "small-c-catholic" parish in the diocese. We had more Blacks and Mexican Americans than any other parish. We had the biggest banker in Iowa and a woman who was penniless coming to communion in line next to each other, and they were all Catholic.

An African American couple from Washington, D.C., were eucharistic ministers at another parish, which means they gave out communion. White people coming up in line sometimes changed lines to avoid them. I asked them to come to Sacred Heart. It was a whole different ballgame. They were a model couple, and the man became the president of the Parish Council.

Father Appo, who worked for me, was a Josephite from the Congo. We recruited him from London. He was so proud that I could pronounce his name, Apolinaire Shapamba. He did a lot of work with

African Americans. That guy had such dignity. He acted like a bishop. He taught French in our school and later became a pastor and coach in a small town in Iowa. His soccer team never lost a game, and he became a local hero.

Two men came to the cathedral to ask for help getting jobs. They had been baptized in Nepal, but I discovered that they were confused about what faith they were. They didn't know about denominations until they came to the U.S. They went to the Episcopal Church next door because it looked most like their church in Nepal. I asked them, "What did you call the pastor where you went to church?" They called him "Father." I asked, "Did he have a wife?" No. "Did he talk about Mary?" Yes. "Did he talk about confession?" Yes. I told them they were Catholic. They told me they converted and were baptized because of "those bloody sacrifices" of other religions. They rode a bus for hours to get to the site of their baptism. Compare that to people who don't want to drive fifteen minutes to go to Mass on Sunday.

Those two brothers worked at a gas station that paid very low wages. I intended to turn the employer in to the Labor Department because he was cheating them, but they said, "Oh no, don't touch it. We work for low wages, but we're saving our money to start our own station." I backed off. They were so industrious. They started gas stations of their own all over the Quad Cities.

All the modern Popes have talked about evangelization. Our evangelization started with a homecoming. We put up billboards around town saying: "The people of Sacred Heart Parish invite you to come home for Christmas." We also did it for Easter and included times of the Masses. The advertising cost thousands of dollars, but if we got one or two families that became regular members, their contributions paid for the billboards. We also advertised on the radio. WVIK, the public station, was very inexpensive. We advertised there for so many years that I knew the first names of the people at the radio station. The two motions of the gospel are "come and see" and "go and tell," and that's what we were doing.

I learned about the Rite of Christian Initiation of Adults from a Lutheran minister who said, "This RCIA thing is great. It's going to renew the church." I didn't know much about it, but our Religious Education Director kept bugging me to go to a meeting about it. As soon as I could clear my calendar, I went to several meetings near Chicago. The priest who led them was fantastic. We sent other people, and they came home so on fire.

"The Rite of Christian Initiation of Adults is a process through which non-baptized men and women enter the Catholic Church. It includes several stages marked by study, prayer and rites at Mass. Participants undergo a process of conversion as they study the Gospel, profess faith in Jesus and the Catholic Church, and receive the sacraments of baptism, confirmation, and Holy Eucharist. The RCIA process follows the ancient practice of the church and was restored by the Second Vatican Council as the normal way adults prepare for baptism. In 1974, the Rite for Christian Initiation for Adults was formally approved for use in the United States." [42]

This rite was used for the first seven centuries when millions of pagans came into the Church. There are enormous baptisteries in Europe, like St. John Lateran in Rome. Thousands of people came in as a group and were received as a group. Later, they abandoned this approach in favor of individual instruction. The convert gets to know the priest very well through one-on-one instruction, but with the Rite of Christian Initiation of Adults, you are part of a community. Vatican II helped bring the rite back. It's how the church in Africa has grown so fast. People are introduced to the whole parish at the beginning, and the whole parish prays for them. They are brought in as a community and welcomed by a community.

We had a welcome night, especially for fallen-away Catholics, with snacks and non-alcoholic drinks. The most recent group hosted the event. We told them the history of the parish and gave them a tour of the church. The bishop welcomed them, and each person had a sponsor. Those who were brand new went into the Rite of Christian Initiation of Adults, and those who had wandered away got into a shorter coming home course. We called this whole thing "Come and See--Go and Tell." It wasn't really a program. It was an approach. When Jesus said to Andrew, "Come and see, "Andrew went and got his brother Peter. *(John 1:39-40)*

As part of Come and See-Go and Tell, everybody told their story, and I still remember a lot of them. Some needed to go to confession and clean up their past. Some needed instruction. Some people were baptized but had no first communion. We started where they were and helped them move forward. The teams who acted as sponsors got so much out of it that they became much better Catholics. We had larger classes than parishes three or four times our size. We ran that for many years, and a lot of people came into the Church, but there was one big problem. Participants experienced community very deeply, but after baptism they didn't experience community in church. Our African American mailman went to the Rite of Christian Initiation of Adults and was joyful through the whole thing. He was baptized, and he came to Sunday Mass, but without that group experience, he didn't have the community he valued.

People sometimes ask about the size of the congregation. We kept track, but I don't remember the numbers very well. When I came in 1985, my guess is that there were three hundred fifty families. The capacity of the church is over eight hundred people. We had several Masses, and families were big in those days. One family could fill a pew. I knew a family that had twelve children, and another had thirteen. They sat in front because they wanted their kids to pay attention. Some people came from outside the neighborhood. Before Vatican II, the neighborhoods were street by street, and the joke was: "The Catholic Church has divided the world into big squares and little squares." The big squares were dioceses, and the little squares were parishes.

The Pope Turned to Laugh

In 1993, I got three months off for a sabbatical after thirty-seven years, and I went to Rome with a group of thirty-nine priests from all over the country. It was a great experience. I should have done that when I was younger, when I was in seminary or early in my priesthood. Professors came in from all the universities in Rome and brought us up to date on what happened after Vatican II. They lectured off the top of their heads because they didn't need notes after teaching for years.

I only left the cathedral for three months. If I left longer, I would have to give up the parish. I got a St. Ambrose University professor to take my place on Sundays. I understood that the people might love him so much that they wouldn't accept me when I came home. That didn't happen, so it was a miracle.

One day we went up to Pope John Paul's private quarters at the Vatican. We walked up those big stairs to what they call "the mansion" and had Mass with him in his private chapel. We were shoulder-to-shoulder in that small chapel. The sisters who worked on his staff were in the back row. The Pope knelt at the prie-dieu, his private kneeler. He had the same books I use, the daily missal, the breviary, and another book.

After Mass, we went next door to the library where each one of us met him personally. When I had my chance, I said, "Holy Father, Davenport needs a Bishop. Our bishop retired." He said, "Not yet." A couple of weeks later, the decision was announced, and it was my classmate Bishop Franklin from Dubuque. The Pope gave us each a little case with a rosary in it. When I got mine, the priest behind me cracked a joke, and the Pope turned to laugh. He got distracted and gave me another one. He said, "Well, have two." It was providential because I brought those home for my sisters Lucy and Katy.

I agree with people who think Pope John Paul II was the man of the century. He was responsible in many ways for the fall of Communism.

Congressman Jim Leach told me Reagan got the credit, but as Chairman of the Banking Committee, he knew the Russian economy was falling apart even before Reagan was elected. There was a military build-up, and they couldn't keep up. Gorbachev went for a walk in the woods with Reagan and said, "Why don't we just both disarm?" It was a total surprise to Reagan. The Pope's trip to Poland was the turning point. He identified with the labor movement, and when he went to Poland, the people mobbed him. He inspired the people. That trip was the turning point.

Pope Francis refuses to live in the papal mansion, which is called "the castle." He lives in a hotel room on the ground level. When he was elected, he went to pay his bill, and he said, "You will have trouble finding my name because I signed in under a different name." The man who owned the first Mississippi River gambling boat in Davenport built that hotel to house the cardinals when they come for meetings. He was a shrewd investor, but he and his wife lived simply in a four-room house in Pittsburgh, Pennsylvania.

On that trip, we also went to the Holy Land, a place I never dreamed I would see. It was a great moment on the bus when we rounded the mountain, and I saw the Sea of Galilee. So many things I had read in the gospels came to mind. I realized I could lead a trip like that, and I led a couple of them with Catholics and Protestants together. I went once on crutches after hip surgery. One Lutheran said, "I'll never go to the Holy Land again unless Fr. Mottet leads it." Another one said, "If it weren't for the Catholic Church, all these places we've visited, and these shrines wouldn't be here." I got free flights based on the number of people I took, and I passed those around to my family members so they could go at half price with my credits.

I Think Miss Pat Is Having a Kegger Down There

If we didn't take care of problems quickly, we lost people. They usually fell away because of some obstacle, not because they didn't want to be Catholic. They lost interest. We believed they wanted to come back to the sacraments.

Exciting music and a sound stage is part of the reason megachurches are such an attraction. A priest in the Chicago suburbs tried to match this, and he was very successful. Our folk music Mass at nine o'clock was always the best-attended Mass, especially for younger people, but I don't believe music is the end all and be all of worship. About the time I retired, I noticed that all the Protestant churches in the neighborhood started folk music services. A friend of mine, who began Lutheran and finished Methodist, started country music services. He put it on the billboard out front and wore a cowboy hat. I don't know how it turned out. I can never figure out how people move from one church to another. I studied the Lutheran reform, which I call "the revolution," and I know how the splits came: If you don't agree, just go your way. That is why there are thirteen thousand denominations today.

One of the greatest things we ever did was an outreach to the whole neighborhood. We found the biggest house on each block and got that family to invite all the neighbors in the parish to come together once a week for nine weeks. We only had one block that refused to do it. It was a great way to get to know the neighbors in the parish because you spent time with them and prayed with them. It was like the cell groups priests and nuns developed in Latin America, which spread like wildfire. They listened to the poor. Communists had small groups that they called "cell groups." We met in homes and had plenty of coffee. If the communists can take over the world, we can too. Trying to transform the world is contagious. It reminded me of my Young Christian Student days.

We divided up the parish and worked strategically where we had families. It was well-planned. We thought of those meetings as retreats, and some people were baptized with the Holy Spirit. One of the best retreats was in the home of a parishioner named Pat. A student from our school walked by while we were singing. He went home and said to his dad, "I think Miss Pat is having a 'kegger' down there." His dad walked over there and said, "No, those are religious songs. They're not having a kegger. They're having a retreat."

Those meetings were a simplified version of the Life in the Spirit seminar. I think the greatest need in the Catholic Church today is to understand the role of the Holy Spirit in the church and in individual lives. It was essential to have at least one Life in the Spirit seminar every year, if not two. It was the engine that drove the renewal of the church. The Life in the Spirit seminar was borrowed from the Pentecostals and adapted to Catholic theology and Vatican II.

A Life in the Spirit Seminar is completely different from Fr. Mottet's experience with the Methodist minister who prayed for him for the baptism of the Holy Spirit. "The goal of the Life in the Spirit Seminar is to help people find a new and fuller and better life as Christians by laying or strengthening the foundations of a truly Christian life."[43] It consists of seven sessions over seven weeks: 1) God's Love, 2) Salvation, 3) The New Life, 4) Receiving God's Gift, 5) Praying for Baptism in the Holy Spirit, 6) Growth, and 7) Transformation in Christ. Since it is a group experience over several weeks, in incorporates the community-building possibilities that Fr. Mottet valued in the Rite of Catholic Initiation of Adults.

We also had an Andrew Dinner two or three times a year. The bishop hosted a very simple dinner and invited priests, seminarians, and people in the diocese who were interested in the priesthood. Priests told their stories, which made it clear that they were real, normal people. The vocation director said we always got at least one seminarian from an Andrew Dinner. One of the last ones we had was at Sacred Heart. A Vietnamese man showed up. We didn't even know he was interested. Then a doctor from the Philippines, who was doing research at The University of Iowa, came. He told the university chaplain that he would rather be a priest than a doctor. The chaplain brought him to the Andrew Dinner that same day. Those two were both eventually ordained.

There was a saying about nuns and priests: "MA and away, PhD and flee." They go to graduate school, and you never see them again. Something like that happened with marriage preparation. We married them and never saw them again. We came up with a solution to the problem. We started a program for marriage preparation based on the

Rite of Christian Initiation of Adults, and people stayed. They became part of the parish and came to Mass.

The First Gated Community in the Inner-city

We lost money on most of the houses we fixed up, so we had to get grants. If you could make money in that neighborhood, the big realtors would be making it. Interfaith Housing got grants to prime the pump and impact the neighborhood.

In the early nineties, I had a plan for senior housing across the street from the cathedral. From my travels, I knew that senior citizens are politically and religiously active. When I visited parishioners at Kahl Home, I met people I knew from all over town. Senior housing would attract people who are active in the church and go to Mass every day, and it would attract the families who visited them.

The real opposition started in the late nineties when we got a housing grant from the Regional Development Authority. A woman from the neighborhood went berserk when she learned that we planned to build Cathedral Heights across the street from the cathedral. She didn't want the Catholic Church to be able to use that money, so she got a lawyer and started a group called "Lincoln Neighbors."

Fr. Mottet's Cathedral Heights proposal was a multi-unit housing project, which was a departure from his previous work rehabilitating single family homes. It may have been based on the senior housing proposal that Bishop O'Keefe had quashed. In 1993 at the mandatory retirement age of seventy-five, Bishop O'Keefe retired.

We had a developer who had a successful record of getting tax increments, and he always answered his phone. I told him Interfaith Housing wanted to do something in the Sacred Heart neighborhood, and he agreed to do it. When we had our first meeting with him, the lawyer for Lincoln Neighbors showed up. I should have said, "What's your name? Where do you live? Why are you here?" I'm sure he didn't live in the neighborhood. He treated the meeting like a courtroom, and I was the defendant.

Before that woman openly opposed us, I tried to talk with her, but I could see it was a hopeless case. Her passion was protecting their property, and it would never match mine. They don't own the neighborhood. Sacred Heart Cathedral was there a hundred years before they were. Another organizer tried to talk with her, but he was just giving Lincoln Neighbors power. The rule in organizing is that you don't give power to the other organization. You form and develop your organization to build power, and you never choose an issue that will divide your group. That is very important. Rich people don't want the poor to organize because it gives them power.

Fr. Mottet knew good intentions weren't enough. Analysis of power is necessary for an organization to competently acquire and use power. Without this analysis, the organization gets into fights without a chance of winning or fights against targets that have no power. Analysis of power is based on how things are actually done, not on how they should ideally be done.[44] Aversion to the use of power is often an avoidance of responsibility. Power is the ability to act.

Those are the kind of tactics they used. They brought in people who had no business being at our meetings. Our developer was there, and he could see where the meeting was going. He said, "I'm out of here. I can work north of Locust, make twice as much money, and not have to put up with this flak." Pointing at me he said, "If you want me to work, I'll work with you," and he walked out. That was the end of the program. Priests are trained to bring about reconciliation, not to fight in court. I had two lawyers in the congregation, who could have torn apart the opposition if I had hired them. I regret that I didn't, but I didn't think of it. I'm an expert at getting ideas two hours late.

I think my opponent attacked me because she hated the Catholic Church and what I was doing, but Interfaith Housing was a separate corporation. It was not operated by Sacred Heart Cathedral. She was offended because we held meetings in the rectory, but when we started Interfaith Housing, we didn't know what we were doing and had to meet weekly. One time she brought a witch to a meeting. In fact, witches wanted to join Quad Cities Interfaith, but I resisted. We were criticized for not being open, but the Protestant churches would have scattered like crazy. If it weren't for that, I would have looked the other way and let them in if they wanted to work for justice.

This is another example of Fr. Mottet's commitment to the concept of public relationships. Narrowly based organizations that work only with other organizations that agree on all significant issues are unlikely to gain enough power to make changes.

When the woman ridiculed me and wrote a nasty letter to the editor, the controversy became public, and our meetings became confrontational. She thought she owned the neighborhood because she and her husband owned a big house there. They had the connections to pressure other organizations not to work with us. After I retired, she had the gall to expand Lincoln Neighbors to include Sacred Heart Cathedral. That required permission from the City Council and street department because they had to change the street signs.

Fr. Mottet's opponent and her husband actually had goals that were similar to Fr. Mottet's, and they had a reputation in Davenport for philanthropy and work for affordable housing. Either Fr. Mottet misread the woman in his one-on-one interview, or he uncovered interests and passions that were not part of her public reputation.

Interfaith Housing worked closely with the East Davenport Development Corporation. A friend of mine, the Pastor of Redeemer Lutheran Church in Bettendorf, also started a housing program in West Davenport called Ecumenical Housing. He was on the board of the Regional Development Authority, so I worked with him to get housing grants.

Through United States Senator Tom Harkin, the East Davenport Development Corporation unexpectedly got a half million-dollar grant. When I got the call about it, I was dumbfounded. There was a shortage of housing for middle-income people, and we were prepared to bring in a company that had a great reputation for their work in

Des Moines. When Senator Harkin's office called the city and asked if they had any good housing programs, they said, "Yes, we have a great program, and they are already talking with the company we want to bring in."

Our contractor planned to introduce a new inner-city model that would build community. It included a playground for children. Residents would agree to abide by certain rules when they moved in. My opponent, that same woman, called it "the first gated community in the inner-city." She didn't mind being mean or dishonest.

This housing project may not have been completed. There is no public record of a federally funded housing project in Davenport between 2000 and 2010.

Chapter 15

They Called It Black Friday

Good intentions don't always get through, even if they have the potential to change history. One of them was outreach to African Americans. At the Catholic Bishops meeting after the Civil War, two bishops said, "We ought to reach out to the freed slaves. There's a great opportunity there." They were voted down, and that's why there are so few African American Catholics in the United States. Here in Davenport, two young assistants at Sacred Heart Cathedral wanted to reach out to the African American community in the neighborhood, but they were shot down too. I wanted to bring in African nuns and send them through the neighborhood. I even raised part of the money, but Bishop Franklin said, "We're talking about combining some parishes, so hold off until that happens."

We had a wonderful school with terrific teachers, and the kids did well, but we couldn't keep the enrollment up. We spent twice as much per student as the other Catholic schools because our enrollment was so low. One year we even had no tuition, but we attracted only one family. Families wanted to send their kids to public school because everything was free with all the frills and no worries. After Vatican II, we had to have a finance council of experienced lay people, and they said we had to close the school.

We combined Sacred Heart, Holy Family, and St. Alphonsus schools into All Saints School, which is very strong to this day. The first year, the eighth graders earned five presidential awards, and four of them were from Sacred Heart. Catholic schools are some of the best schools in the country, but so many people don't value Catholic education enough to make the financial sacrifice and pass up the frills of public school. Closing the school was a very painful thing.

After we closed Sacred Heart School in 2004, we had an idea for using the building. We wanted to use the space for seniors and for the parish. We had an agreement for a one-hundred-thousand-dollar grant to install an elevator. There is a huge amount of room in the building, especially in the auditorium. If the nearby Rock Island Arsenal were under attack, I would tell people to run to Sacred Heart School and be safe because there is so much poured concrete in the building. Someone had pledged the money, but the parish wanted the building torn down instead. I think it is still standing.[45]

Shake and Bake

At age sixty-eight, I had a kidney transplant. I was balancing Sacred Heart Cathedral, Quad Cities Interfaith, Interfaith Housing, and other things. For eleven months before the transplant, I was on dialysis with a tube called a "fistula." When I started on dialysis, all kinds of rumors started in the parish. Some thought I was dying of cancer, and they tried to guess what priest would take over the cathedral. I decided to give them the facts. I wrote a letter every Sunday for the bulletin and told them what happened at dialysis. When one woman left on vacation said, "Be sure to clip those letters while I'm gone. I don't want to miss one."

I was in an office at the University of Iowa to arrange for the kidney transplant. The nurse I talked to had just gotten a call from a woman who wanted to give me her kidney. I was floored. The potential donor was a nurse from Sacred Heart parish. Her family claimed I did something for them, but I couldn't figure out what it was. I had thirty offers of a kidney, but I don't know how many of them were serious.

Ben offered a kidney, but he had the wrong blood type. My sister Katy's five children were all willing to donate a kidney because of their love for her. I said, "You sure raised those kids right." The first one to offer got within two weeks of the surgery, but they eliminated her when they found a small tumor behind one of her kidneys. She is now in China. Her brother Stephen was next in line to be the donor. He worked for a computer company in the Twin Cities area and had to wait five months to get time off.

A parishioner said, "Your homilies have improved since you've been on dialysis." I'm sure there was spiritual growth because I had more time to think about my homilies. I was on a limited diet, especially water, but I sucked a lot of ice cubes.

My kidney transplant was on my mother's birthday in September of 1998. The surgeon was seven months pregnant. Katy gave her a copy of the diary I wrote for the parish bulletin, and she published it for all the doctors in the department. They said, "We seldom hear from the patient's point of view." I had always gone into surgery alone, but this time I went in with my nephew Stephen. He picked me up, and we went to the hospital together. We were like a team. Ben was in the healing ministry, and he prayed over the surgeon before Stephen and I went into surgery.

After the kidney transplant, they used an experimental drug. I had a reaction to it that put me in intensive care for a couple of days. I had a tube down my throat, and I couldn't talk. When my family visited, I squeezed their hands to let them know I was still alive. The name of that drug is OK23, but it wasn't okay for me. The nickname for it is "shake and bake," and I did both. I had more dialysis because the kidney didn't kick in right away. They decided that Steven was so healthy the kidney thought he was asleep, but it finally started to work.

The doctors at the University of Iowa Hospital worked as a team. I saw several doctors who consulted one another, and sometimes there were students. It reminded me of when my mother was taken to University Hospital when I was seven. She complained that a doctor walked in with several students, and said things like, "This is not very painful." She wanted to hit him over the head. When I was discharged, I stayed in an extra room at the Catholic Student Center because I had to go back for treatment every day.

I had a problem with the prednisone they gave me. It killed the blood supply to my hip. After I came home, it felt like I had gravel in my hip. It was so painful I couldn't walk. When I went back to the doctor, a professor came in to tell me I would need surgery, but it couldn't be scheduled for three months. I went to a doctor in Davenport who could do it in two weeks. The surgeon thought he had run into infection, so he stopped, sewed me up, and called a specialist who said, "If they had continued that surgery, you would have died." They gave me a couple of weeks to heal up, and they went in again.

I had my left hip replaced within the first year, and they said there was a twenty percent chance the prednisone would affect the next hip. My other hip was also affected, and I needed another surgery. I like to joke that I won both prizes and should go into gambling.

Every time I go into surgery, I say the same prayer Jesus said on the cross: "Into Thy hands, Lord, I commend my spirit." The first time, I had some fear going into surgery, but I got used to it. Seventeen years later, the kidney Stephen donated is still working. They didn't remove my right kidney, but it's asleep.

We put a bed in my office because I couldn't climb the stairs at the rectory. Fr. Tom told Bishop Franklin he didn't think I was going to make it. I had thirteen major surgeries: four for cancer, four for kidneys including a transplant, and three for hips. One was for an infection, and one was a knee. I count things like putting in a pacemaker and five or six stints minor compared to cutting you open. With those minor things, you go home the next day.

After I got the kidney transplant, it was like I was let out of prison. We have mandatory retirement at seventy-five, and I was sixty-eight. I said to Bishop Franklin, "I will sign on a year at a time depending

on how I feel and how things are going with the parish." I came home
fired up with all kinds of plans. At Sacred Heart they called me "the
bionic priest." Sometimes the medication made my voice raspy, and
at evening Mass I sounded like "the godfather." I said, "I gotta get
those godfather lines down."

Who Ever Thought It Would Come to This?

I knew I would have to talk about the sexual abuse scandal, so I had
notes ready. The most important thing I want people to understand
is that I was taken totally by surprise when the sexual abuse scandal
became public. It was a shock. I had no idea it was going on. Seminary
classmates stick together, but even classmates didn't know that priests
in their seminary class were involved.

Our bishop was falsely accused and Cardinal Bernadin was falsely
accused, but there was never an accusation against Msgr. Menke.
When the news about sexual abuse by priests came out, I had been
back at the Cathedral for a year or two. A friend gave me a book based
on the Boston experience, which was intended to make it look like I
was part of the cover up. It quoted from a homily where I said,
"Sexual abuse is not going on here."

*Fr. Mottet's tenure at Sacred Heart Cathedral were bracketed by the clergy abuse
scandal, which began in 1985. A year after his retirement, the Diocese of
Davenport filed for bankruptcy. Fr. Mottet was never accused of sexual abuse or
of covering up abuses by other priests, but he was profoundly affected by the abuse
scandal. By early 2016, when we talked with him about the scandal, he had dealt
with the pain it caused for over twenty years, and his views had solidified. There
were obvious questions we didn't ask, and we wonder why we didn't probe more
deeply. He had a blind spot. We did too, perhaps for some of the same reasons.*

Msgr. Feeney, a previous pastor, sexually abused boys, but I didn't
know about it. He was from a prominent family that owned Feeney's
Grocery. He was well known because he went to school in Europe.
When I travelled the country, people said, "Oh, you're from

Davenport. How is Fr. Tom Feeney?" I said he was fine because I didn't know what had gone on.

We all knew Tom Feeney drank too much. He went away for treatment for alcoholism at a place called "The Guest House." One of the principles of the AA twelve-steps is to apologize to the people you hurt. He spoke honestly from the pulpit about recovering from alcoholism, but nothing about abuse. He even went to the mother of a boy he abused and apologized, but the abuse didn't come out then.

Unfortunately, this scandal brushed off on the younger Feeney, a nephew, who was not involved in abuse at all. He was a pastor and worked in a chancery. I taught him in high school. He had a great sense of humor and was very well accepted by people in Davenport, very bright and witty.

I remember a priest who called me from West Liberty, Iowa, because his brother had been abused. Abuse affects the whole family. He said, "I want to talk to you about Msgr. Feeney." I thought it was just gossip, and I didn't call him back. The boy who was abused had worked as a volunteer in our Social Action Department, but he never said a word about this. You would think I would learn. I would have gone to the bishop if I had known. That priest was the guy who took us to court, and that led to the bankruptcy. I remember the day of the court hearing. When they broke for lunch, the priest from West Liberty walked with the group of people who had been abused. They were part of the Survivor Network of Those Abused by Priests. He always appeared in court with them. He was a fine priest and a friend of mine.

It isn't surprising that the young volunteer in the Social Action Department didn't say anything about sexual abuse. It is common for victims of sexual abuse, especially those abused by clergy, to be in a position where no one believes their allegations. This is one of the factors that makes it possible for abuse to go on for an extended time and then be covered up for years. Even for parents of abused children, it is difficult to believe that a priest could commit the abuse.

One of the priests who was the worst was Janssen. He always had a carload of youth and kept doing strange things. I thought he was wacko, but I didn't know he was doing this stuff. He had worked as a lifeguard at an expensive private club in Davenport. Those people must have gone ballistic when they found out about the scandal. Now it is a policy that you cannot be alone in a car with a youth. If you're in a meeting, you can't drive anyone home. It is strict.

Another priest who was accused was Wiebler. I taught with him and thought he was a great teacher. He was so creative. I had no idea he had this problem.

Bishop O'Keefe was accused, but the two women who accused him had criminal records and mental problems. The cases were dropped, but he had to go through that. The lawyer against Bishop O'Keefe was a guy named Anderson. He went all over the world prosecuting cases and even brought a lawsuit against the Vatican. He was hungry and unscrupulous.

If you are a priest, you are guilty until proven otherwise. I remember being at a meeting of social workers, mostly women, and word association was brought up. One of the words they used was "priest," and the association they immediately gave was "abuse." I was shocked. I know families who asked their sons and brothers not to wear the Roman collar when they were out in public. Some didn't, even in the hospital where it serves as identification, but I always wore mine. I was asked to speak at the First Christian Church two blocks away. I said, "I know you have one question you are afraid to ask, and it is about the sexual abuse scandal." I spoke freely about it.

Information about the cases of specific priests who were investigated is available at bishopaccountability.org. Father Mottet knew two of the guilty priests personally, and he easily acknowledged their guilt, but dealing with accusations against church officials he had long admired was a different matter. He had a mostly positive relationship with Bishop O'Keefe, was dismissive about the accusations against him, and expressed sympathy because of the unjust treatment he received.

In 1992, Bishop O'Keefe was charged with abuse of two Minnesota women in the early sixties. The cases against Bishop O'Keefe were dropped in 1993 because the accusations made by the two women were based on repressed memories that came to light during therapy. The psychiatrist's license was suspended after former patients successfully sued her for planting false memories of abuse.[46] However, "O'Keefe acknowledged before his death that he was told of some instances of abuse and chose to relocate the accused priests, rather than report the abuse to authorities or take action to have the priests defrocked."[47] Bishop O'Keefe's name was removed from the library at St. Ambrose University in 2007 at the request of a survivor of sexual abuse. The survivor said he reported the abuse to Bishop O'Keefe, who failed to take action.[48]

Cardinal Bernardin was falsely accused, but when the person who made the accusation was dying of cancer, Bernardin went to his home and had a home Mass. There was a reconciliation. He was a great model of the forgiveness point of view. Later, the way Bernardin faced his own death from cancer was a model.

When the story of Cardinal Bernardin broke in Chicago, you can imagine what happened. Here is a big fish, and he had been President of the Bishop's Conference. He spent all morning in his office talking to lawyers. They told him to fight it, but he said, "I'm going to go down there to meet the press." He said to the press, "I have tried to be faithful to my celibacy all my life and follow the commandments. I have never abused anybody." The press respected him because he faced them head on and told the truth.

Fr. Mottet admired Cardinal Bernardin, who received the Pacem in Terris Award in 1985 before the sexual abuse lawsuit in 1993. In the scandal, Bernardin was proactive on the side of victims. He was exonerated of all charges, but he "also helped cover up for sexual abusers, according to internal archdioceses documents … that show how the archdiocese tried to contain the scandal."[49]

When I went to Washington, D.C., for a meeting, people I talked with people said that the Catholic Church had lost its credibility to speak on issues like war, peace, and social justice. It was painful for Campaign for Human Development staff members to go to work. The bishops didn't have as much power to speak on social issues as before. In the news, it looked like everything was a cover-up. In some cases, it probably was, but lawyers and mental health authorities gave the bishops bad advice. Often what looked like cover-up was just following professional advice. They were trying not to harm the church. For thirty years, we missed opportunities to turn the sexual abuse situation around.

Every priest is warned in seminary to go to confession once a week and have a regular spiritual director. If they had followed that advice and been honest with their spiritual director or honest in the confessional, sexual abuse would not have happened. Apparently, they didn't do those things. This is quicksand. Secrecy is a weapon of the devil.

People have asked what I was doing when all this took place. They even brought it up when I received the Pacem in Terris Award in 2008. I was living with and serving the poor and homeless. I was making sure people had housing and civil rights. I had no idea this was going on. Most clergy are afraid of the press and avoid the press, but if you avoid them, they think you're hiding something. Since other priests wouldn't meet with the press, I had them at the cathedral all the time. That was easy for me because I spent seven years holding press conferences.

There is always some level of opposition to the Catholic Church. I faced it as a child and young man. The abuse scandal made that worse. It gave opponents all the fire they ever wanted in the social justice area. People in the congregation were not affected as much as I was. I had to deal with the issue every day. If anyone was anti-Catholic, this made them feel they were right all along. It was also a painful cost in money. It has been an uphill battle from then on. It still comes up for Pope Francis.

What might explain Fr. Mottet's blind spot about the sexual abuse scandal? Maybe his early experiences of anti-Catholicism made it easy for him to suspect that rumors about Catholic clergy were more of the same. Perhaps his intense focus on rebuilding the Sacred Heart parish and neighborhood kept the rumblings about sexual abuse from rising above the level of gossip in his thinking. His understanding of priesthood as "in persona Christi" probably made sexual abuse by priests unthinkable to him, and his deferential respect for bishops made it natural to defend them. The unthinkableness of clergy sexual abuse may have kept him from ever coming to grips with the enormous and often lifelong damage inflicted on victims.

No one dares to mention whether there is any connection with homosexuality because it's not politically correct. People like to point to problems with celibacy, but psychologists say there is no connection between celibacy and homosexuality. Most sexual abuse takes place in the home, sometimes even involving married couples. In seminaries, men with homosexual tendencies were asked to leave even if they hadn't done homosexual acts. Now there are professional football and basketball players who are homosexual, but in those days, you were out if you acted in an effeminate way. It was very unfair. We were taught to not make judgments, but that was a rash judgment that could be very damaging. The church says homosexuality is a disorder. I taught with a priest who had those tendencies. We knew his mother had died when he was very young, and we wrote it off to that. He was very talented.

I believe the Catholic Church has fully addressed the abuse problem. We have done a better job than most churches, but yes, there was some cover-up. The Lutherans, who sponsored a camp north of town, asked us to train their staff because they knew how we responded. Every priest, including the bishop, had to have a criminal record search. No one can be a lay leader or work with youth without being approved and trained. We trained every parish. There is accountability. Reports must be submitted. I don't know of any organization that has done a better job of responding.

I believe there is less and less abuse, but since we are dealing with human nature, there will always be some cases. The Davenport Diocese hired a university to check every year to make sure the regulations were followed, and in their report, the diocese came off well every year. We were trained and tested on our knowledge of sexual abuse prevention. It was time-consuming and kind of a pain in the neck, but we knew why it had to be done. Even if your mother or sister was riding in your car, she had to be in the back seat. The rules were strict. There is so much accountability now.

Two years after Fr. Mottet's death, a major sex abuse scandal in Illinois hit the news. The Illinois Attorney General charged that six Illinois dioceses failed to disclose at least 500 sexual abuse cases involving priests. In the following months, six dioceses released names of 180 priests who were credibly accused of abuse, but "the Church did not notify the police or the Illinois Department of Child and Family Services about the hundreds of other cases. [50]

I remember the day of the clergy meeting at Ambrose in 2006 when we found out that the diocese was being sued and was going to take bankruptcy. I said, "Who ever thought it would come to this here?" We had sacrificed our lives and lived simply. We were crushed. People asked me how we dealt with it. We prayed more and talked more to other priests. We thanked God for His grace. There, but for the grace of God, go I. We understood that anyone else could have fallen. That was our attitude.

"Bishop William Franklin said that the diocese was left with no other alternative to settle more than two dozen claims against priests accused of sexual abuse. He said the move would ensure the financial health of the church. At that time, the diocese had already paid over ten million dollars in legal suits filed against priests. New claims that led to the bankruptcy were against Sioux City Bishop Lawrence Soens, who was accused by former students at a Catholic high school in Iowa City."[51]

Dan Ebener, who followed me as Director of the Social Action Department, called the day the bankruptcy was announced "black Friday." The diocese laid off a lot of people, and he lost his staff. He couldn't even afford a secretary. Later, he said we were better off because we had such qualified volunteers who worked almost full-time. We could never have afforded to hire people like Loxi Hopkins and Glen Leach. Our weekly Social Action team meetings had such talented volunteers around the table.

With the poverty in the neighborhood and my background in social action and community organizing, Sacred Heart was the perfect appointment for me. Every year priests get a letter asking whether they want to move somewhere else. I always said, "I'll do whatever the bishop wants, but I can't think of any place I would rather be." I stayed because it was inner-city.

A lot happened in those twenty years at Sacred Heart Cathedral. When I first went there, people were afraid to come into the neighborhood during the daytime, let alone at night. I knew we had to build up the parish. Eventually, the congregation grew to about nine hundred families. We made a big impact on the neighborhood through Interfaith Housing and Quad Cities Interfaith. Thirty churches worked together. People lost their fear.

PART FOUR

Healer

In 2015, Fr. Mottet moved to Kahl Home where he did his best to adjust. He was still mobile with his walker, but it got harder to get his large shoes into the passenger side of our car. I took him to a Rock Island school to speak with six graders, where he was an instant celebrity because he knew Martin Luther King, Jr. personally. Wherever we went, people recognized him and wanted to greet him. Despite his failing health, he was good humored and always happy to tell his stories.

How did Fr. Mottet manage to preserve his legacy and finish so well? Part Four follows him through loss and frustration and into new opportunities to fulfill his vocation. Although this part of his life appeared, on the surface, to be fundamentally different from his life as a playmaker, organizer, and developer, his role as healer had the same earmarks. He conducted healing Masses across Iowa and reluctantly became an exorcist. At age eighty-six and in the last months of his life, he prayed and worked toward what he called "the greatest miracle of my life," an economic development initiative with the potential to provide jobs and justice for workers, particularly veterans. Always a citizen lobbyist, he continued to raise his voice for justice through letters to the editor in The Quad-City Times. In some sense, he had come full circle, still connected to those obscure days in the Ottumwa farmhouse where he read Labor magazine and weighed the voting records of Iowa legislators. He was still ready to take on the world. He was known, admired, and loved everywhere he went, and remarkable people called him their mentor. It felt good to be around him, and we kept hoping he would rub off on us.

In the last years of his life, his niece Theresa Mottet interviewed him on their long road trips. She called him "my cute uncle.". They went twice to the Medjugorje pilgrimage site in Bosnia and Herzegovina, which is known for apparitions of Mary. When I asked Theresa about her relationship with Fr. Mottet, she said:

> When my father passed, the only thing I took out of his office was a picture of this drop-dead-gorgeous priest. I didn't really know Marvin, but my family had stories about him, like his bringing Mother Teresa and Martin Luther King, Jr., to Iowa. It was time for me to get to know this man and ask him questions. God had a hand in it. I scheduled a business trip to Davenport. After our first dinner together and a few days with him, my gut told me Marvin's story needed to be told. I had no idea how it was going to happen, but I wanted to spend quality time with him and record him. Meeting him opened up a whole new part of my world. It was a rich experience. It's important for his story to be told because of his impact and his devotion to the underserved.

A few weeks before his death, Fr. Mottet asked us to keep his photo album for use in his book. A photo of him, the one on the book cover, is on the wall above my computer screen. I see his broad, square-toothed smile as I write. He's in his fifties and dressed in his clerical collar. His thick brown hair has mostly disappeared, and his gray moustache and beard are neatly trimmed. He looks as if he has just told one of his funny stories or as if he just said, "I love what I'm doing." No wonder people felt so at ease with him.

Chapter 16

If You Stay in Healing Long Enough You're Bound

to Run into Exorcism

I was the Pastor of the Cathedral for twenty years from 1985 to 2005, which is unusual. It was inner-city, and not many people wanted it. I worked hard, and I loved it. With six months to go before mandatory retirement at age seventy-five, I resigned. Another priest had raised a big stink about retiring at seventy-five, but I wasn't going to do that. My opponent kept attacking, and I didn't want to spend the last six months fighting bigots and turncoats after a woman in our parish turned traitor and supported her. The attacks and betrayal at the end were the cross before the crown.

When I retired in 2005, I had been preparing for a while. About twelve years earlier, the diocese required every priest to purchase a long-term health care policy. That was wise. I was turned down by two companies because of the kidney transplant. I had to have help from one of my classmates to finally get a company to take me. I take a ton of medicine, so I had to get together all that medical and insurance information.

I've had an exciting life for a priest. I thought I would never go to the Holy Land, but I went several times. I liked to lead pilgrimages. As the leader, I made the arrangements for all those people, and I got to go free. I loved those places. I didn't think I would ever get to Europe, but I went to Fatima, Lourdes, and twice to Medjugorje. I remember my first plane trip to Europe. I looked out at all those tile roofs, which came from the Muslims in Spain, and I felt a deep joy. The plane was circling around where my ancestors came from.

Fatima in Portugal, Lourdes in France, and Medjugorje in Bosnia are pilgrimage sites where apparitions of Mary have occurred. A spring of water at Lourdes is also associated with miraculous healings.

Besides the cancer early in my life, I've had other close calls. I was driving home one Easter Sunday. In those days, the highways weren't as flat, and you couldn't see over a hill. As I was passing a car, another car came over the hill, and I was in his lane. He turned off just in time, or that could have been the end of it right there. Another time, my heart went into atrial fibrillation while I sat at my computer. I put my head down because I thought I might be having a heart attack. I remember thinking: "Maybe this is what it feels like to die." It happened again as I drove home from Ben's wife's funeral. Near Columbus Junction, I felt it coming on, so I pulled off the highway. I was taken to University Hospital, and I had to call someone to get my car.

When we began work on his book in 2014, Fr. Mottet had been retired for nine years and had become somewhat frail. He still had his car, but it was no longer safe for him to drive. He was always ready to go, but it became increasingly difficult for him to get into a car as a passenger. He used a walker because he had fallen a few times. His gait was slow and shuffling, but his mind and smile were quick. The long-legged, scrappy high school basketball player, with his determination to get the ball in the hoop, was still there.

After his retirement, Fr. Mottet was satisfied living in his apartment at St. Vincent's where he could still be part of the action. He had a greenhouse built and took delight in his garden. He mentored and advised young social justice leaders. He was still involved in Quad Cities Interfaith and Interfaith Housing. He crisscrossed Iowa to conduct Healing Masses and pray for the sick. His focus on

I Don't Have a Clue

Someone asked me how many healings have happened in our prayer services or healing Masses. My answer was: "Just enough to keep me going." The Catholic Church is careful about calling a healing a miracle. I think they are overly careful at Lourdes. They have a whole committee of doctors, and very few healings meet the guidelines. We know a lot more healing goes on.

Around 1973, a woman I had never seen walked into my office. She had been sent by a Humility nun. Her fifth child was born a blue baby with Downs Syndrome, and they thought he would die. When she walked in with the baby, she said, "This baby has never cried." I prayed in tongues, and the baby started screaming bloody murder. I said, "Don't worry. I'm not hurting him. I think something is happening."

I didn't understand at the time, but I checked later and learned the baby was baptized in the hospital by a nurse when it looked like he would die. Lay people can do that. They just use water and the right words. The woman moved to Dubuque, and I didn't hear from her for twenty years. One of our parishioners, a blind man who served on the Governor's Commission for the Handicapped, went to a meeting in Dubuque where he met that woman. She told him the story of her son. When I heard it, I said I'd like to see her. One Sunday afternoon, the doorbell rang. I went to the door, and there was the baby's mother with this guy about six feet tall. She told me the story. After we prayed for him, he still had Downs Syndrome, but he didn't have a lot of the typical symptoms. He was way above average. He had a driver's license. He was best man for his two brothers' weddings. He worked at the Hy-Vee grocery store, and everybody in town knew him. She told her story twice at our Healing Masses.

I remember another woman who played the organ at Kahl Home and at Healing Masses. She was healed of lung cancer, and she gave her witness.

My younger brother Ben was in a car wreck and was thrown from the car. He landed on his head in a ditch. Since there was mud in the ditch, he didn't break his neck. Then he injured his back at his job and couldn't get disability insurance. I told him Fr. Francis MacNutt was having a weeklong healing conference in Dubuque and said, "Why don't you go up there?"

Francis MacNutt was a famous leader in the Catholic Charismatic Renewal and known for his ministry of healing. He later left the priesthood and the Catholic Church to marry.

Ben thought that was crazy. He had been a Catholic all his life and had only heard of healing at Lourdes. Fr. Ed O'Melia, who was not yet a seminarian, went with him. The healing Ben got at that conference changed his life. He was the hell-raiser of the family. When he came home and told my sister his story. she said: "If you're so smart, you can pray over my hands. I've had trouble with these scales on my hands for years." He prayed over them and said, "Thank you, Jesus." From then on, Ben was in the healing ministry.

My high school basketball coach worked for Deere and Company in Ottumwa. His granddaughter had a very troublesome illness, so he retired and moved to Davenport to be near her. He called and asked me to pray for her at the house. I went and prayed the Sacrament of Anointing of the Sick. After that, the family came to the healing Mass where a lot of people prayed for her. Her parents took her to the University of Iowa for an exam when she was about nine or ten years old. The doctors said, "We looked at her x-rays, and we can't believe that she ever had that condition." I can't remember the details. She had to take medicine, but she went on to become a champion swimmer at a college in Illinois. I wanted her to witness at the Healing Mass, but her grandpa said she was too shy.

There is a formula for integrating the Anointing of the Sick in the Mass. I used it during healing Mass, which was every first Friday. Medical people left the hospital in the late afternoon and came to the five o'clock Mass for that anointing.

I knew what people were going through and what they were praying for. A young man who had mental illness came from across the river, and I anointed him every first Friday. The Priest who took over after me hired a deacon as liturgist. He cut out the Anointing of the Sick and just said a general prayer. He didn't think the Anointing of the Sick was appropriate for Mass, but I knew it was. I was angry about that. After they cut that out of the Mass, the young man jumped off the bridge into the Mississippi River. Luckily, a couple of fishermen bailed him out. All he did was hurt his shoulder and arm. I asked why he did that. He said, "I wanted to be with the Lord." Without the Anointing of the Sick in the Mass, he jumped off the bridge. He was married and the father of five children.

When people experience the power of the Holy Spirit in healing or deliverance, they realize that God's power can change their lives. They can get off drugs or booze. They can be healed. That brings them into the church, and it brings fallen-away Catholics back to the church. Any medical doctor will tell you if you get your head and heart straightened out, the psychosomatic effects in your body will straighten out too. The deepest healing is spiritual, and it can lead to physical healing.

There are several levels of healing: physical, spiritual, mental, emotional, and psychological. When we started the Healing Masses, we passed out a page to the new people to explain what the healing Mass is and what it isn't. We don't heal anybody. We pray, and Jesus heals. When I pray for healing, I mention Martin de Porres and Juan Diego, the Aztec Indian that Our Lady of Guadalupe appeared to. Of course, I ask the Blessed Mother. She is the best intercessor.

Remember the man in the Bible who was brought to Jesus on a stretcher? That man just laid there. The other people had the faith to bring him. Sometimes the faith is in the people who bring the sick person, like the mother who brought her Downs Syndrome baby, or the nun who said, "Take him to Fr. Mottet." It's amazing how people come, but someone must have faith.

People always want to know why Jesus doesn't heal in some cases. The best answer I have is that I don't have a clue.

We wanted to see Fr. Mottet in action, so we attended a Healing Mass in Rock Island. A family several rows ahead of us brought their adult daughter, who had a severe disability that caused large involuntary movements. During the Mass, she occasionally cried out. When the time came for the priests and members of the healing team to pray for people, Fr. Mottet went straight to that girl. He prayed for more people and finally reached the back where we were sitting. He leaned toward us in the same way he leaned in to hear people's prayer request, but he said, "My back is killing me." Without thinking about Mass decorum, we put our hands on him and started praying.

Hispanics are so open to healing. They call other people around the states of Iowa and Illinois, and big crowds come. Hispanics are five times as likely to be charismatic as Anglos. They bring water, salt, or oil to be blessed at the Healing Mass. We call these things sacramentals, and they are very powerful. It fits Hispanic culture and spirituality. A lot of people have lost this trust. I had a Healing Mass at the Indian Reservation in the Dubuque Archdiocese. The pastor expected a hundred people, but four hundred came. Many were Hispanics. When I went to Ottumwa, people came from as far away as Mason City, which is a drive of several hours.

We had standing room only at the healing Mass in Columbus Junction. Word gets out in the Hispanic community, and they all come. After Our Lady of Guadalupe appeared in Mexico, the Franciscans baptized ten million Aztecs. She has become the patron saint of the pro-life movement because they stopped human sacrifices after she appeared. Blood flowed out of those temples, and some of it was their own babies.

I was surprised to receive the Pacem in Terris Award in 2008. When I saw the crowd, I said to the bishop, "We've gotta take up a collection." I knew the caliber of the previous recipients because I either wrote them, called them, or asked a favor from someone to get them here. Six were Nobel prize winners, and two are up for canonization. In my speech, I said, "I gotta get a lot smarter or a lot holier in a big hurry." I explained that the award was about what we've been able to do together and about how much is left to do. It was a chance to recognize people who worked with me and the organizations we started. I said, "I have a reputation of not being afraid to ask people to work or ask them for money."[52]

In October of 2009, Charles Toney died. Toward the end of his life, I gave both him and Ann the Anointing of the Sick every time I visited them in their home or in the nursing home. On Sunday afternoon, I took them things they liked from Bishop's Cafeteria, and we had a meal together. I could talk with them if I could get them to eat a meal. When Charles was watching a football game, you couldn't talk to him. I was so tired when I went home one Sunday that I fell asleep, went through an intersection, hit a stop sign in someone's front yard, and destroyed my car. All I got was a sore thumb and a black eye.

room. He still had the appearance of a powerful man. We could see the respect and affection between them, and it felt sacred to be in their presence.

In our interview, Bill Cribbs said, "I never heard Father Mottet say a bad word about nobody or a cuss word. He didn't talk all the time, so when he spoke, he had something to say, and you listened." When we asked Bill what he learned from Fr. Mottet, he said, "Friendship is the main thing I learned from him. He was very patient. If things didn't work out exactly the first time, he tried another method. He never judged people." We offered to leave because we thought Bill was tiring, but he wanted to go on reminiscing about those days at the barber shop with Charles Toney, Jack Schneiders, and Fr. Mottet.

No One Else Wanted the Job

My first exorcism was a single mother of two mixed-race children who lived a couple of blocks from the cathedral. A priest, who knew I was in healing ministry, thought I could help her. I took another priest with me. First, we blessed each room with holy water and put exorcised salt in the corners because Satan can't stand blessed objects. I said, "Now we'll bless you." When I sprinkled her with holy water, she screamed, fell on the floor, and said, "That burns." I thought, "Uh-oh, I've got a real case. This is real possession."

Her reaction was a sure sign, but I didn't have permission to do an exorcism. I went to Bishop O'Keefe. It was 1993. He had retired and was down on the floor packing his books while he waited for the new bishop to arrive. I said, "I think I've got a real case. Has anybody asked you for this permission before?" He said, "Not in thirty-five years." That's a problem. As a result of our theology and seminary training, we dropped the whole thing, but Bishop O'Keefe gave me permission.

Nobody wanted this job. I'm sure some people thought wacko Mottet is at it again. Most priests respect exorcism because they know they don't want to do it. Priests called me from all over the diocese, so the word was out. I accepted this job reluctantly.

Fr. Mottet was reluctant, but willing. Some people are squeamish even hearing about demons and deliverance. When I talk about Fr. Mottet and mention his character qualities and achievements, I see the look of surprise and skepticism when I say, "He was an official exorcist." To him, it was simply part of his job. He was businesslike and undramatic about it. It was a continuation of the work he had always done for justice and better lives for oppressed people.

When Art visited him in his apartment in 2009, Fr. Mottet offered, in a very matter-of-fact way, to show Art his exorcism kit, a soft-side zippered bag slightly smaller than a briefcase amid other books and papers cluttering the apartment. There was nothing secret or mysterious about it. Art saw that it contained books, papers, and some small containers that probably contained holy water and exorcised salt. It was a tool of Fr. Mottet's trade. He explained some of the theological and procedural aspects of deliverance, but his motive for studying and practicing deliverance and exorcism was that he saw it work, and people's lives were changed.

An African American man, who lived in an apartment on East Locust, often called the chancery and said, "I got demons." Bishop Franklin got tired of the calls and gave me standing permission. When Bishop Amos came, I asked if he wanted me to continue, and he said, "You just go right on with what you're doing." Now he has appointed a younger priest to be the contact person when a phone call comes to the diocese. The new exorcist is in training, and they keep his name secret to protect him.

I had no training, but I learned on the job. I call it "dumbing through." There was nowhere to go for training. I couldn't find a book to read. In the past, priests attended a workshop in New England, but that ended. Luckily, Dr. Margaret Schlientz, a psychologist in Milwaukee who was in charismatic renewal, started an annual conference and a school of exorcism.

One of my favorite teachers had become an exorcist in New York. When I was in his class, some French speakers from Canada were in our group. He said some words in French, and they all laughed. He was an entertaining speaker. He wrote a long Greek sentence on the board and said, "That's why they call me Fr. Nerd." He told us the rite of exorcism is in Latin, and we should only use it in Latin even though it has been translated into Spanish and French, and an English translation was in progress. It must be official with no theological errors. His main caution was: "Don't do this alone."

I'm convinced possession is a mockery of the incarnation. Lucifer revolted when God revealed the incarnation to the angels. It was too much for him to accept that one of those crummy human beings on earth could be united with God. They revolted and sinned. They hate Jesus, and they hate the Blessed Mother because Jesus took his flesh from her. They think, "If you can do that, I can do that," so they get into human beings and use people's voice and power and even give them extra power.

People are hurting badly. They start out wanting deliverance, but the demon works through them to fight against it. In one case, it took two strong men to get a person through the church door.

One woman came with a steak knife under her sweater. She insulted me and started to attack me. The man who brought her threw the knife across the chapel, and I didn't even see it. I had told the janitor, "If you hear screaming and noise coming out of there, don't let anybody in. Keep the door locked. Don't worry about the hollering because we know what we're doing." The woman finally calmed down. The guy who brought her met her at a detox center. Someone there said, "Call Fr. Mottet." It was one of the earlier cases, so it's hard to remember, but I think she eventually straightened out.

Since we were told never to do this alone, I have several team members. One of the first was a woman who called me after she got kicked out of the Baptist Church. She's the wife of a farmer over sixty miles from here, and she has six children. When she was Baptist, she led mission trips to Mexico where she ran into demonic activity and did deliverance. I said, "You were fighting Satan with a butter knife." She and her whole family became Catholic. I talked to her endlessly to answer her questions. Now she is helping a priest develop teams all up and down the west coast.

When I get a call, I ask the person permission to take notes as they tell their story. If they have a computer, I ask them to send me an email because it's hard to get all this over the phone. While the team members listen to the person's life history, they make notes of what comes to their minds. Some people get words of knowledge, but I don't. I get hunches. It is all confidential, like confession is. Team members show me the notes on their pad, and I pray about those things. I am the only one who addresses the demon personally because the other team members aren't appointed by the bishop. I don't feel in danger because I'm with a team. Sometimes I have three or four team members, but I must have at least one. They have work lives, so it depends on who I can get. I usually need to make several calls. It's important to get a mental health professional on your team, but most priests are too quick to send people to the psychiatrist.

I think women are more open to these gifts than men. Men seem more analytical, and women seem more receptive. When I first started praying, a gifted woman on my team said, "This ain't gonna work." Then I switched into Latin, and she said, "Wow! That was powerful." Some people can hear the demons screaming and hollering.

One time they prayed over me at the Eagle's Wings retreat on the outskirts of Davenport. A woman heard a demon say, "We want to kill him, but she won't let us." The Blessed Mother stopped them. I have always felt protected by the Blessed Mother. Once when I prayed for a woman, she had a vision of a demon that was scared of me. Demons are more afraid of Jesus, the Blessed Mother, and priests than we are of them. Demons are creatures, and they are scared to death.

Even when a person thinks he or she has a demon, discernment is necessary. People always think the worst. It's amazing how they find the names and phone numbers of exorcists. Any exorcist gets calls from all over. If the call is from another state, I check my list to find an exorcist in that state. For a long time, there were only fourteen exorcists in this country, but now I think it is up to fifty-five. There are one hundred dioceses to go. An archdiocese should have more than one. Rome has six or eight, and they have several discernment teams to make sure they only send real cases to the exorcists. People in the charismatic renewal will usually know someone or fish around to find someone. I've gotten calls from England, Australia, Canada, and twelve dioceses in the United States. I get a lot of calls from Canada.

A man from the western part of the state was brought to Ottumwa by his girlfriend. A trained deacon said, "This guy won't let me pray over him." I prayed for him, but he resisted. I took him into the sacristy to have more privacy, and there was a big reaction. I learned that they were baptized several years earlier but had never gone to confession. I told the girlfriend to take him to confession as soon as possible. The sacrament of confession is more powerful than an exorcism. Exorcism is only a blessing, but Christ acts through the Sacraments. People need to realize that a lot of things can be taken care of by regular confession. Since people don't go to confession, we still need exorcism.

I try to go to confession once a month. When we were ordained, we were told to go once a week. I think we overdid it. Once a month is good unless there is some other problem. Some people go with a list. I don't because it is clear to me what I need to confess.

Two pastors in Ottumwa didn't believe in this. When Hispanics went to them with a problem, they said, "We don't believe in that stuff. Go to Ben." I said to Ben, "We're just doing deliverances. We're not doing exorcisms because we don't have permission from the bishop."

I went with a team member to the house of a lay woman in Rock Island, and even the cat had a problem. Demons can get into animals. We cleaned out that whole house. I got a lot of calls like that. It is called "infestation," which is different from possession. You must discern. Catholics believe in purgatory, which Luther rejected, but there are restless souls trying to get attention. Sometimes doors, cabinets, or windows open, or you hear tapping on the walls, but if they aren't doing evil things, they aren't evil spirits. Before I pray, I ask, "Has anybody died in your family recently, or do you know what went on in the house. Could someone be trying to get your attention?"

St. Augustine thought most ghost stories could be attributed to angelic visions, but St. Thomas Aquinas explained the phenomenon of ghosts this way:

> According to the disposition of divine providence, separated souls sometimes come forth from their abode and appear to men . . . It is also credible that this may occur sometimes to the damned, and that for man's instruction and intimidation they be permitted to appear to the living. [53]

A Lutheran minister in the west end of Davenport called and asked me to help him when they started seeing and hearing things in the house. I asked him to do a history of the house: who built it, who lived there, and whether anything unusual had happened there? I've had houses where doctors did abortions and where murders took place. You want to know what you're praying about.

A family in the parish bought a house where their three little children saw ghosts. Their father investigated the history. A hundred years earlier, a man came home from the Civil War sick with flu. Three children caught it, died, and may have been buried in the back yard. I helped him clean out the place, and the children ran to me at school to tell me they didn't see the ghosts anymore.

I had a call from Peoria about a house where they kept slaves before the Civil War. You can imagine the suffering that went on in that house. A woman, who was a fallen-away Catholic, bought the house and was fixing it up with the help of a non-practicing Catholic. A little kid from the neighborhood said, "You bought the haunted house, didn't you." They knew nothing about that. A priest in Peoria called me, and I went. If it is a Catholic family, we have the Mass, but if not, we just say the prayer and the Our Father, and sometimes that does it. We went through and cleaned out the house, and then we had Mass because they both had Catholic backgrounds. They started praying the Rosary every day and going to Mass every Sunday. They came back to Church in a hurry once they encountered the supernatural.

It's All About Removing Evil

While I was in Rome for a conference, I met and talked with Fr. Amorth, the best-known exorcist in the world. I sold hundreds of his book *An Exorcist Tells His Story*. I got to meet him because of M&M's. One of the conference organizers had studied in the United States. He asked me to bring him "some of those little chocolate pills," and I did. When I met Fr. Amorth, he said, "I've prayed with seventy thousand people, and ninety percent did not need exorcism."

They needed deliverance, which is for lower grades of demonic activity: oppression, obsession, and temptation. We all suffer from temptation, the lowest grade. Deliverance is nothing like exorcism. A lot of people need deliverance. It helps. Deliverance is extremely common in Africa. When American missionaries went to Africa, the Africans had to teach them. Most cases of demonic activity are low grade. The higher grade, possession, is quite rare, and it needs exorcism.

St. Thomas Aquinas said, "Take care of the natural before you go into the supernatural." If it's physical or psychological, take care of those things first. Signs, like unaccounted for knowledge and excessive strength, let you know deliverance is needed. If a child can throw an adult across the room, you know. People who are addicted to gambling, alcoholism, pornography, or theft may need deliverance. I dealt with a man about pornography addiction. He tore up my chair and came at me like a bulldog, so I prayed the deliverance prayer. Fluency in a foreign language is a sign, but I haven't run into that much. That is different from the gift of tongues, which is from the Holy Spirit.

Even in Rome there is disagreement about the appropriate steps to take. I've asked them to make up their minds. Most of the disagreement is about whether the whole team should pray the prayer of protection before a case. They worry about whether someone might be attacked because he or she doesn't have holy orders, but I have the whole team prayed for, and I am never worried.

Our genealogy may affect us, so It is valuable to review the family tree. We thank God for all the good qualities in our family line, but there are also negatives. Maybe there is a lot of cancer, or something physical, spiritual, mental, or psychological. There might be a lot of alcoholism or maybe abuse of some kind. Some of these things have gone on for generations. We ask God to cut off and heal any negatives that come down the family line. This is called "inter-generation healing," and I have found it to be very powerful. Sometimes we have a generational healing Mass with a small group or family. In African American families, some of the wounds go back to slavery days.

The exorcism rite is a public prayer of the church, not a sacrament. It calls on all the saints and angels of paradise to come. The rite usually takes a minimum of two hours, but it can be three or four hours or several sessions. In Rome, they sometimes drag on for months and years, but Americans want everything to happen right now. Some people have visions during an exorcism or hear things. Demons know who is present. I heard, "Oh, not her. She is the cause of all my troubles," referring to the Blessed Mother. The exorcist just tells them to get out.

A lot of people, even priests, don't believe in exorcism. This view grew out of the Enlightenment that began in the late seventeenth century after Luther's revolution. In seminary, exorcism was mentioned, but we weren't instructed about it. In the early church, bishops and popes didn't allow pagans to be baptized until the demonic manifestations stopped. One third of the priests in Rome were exorcists, and they did exorcisms all the time. They had to do a lot of them because so many pagans were being baptized. The bishops ordained exorcists even before priests because exorcism was a minor order. Exorcisms or deliverances were on the last three Sundays before Easter, which are called "scrutiny Sundays," because the pagans were going to be baptized at Easter. A minor exorcism was part of the baptism ritual in the early church. It is still part of the Rite of Catholic Initiation of Adults, but most people don't recognize the exorcism rite.

According to the United States Conference of Catholic Bishops website: "Minor exorcisms are prayers used to break the influence of evil and sin in a person's life, whether as a catechumen preparing for Baptism or as one of the baptized faithful striving to overcome the influence of evil and sin in his or her life." As Fr. Mottet liked to say, "It's all about removing evil."

We are waking up, and things are changing. Dr. Margaret Schlientz started an annual conference in Canada that later moved to Mundelein Seminary. I have made nine out of ten of those meetings, but my health keeps me from going now. She always kept the bishops involved. You are required to have a letter from a bishop saying you are part of a team. Dr. Schlientz took down the names, addresses, and phone numbers and checked whether a bishop had written a letter. She tried very hard not to get the bishops riled up. Dr. Schlientz sends out those lists marked "confidential." When I get a call from another state, I look at the list, and if I find a priest from that state, I give him the phone number. If he can't do it, he will know someone who can. Dr. Schlientz also started a two or three-year course on exorcism at Mundelein.[54]

There is a controversy about whether a Christian can have a demon. Of course they can. I run into Christians all the time who invite them in and then get trapped. Some denominations say, "Once saved, always saved." It is a mistake to think that you cannot fall into serious sin. Satan is always looking for an open door, and he has just enough knowledge and power to get you hooked. Pope Paul VI said we have gone too far in denying the existence of Satan. Satan is real. Some people say Satan is behind every bush, but he is behind a lot more bushes than you think he is. A voodoo priest with specific knowledge or power charges a person a few hundred dollars to put a curse on someone. Then he charges that person a thousand dollars to take the curse off.

The Masons once put a curse on me. A priest I knew in Peoria sent a brother and sister to us for prayer. The sister had a dramatic change within twenty-four hours, but not the brother. When I questioned him, he told the team about the day he became a thirty-second degree Mason. He started to cry, and he apologized to his sister. Someone on our team, who had family members who were Masons, knew how to renounce the Masonic vows. We went through the vows one by one. The brother and sister were supposed to come back for another time of prayer, and we intended to get a psychologist involved, but they didn't come. The priest from Peoria called and said, "The Masons are trying to get information on you, but I refused to give it to them. They want your address and phone number."

Shortly after that, a friend called and said, "We're having a lot of trouble in our house." When he investigated, he found out it was built by a thirty-second degree Mason who lived there for a while. I went there to pray on a snowy winter night. They didn't hear me at the back door, so I went around to the side door carrying all my material and my briefcase in my right hand. I tripped, fell, and took all the force of the fall on my left arm. We prayed then, but I think it was more than a fall. It was a push. It still hurts to this day, even after physical therapy. Several years ago, at the Mundelein conference, I told the story to a monsignor from Pennsylvania. He prayed to break the curse, but my arm still bothers me. The Masons are anti-Catholic. A faithful Catholic cannot become a Mason because of the promises they make.

The Rite: The Making of a Modern Exorcist, published in 2011, tells the story of a priest from California, who went to Rome for training as an exorcist. The author accompanied him to his classes in Rome and followed the Chief Exorcist of Rome for a week. After the book was published, the film *The Rite* came out. By Hollywood standards, *The Rite* is rather modest. It wasn't as scary as some people thought it would be, but when I got home after watching it, there was a phone call from the priest who is the subject of the book. He said, "Since this movie came out, I've had a tsunami of phone calls. I just got a call from Des Moines. Can you handle it?" We all worked from that list of fourteen priests who were at the conference in Mundelein.

When I was in Rome, ABC News wanted to do a story on exorcism. They asked if they could interview me, and I met them for lunch at a restaurant. I love the restaurants of Rome. The head honcho of their Rome office interviewed me for thirty minutes. He said, "You've been into social justice most of your life, and that's kind of left wing. Now you're in exorcism. Isn't that right wing?" My answer was, "It's all about removing evil." I hoped they would just use that one line, but the producer called to tell me that I was mostly cut out of the program. They filmed a Protestant minister who did exorcisms on television. The people involved were jumping all over the church and each other. That kind of public display ruined it.

I got four words and about ten seconds, but they used my picture in the promotion and apparently my name. People at St. Vincent's got all excited and advertised that Fr. Mottet was going to be on an ABC special program. It caused quite a buzz, but it was ten seconds. I once got a call from Oprah Winfrey's organization about filming an exorcism. I said, "You'll never find a Catholic who will do that. It's private like confession."

Chapter 17

Use Your Power While You've Got It

fter hearing Fr. Mottet's stories about the restoration of Sacred Heart Cathedral and his initiatives to develop the neighborhood and make it safe, we were eager to see those places for ourselves. As we drove through the Sacred Heart neighborhood, familiar sites flooded Fr. Mottet with memories. Even though it was difficult for him to walk, he got out of the car at Project Renewal to walk around. He sat in a chair outside a house that had been the Thomas Merton House. On a street near St. Ambrose University, he said, "I cleaned out that house," meaning a demonic infestation.

Fr. Mottet took us for lunch at Café on Vine, which he helped start in 2007 through Thomas Merton House, Inc. Over four hundred eighty thousand free meals have been served with no questions asked. The official name of Thomas Merton House, Inc. is now "Café on Vine, Inc." Lunch there was like a family reunion. Everyone was delighted to see him. He bragged that it was the best lunch in town.

Our tour of Sacred Heart Cathedral was our favorite stop. It had a returning-home quality like our trip to Ottumwa. We didn't know then that we would make only two more trips there, one for the Easter Vigil and one for Father's funeral.

When Fr. Mottet moved to Kahl Home, the most luxurious place he had ever lived, he struggled with helplessness for the first time in his life and a rare taste of

I had to do a lot of paperwork to get ready to move. It costs ten times as much to live at Kahl Home as at St. Vincent's. I knew this day would come, but I was surprised it came so soon. I tried to stretch it out a little bit, but whatever God wants is going to be okay. Kahl Home is a nice place run by Carmelite nuns.

When I left the Cathedral and moved out of the rectory in 2005, two janitors went up and threw everything in boxes. It took me years to sort stuff and give it away. They threw out my shoes. I had snow boots with treads on them, and now I can't find them.

My niece Pat, a retired schoolteacher, lives in Oskaloosa, Iowa. She is my sister Katy's oldest daughter. She is trying to take the place of Katy, who was kind of the switchboard of family news, and I commend her for it. She has the photos that are in a big black scrapbook with all my records from high school, college, and ordination.

I have a lot of help from a woman named Carol, who is supposed to be dying of cancer. A prayer group of four or five women pray for her, and people wonder if a miracle has happened. It is remarkable that she can be up and around and help other people. She calls me to let me know when a former Sacred Heart parishioner is dying in the hospital and says, "I'll pick you up if you want to go over." One of the women she worked for appreciated her so much that she left her a home on Forty-sixth Street when she died. I used to go to that house to give the sacraments to the woman who owned it. Carol just continues to work in ministry.

It's Easier to Drop Dead at Saint Vincent's than to Move Out in an Orderly Fashion

I told you about the scripture that haunted me: "If you give up one family, you'll get a hundred more." *(Matthew 19:29)* I have had a lot of company lately. Dennis and Patty Little were here yesterday. Someone else came in and asked the person at the front desk if they could visit me, and she said, "Oh, Fr. Mottet is all over the place. He's in and out, but if you can find him, he'll be in room 129 south."

I am disorganized now, and I'm so isolated. I don't have any Christmas cards, and I can't find stamps. I called Ann down at Project Renewal because they put out thank you cards the kids make as a fundraiser. I asked her if she would send me some, and I will pay her for them.

Doctors and nurses keep me alive with pills. There is nothing worse than getting those things caught in your throat. I get a blood test every three months because of the kidney transplant. If something is out of whack, they call the nurse at the station and say they want me to drink all that water. I'm doing my best.

I unloaded on Bishop Amos in a letter about moving here. He answered that I cannot come back to St. Vincent's, but I can move to some cheaper place if I like it better. I wrote back to thank him for his letter and tell him I don't blame him, but I still blame other people who were part of it. It's easier to drop dead at St. Vincent's than to move out in an orderly fashion.

I saw Bishop Amos at the Easter vigil last week, so it's all cleared up, and I feel better. Even my medical doctor said, "You've got to tell somebody. Get it off your chest, or you'll wake up every morning thinking about it." I knew I couldn't take the poison of staying angry, but the move here was rough. The problem isn't this place. It was being rushed out of St. Vincent's with everything in disorder. Glen Leach promised me that he and Loxi Hopkins won't let a scrap of paper go away until they have looked at it. That makes me rest a little easier. I am at peace with it now.

Gardening was a theme throughout Fr. Mottet's life. When he and his niece Theresa came for dinner at our home, he arrived with a bag of spinach, Swiss chard, and other leafy vegetables from his garden at St. Vincent's. On one of our trips with him through the neighborhood, we stopped to admire his garden and take photos. He had a small greenhouse with a high raised bed that he could reach without bending low. He was proud of his garden, but he held material things loosely, and he sold the greenhouse after he moved to Kahl Home. The administrator there was willing to install a vertical garden that he could reach easily, even from his wheelchair, and we tried to interest him, but he declined the offer.

It Would Be the Biggest Miracle of My Life

I'm still praying for big miracles. I would like to see them before I die. I almost gave up on the idea of starting a worker owned co-op, but now I'm trying again with Jim Orr, one of my students from Assumption. He is an inventor. He used to work for the CIA, but he resigned for conscientious reasons. He called me one day and said, "Do you remember me?" He was surprised when I did. He reminded me of the day when I threw him out of class. I told him to take his books and go for a walk. Later he asked if he could come back, which took a lot of humility.

When I visited the Mondragon worker owned co-op in Spain, I hoped we could translate that to the Hispanic culture in this country. Worker owned cooperatives bring democracy to the workplace. Each worker gets a vote. The key to success is good management.

I introduced Jim to Mondragon via the computer. He took to the idea of worker owned coops right away when he learned that Mondragon has ninety thousand employees. In case one of us dies, Jim asked me to write a statement that his inventions are only to be used to start worker owned co-ops. We don't want the project to be for someone to get rich and send all the jobs to China. Jim calls this thing "the Mottet Initiative." It was written up in *The Catholic Messenger.*

I'm sworn to secrecy about Jim's invention. I told him that if we can pull this off as a worker owned co-op, it will be the biggest miracle of my life, and I've had lots of miracles. I said, "We better get going because I don't have much time left." His invention could make him a millionaire. He was offered a quarter of a million by a group of investors, but that's a small amount.

I'm having lunch with Jim tomorrow to pray for an open door. He calls me "the rogue elephant," because I always uncover another contact. Some people call that stubbornness. We're looking for people who have a passion to bring jobs to those in need. He made a DVD about his invention, and he has shown it to congressmen, investors, and businesspeople. He recently contacted the Veterans Administration, and he is going to Washington, D.C., this week to meet with an army general because there are so many unemployed, homeless veterans. Mayor Bill Gluba has helped open some doors for him.

Jim had what I call an epiphany experience. He always wanted to drive a truck, so he got in the trucking business when he got out of the military. He worked at the Eagle warehouse in Milan, which I picketed during the grape boycott, and he noticed a stack of groceries in the corner. He asked his boss what would happen with the groceries, mostly bent cans and broken packages. They were going to be thrown out after the company representative recorded credit for them. Jim asked if he could have them for the poor.

He asked the social worker he dated to introduce him to a family in dire need so he could give them the groceries. She told him about a family along the Mississippi River in Buffalo, Iowa. He had driven by those four-room cinderblock houses many times. He pulled up, walked through mud to get to the house, and knocked on the door with the groceries. The woman who came to the door was pregnant and had a baby hanging on her leg. She had cancer or some illness.

He said, "May I come in? I've got some groceries in the car. Can I bring them in? I work in a place where they're going to be thrown out." Her husband came home in his overalls and sat down. Jim could tell they were very poor. Then the man said, "May I wash your feet? No one in my life has ever done for me what you've done for us." That's right from the gospel. You never know what's going on behind a door. There may be tremendous poverty, illness, or despair.

Jim has never gotten over that experience. I asked him to talk with everyone at Social Action about his experience. We want people to have an epiphany experience like that in every classroom and in every homily. When people help at Project Renewal or work in a soup kitchen, they experience that.

I will be with Jim and his wife this Christmas. When Thanksgiving, Christmas, or Fourth of July come along, the people I used to go to, like the Toneys, are now deceased. Jim has taken over. *Jim Orr passed away after a brief illness on May 27, 2021.*

The other family that invited me is a mother and her eleven children. A few years ago, when her adult children wanted to plan a trip, they went to a travel agent and said, "We can't get our mother out of the country, but if Father Mottet goes with us, she'll go." The travel agent and I met at the Café on Vine for lunch, and I agreed to go. It was a delightful trip. They are a good family, and that mother raised them right.

If You Get in a Pinch You Can Call on Me

They don't have a chaplain here now. A priest from Ottumwa was chaplain for about ten years. During World War I, he was an infantryman and later became a chaplain. He was able to work in a parish without a salary because his military retirement was so good. When he got too old, he went to St. Vincent's, and there hasn't been a chaplain here since then. Six priests are residents, so they can always call on one of us. I'm probably the healthiest one.

You always need to be ready to serve. I was in the hospital for surgery, and a nurse came in and said, "Someone is dying down in the emergency room. Can you come? The chaplain is out for the evening, and he put your name on call." I put on my bathrobe and went down to the emergency room and gave the rites and so forth.

I was drafted for Saturday Mass when a priest didn't show up. They were scraping the bottom of the barrel. Another time Sr. Teressa, the little nun who runs all the time, came to me in the hall, and asked me to come and anoint a dying woman. I went and gave her the last rites, but I had her book, not mine. Mine is all marked. The priest who makes assignments for Mass here came the next day. I told him I was drafted for Mass. He had already heard about it and about the dying woman. Word is getting out. I told him, "If you get in a pinch, you can call on me."

I've been scheduled to celebrate Mass eight or ten times. I usually know ahead of time, but sometimes they ask me to come without notice. I always have a homily ready. I meditate on the scriptures every day and take a few notes like I've always done. I have to get my little points in there too. Sometimes Catholics are criticized because we can't quote chapter and verse, but the whole day is the scriptures.

I have my breviary with me all the time, so I meditate on scripture all day long in the Liturgy of the Hours. We have the Old Testament reading and the New Testament. We pray seven times a day. I do most of mine. If you don't get up at four o'clock like the Trappists, you can read those scriptures the night before. It includes reflection on the scripture reading by a father of the church. Every hour has something from St. Paul or the Acts of the Apostles or the gospel. I still underline a lot.

According to the United States Conference of Bishops website, "The Liturgy of the Hours, also known as the Divine Office or the Work of God (Opus Dei), is the daily prayer of the Church marking the hours of each day and sanctifying the day with prayer." There are five hours: Office of Readings, Morning Prayer,

I had a Christmas homily ready, which I didn't get to give. The young Vietnamese nun asked me to take the four o'clock Mass. I said I would do it, but when I got there, Fr. Deo was suiting up. The next day they had another priest who had been ordained sixty-one years and could hardly walk and talk.

It is time for the younger generation to take over the healing Mass. They need to stand on their own two feet, which is harder if I hang around. Fr. Ed O'Melia is younger than I am, and he has the advantage of being bilingual, so he is handling healing Masses. About a year ago he said, "I am not the new monarch." He was in the Trappists for seven years, so he is contemplative. He has a trailer, and on his day off, he goes out to a lake or park, and his trailer is his monastery. He says I taught him that you can combine contemplation and social action. A priest in Muscatine, who was in my brother Ben's prayer group in Ottumwa before he was ordained, is very gifted, and he is close enough that he can help.

Fr. Ed O'Melia was the homilist at Fr. Mottet's funeral. He began thinking about priesthood when he was a member of the St. Joe's prayer group. He was pastor of St. Mary's Church, the Spanish-language church in Davenport. Fr. Mottet assisted at St. Mary's after his retirement.

I wasn't planning to go to Healing Mass this Friday night because I would have to stand to pray for people, but I've changed my mind. This morning I realized I should be having people pray over me. A friend usually picks me up, and we go out for supper after Mass.

Three priests hear confessions for an hour starting at six o'clock. Confession, or Reconciliation, is a healing sacrament, and it is right in synch with what goes on in the healing Mass. When Hispanics show up, Fr. Ed hears confessions in Spanish. I can get by in Spanish, but not very well, so I tell them the Lord understands Spanish and all languages. At six thirty, the praise music begins, but the team stays in the confessional until ten minutes after seven because people come late, and there are usually long lines of people.

Kahl Home said I can have a small prayer group here, but I can't do exorcisms. That gives me a good excuse to turn exorcisms down and send them to a younger priest. I get calls, but I refer them. I tell the switchboard at the chancery that if a phone call comes in, it should go to the younger priest who is in training. He is the contact person now. Still, I got a call from Rock Island, and I have a letter on my desk from someone. I'll call them, but I don't know how it will turn out.

Fr. Mottet didn't need attention or admiration, but he needed to be in on the action. He needed to make a difference. He was unable to be a victim or a bystander. His strength ebbed quickly at Kahl Home. He acknowledged this but was reluctant to go to physical therapy or exercise sessions. His voice weakened noticeably and developed a slightly nasal quality. At mealtime, he sat in the dining room with three other priests, but he didn't participate in activities scheduled for residents. Occasionally he asked for a glass of beer during happy hour.

I thought recently about Fr. Simpson, who in 1948 became the first African American priest in Iowa. In those days, if a diocese didn't have an African American parish, there was no place to send an African American priest. That was racist. Now the pastor of St. Anthony's in Davenport is from the Congo. He started at Sacred Heart under my tutelage. We have several African priests who study at St. Ambrose and live at St. Vincent's. If they aren't in class, they're out somewhere raising money. Fr. Deo offers Mass here. He is so lovable and personable that even though you can't understand his English, he is breaking down prejudices by being so approachable.

My friend from Chile called this morning. He is an engineer who has done mining in South America and shipped ore to China. Now he wants to mine precious metals in Tanzania. He wanted some connections in Tanzania, so I set him up with priests who have lived and studied here. He offered five engineers in Tanzania a twenty-five percent cut if they would help him. I called him back and said, "Those precious metals really belong to the people of Tanzania." Companies are moving into Africa and Latin America and buying huge tracts of land to mine precious metals needed for cell phones." I'm talking with a priest from Africa about that. The mining is controlled by gangs, and ordinary people are left out. There is blood money in some of the cellphones because a lot of people are killed in the violence. Some of those countries have public lands where the people farm together. Those lands are being sold, and the real owners are left in poverty.

No one expects to hear an eighty-six-year-old man in a nursing home fuming about conflict minerals, which are mined in areas of armed conflict and illegally traded to finance waring groups, but Fr. Mottet was still attuned to social justice issues and able to see far-reaching implications. It reminded me of the day he said, "Every time I see an injustice, it makes me angry." He didn't stop there. He went on to do something about it. He was never truly sidelined. He was simply behind the scenes.

I watched on TV the mother of a young man who was killed by a policeman in South Carolina. She said, "Jesus is my Lord and my Savior, and I've forgiven that policeman." It was a marvelous witness of faith. The policeman is in seclusion and charged with murder. I wonder what is going through his mind. It was a traffic stop for a taillight that was out. Blacks and Hispanics have always felt targeted.

I had an African American student who was a prisoner of war. After he came home, he worked for the Chamber of Commerce. He went to a house in Bettendorf and knocked on the door, but the people weren't home. He got back in his car, and suddenly three squad cars surrounded him because a neighbor reported a Black man trying to get into a home. My student had a short temper, even in high school, and he blew his stack. He called it "driving while Black."

The police need more training. The Davenport Chief of Police cooperated with Quad Cities Interfaith and a professor at St. Ambrose, who has studied this for several years. He has come up with a plan that can serve as a model. Mayor Bill Gluba called me the other day to say that he is setting up a task force to work on it. If something happens here, like in South Carolina, Davenport will be ahead of the game.

I talked with the Davenport and Bettendorf police, and they agreed not to pick on Hispanics, but recently the owner of the Azteca restaurants was arrested. An over-enthusiastic policeman picked him up for a seatbelt violation, and he had undocumented workers in his car. He employs a lot of people and pays his taxes. We tried to help him, but he got bad advice from a lawyer in Texas. He thought his guilty plea would get him off, but it didn't. He was deported.

The Old Testament says the Messiah will be just, and the church teaches that in the last judgment, everybody sees that God is just. That is important to poor people and people who are discriminated against. Evil gets its comeuppance, and the just get rewarded, but it is not very clear in this life. Only God can create the Kingdom, but we can cooperate or oppose God. When we work for justice and peace, we are cooperating with God. It reminds me of Sr. Concetta. When she got the Senior Iowans together for their lunch of soup, crackers, Twinkies, and a cup of coffee, there was so much joy as they socialized that a visiting priest said, "The Kingdom of God is in there."

I'm Always Preparing for His Coming

As we interviewed Fr. Mottet for his book, we had the privilege of participating in his life review process. He prepared for death by reminiscing about his work and reiterating his message. As the end of his life approached, his memories were a bit random.

When I was a college freshman in 1948 and going to Young Christian Students, I read a thin book titled *Advent.* I can't remember the name of the French theologian who wrote it, but that book had a big impact on me, like *Fishers of Men* did. I've never forgotten it. The author stressed the fact that Advent is a preparation for the second coming of Christ. That has always been standard Catholic belief. I look forward to Advent. It is beautiful and exciting.

In the parish, I used to have a party for the children on the Feast of St. Nicolas on December 6. Someone came dressed up like a bishop, and I said, "This is St. Nicolas." Then I asked them questions. I got candy bars from the food pantry and gave one to anybody who answered a question correctly. The kids loved it. Then I brought in St. Lucia dressed in white with a white alb. She sang Santa Lucia with the rectory full of people. Those are things that you can do instead of putting up the decorations so early. Don't put up the Christmas tree and decorations on Thanksgiving. The Christmas crib should go up on December twenty-fourth.

I preach all the time in the parish that we are not preparing during Advent for the coming of Santa Claus. We are preparing for Jesus' second coming. Santa Claus was the invention of Protestants in New York. They thought St. Nicholas was too "pope-ish." They created Santa Claus, and that started the commercialization. I don't blame businesses. Frank Rhomberg said, "We exist for eleven months, and we make our profit in one month. We sell fur coats before Christmas, and we just survive for the rest of the year."

St. Nicholas and his legend date from the early church and survived through the Middle Ages. St. Nicholas was famous for his generosity, especially to children. The Dutch word for his name was "Sinterklaas," which eventually became Santa Claus in German. Martin Luther changed the date of gift giving from December 6 to Christmas Eve.

I preached on commercialization at the December healing Mass. One week, a woman gave her witness about how she used to love to walk up and down the aisles of the shopping centers and look at all that stuff. Then she realized she was addicted to commercialism. Some of our young priests in Fort Madison got in big trouble when they were first ordained because they taught on commercialization in homilies and told the people that Santa Claus doesn't exist, which upset the parents. They could have taken a little different route. I just avoided that. I preached that while we prepare for the coming of Jesus Christ in poverty and humility to be a servant and die on the cross, we are also preparing for Him to come in glory, majesty, and power as judge. We have to be counter-cultural in many ways to be Catholic.

In a homily last Sunday, I pointed to the crib and said, "Everything you need to know about faith is in this crib," I remember my mother lifting me up when I was a toddler at St. Patrick's to show me, and I realized this is important because she was going to a lot of trouble. The shepherds who heard the good news first were the scum of the earth. They were considered dishonest thieves, who could not even testify in court. They were the least, but they received the gospel first when angels appeared to them. The lesson there is that we should preach the gospel first to the least of these.

The poor evangelize us. They tell us about their problems and about injustices, and they make demands on us. It makes us shape up if we want to be in line with the gospel. Mother Teresa always went to the poorest of the poor. The church has done this in many ways, but not as consistently as we should have. Jesus came to bring good news to the poor,

If you live the liturgy, you cover the important points of Christian doctrine in the scriptures. After Luther, the church took on a defensive role and reduced the scripture to a small diet of readings, but Vatican II broke out of that, and now there are three years of liturgical seasons. The church produced the Bible, and the church should have the right to interpret the Bible. I am still learning things in the Bible, and I will be until the day I die.

Protestants take the Bible and beat us over the head with it. They quote it all the time and use it against the Catholic Church. Some Catholic converts, who were ministers, say there is more scripture on Sunday in the Catholic Mass than in Protestant church services. There are plenty of Protestants who take Christmas very seriously, but people would rather think about the coming of a baby than about the coming of a glorious king and judge, the ruler of everything. That is the main thing, but we don't hear it.

I pray every day: "Lord, help me be ready when You come," not only during Advent, but year-round. I sat with three priests at the dinner table. They talked about how long they have been here. One was just out of the hospital, and another was being rehabilitated. Someone asked me how long I was going to be here. I said, "I'm here until the second coming unless you pray me out of here."

In the early church they thought Jesus would return any Sunday morning at sunrise because that is when He rose. It is a misinterpretation of scriptures to think of end times as a seven-year end of history. St. Paul said that Jesus is coming, but not right away, so get to work. We have been in the end times for two thousand years. Why does the end times last so long? You will have to ask that when you get to heaven. St. Paul said the delay is so that more people can be saved. I mention in Advent homilies and at funerals that no matter when death comes, it will surprise us. Even if we are a hundred ten years old, we will be surprised when the Lord appears. But Catholics get four weeks every year to prepare for His second coming. If we could get that idea across, it would be a revolution in the church and in the world.

People see TV evangelists with signs and so forth, and they ask me what I think about the rapture. It was thought of by an Irishman in the eighteen hundreds. It is a misunderstanding of scripture. The people who teach this usually think all Catholics and Jews should be left behind, but our roots are Jewish.

The Easter Vigil is my favorite service of the whole year. We spend Saturday night in prayer and song. The vigil goes on for two or three hours because we baptize the people we are bringing into the church through the Rite of Catholic Initiation of Adults. That doubles our crowd. There is so much symbolism: light and darkness, people being baptized and confirmed, special music. It goes back to the early Church where they brought in thousands of pagans, and huge baptisteries were built. Art and Suzy took me to the Easter Vigil.

I visited the world-famous Lateran Baptistery in Rome. It was once bombed after a bishop in southern Italy criticized the mafia. The acoustics are so perfect that everyone can hear the priest and the baptismal promises. The water came from the mountains through the Roman aqueduct, and it was cold as the dickens. You can see why they would pray in tongues when they came out of the water.

Everybody thinks St. Peter's Basilica is the Cathedral of Rome, but it isn't. St. John Lateran is. It's smaller, but very beautiful. There is a famous statue of St. Francis out in front. When he went through his conversion, the Lord spoke to him and said, "Rebuild My Church." Because the church building there was falling down, he misunderstood the voice coming from the crucifix and thought it meant a stone building. It's a romantic story. He began a great renewal with thousands of followers who slept out in the fields. Francis decided to go to Rome to get permission for his movement. The pope had a vision during the night of a beggar who was holding up the church. When Francis came into the church dressed as a beggar amid all the pomp and wealth, people tried to move him out of the way, but the pope said, "Let him in." That's how Francis got permission for his renewal that spread all over Europe.

The movie *Brother Sun Sister Moon* shows all of this. We used to show it all the time at the St. Francis Catholic Worker house in Washington, D.C. There are many renewals. Most religious orders grew out of some renewal effort. You can't really understand the Protestant Reformation unless you understand the historical context.

I call Pope Francis a "closet charismatic." He talked about the Holy Spirit every day for his first two weeks as pope. When he was invited to an Italian charismatic gathering, he couldn't go, but he said, "Tell them I love them, and tell them that I was in charge of the renewal in Argentina." You can't get much closer than that. When Pope Francis came along, I said, "This guy understands it even better than Pope Benedict XVI, who was an Augustinian scholar." My card has St. Augustine's saying, "Charity is no substitute for justice." Pope Benedict said the same thing, but he was focused too much on charity. I'm sure Catholic Charities was pumping its muscular arms, but Francis understands you must get at the cause of poverty. The Holy Spirit worked overtime in that election.

One of the reasons Pope Francis is so popular is that he doesn't live upstairs. He lives in a couple of rooms he has down in the hotel. Credibility is important. He lived in a slum in Argentina, and he rode the streetcar to work. Being from Latin America, he can see the foolishness of some U.S. policies. Our policy toward Cuba is just one example.

When Pope Francis was elected in 2013, it was a vindication to Fr. Mottet of the choices he had made and a validation of his work for social justice. We looked forward with him to Pope Francis' speech to the U.S. Congress on September 24, 2015. The Pope honored four Americans as representatives of the American people: Abraham Lincoln, Martin Luther King, Jr., Thomas Merton, and Dorothy Day. Except for Lincoln, they were people Fr. Mottet frequently referred to. He knew two of them personally. Pope Francis said, "In these times when social concerns are so important, I cannot fail to mention the Servant of God Dorothy Day, who founded the Catholic Worker Movement. Her social activism, her passion for justice and for the cause of the oppressed, were inspired by the Gospel, her faith, and the example of the saints." Those were also the drivers of Fr. Mottet's life.

We're in God's Waiting Room

I am the most powerless I have ever been. I can't get to the Social Action staff meetings anymore, but I want to tell them, "Use your power while you've got it."

When I had cancer almost fifty years ago, I felt like I was sliding into home plate. It still feels like that. Some people think I'm doing well, but I don't think I have adjusted very well to this place. The season of Advent helps me prepare. Lent is coming up, and it will be very meaningful. We should live the liturgical calendar. I'm between third and home now. Whatever the Lord wants. The main thing is to contemplate the three divine persons of the Trinity, and that is enough.

Since I retired, I've become more contemplative, and that serves me well. When I was active, I had Mass every morning and Liturgy of the Hours, and I made retreats. I was more successful in social action because I was contemplative. There is a saying: "Act as though it all depends on you and pray as if it all depends on God." St. Ignatius, the father of the Jesuits and the spiritual exercises, said, "Be a contemplative in action." The Ignatian review of the day is like the social inquiry I learned back in Young Christian Students. It gives me a certain cut of mind, so I know when I don't shape up. The Holy Spirit will still be working on me until the last minute. You always review what you are doing and how it fits into God's will, and you pray for guidance for the future, but you can't do just the contemplative prayer part.

"Be a contemplative in action" was one of Fr. Mottet's most important life lessons, and he regarded it as a key to his success. He saw the weakness in social action without spiritual grounding and in contemplative prayer without social purpose and results. By "contemplative in action," he meant acting in a way that aligns with deeply held beliefs and promotes justice; balancing reflection and action; and cultivating the awareness of God's presence while being fully involved in the world.

I look upon Pope Francis as living a contemplative life in action. He teaches by his actions. When he visited the United States, he rode in a little car that spoke volumes to me. Instead of riding in a limousine, he sat in the back seat of a Fiat. Once when I wrecked my car, I had a Fiat from a rental company. The insurance company asked if they had provided me a car, and I said, "It's the next best thing to a car. It's a Fiat." I didn't feel safe in it because it was so small, and I was so close to the road and to other cars.

I often think of my friend Jack Eagan, "mister social action," who did a cool thing when he knew he was dying. He called me one day under the guise that the *National Catholic Reporter* was writing an article about how many priests are foreign-born. That surprised me. I said, "Jack, how are you?" and told him we had two foreign-born priests. Later, I went to his funeral and realized he called all his friends around the country before he died. He had a terrible heart condition. He was so well known that his obituary made the *New York Times*.

When I talk about many of the people I've worked with, I have to say, "now deceased." I ask them to intercede for me. People told me I should write a memoir, but I've only gotten as far as the title: *How Not to Do It.* One of the things I've learned is that truly great people are humble. I've met a lot of great people and worked with some of them. Humility and truth are what you need about yourself, about God, about the world, and about others.

All the plans for my funeral are made. The diocese urges priests to keep our wills up to date and warns us that if we don't leave specific directions, we will get a generic funeral. I knew that would be bad, so I've picked the scriptures and songs about justice that mean so much to me. The wake will be at Sacred Heart Cathedral. It is supposed to be a celebration, but I don't know if anybody will interpret it that way. I have a copy of my instructions here, and the diocese has a copy. I may change it, but so far, I haven't.

I think about death every day and say this prayer: "Lord, help me to be ready when you come." I've been saying that for years. Everybody here is in God's waiting room. You go to the doctor, and you wait, and the nurse comes out when they're ready for you. We are in God's waiting room, and an angel will come out and say, "You're next." I go before the Blessed Sacrament, and I say, "Someday Lord, I'm going to spend all eternity with you." I'm not satisfied with my preparation here. I miss the celebration of the true meaning of Advent, so I'm not pleased. I have learned to wait, but I am not as ready as I had hoped.

I will be buried in the priest circle at Calvary Cemetery. The cemetery was donated by Antoine LeClaire. He and his wife and son were originally buried in the yard of the cathedral. As far as my tombstone, it will be the normal thing, my name and years. I always joked that I was going to put the two feet on it, but I don't have directions to do that. I would like to be remembered as a good priest, a good brother, and a good uncle.

Interviews during the final weeks were meandering, but Fr. Mottet's mind was sharp. He combed his memory for anything important he might have left out. He purposefully handed over responsibilities to others. He suffered in the last months of his life, but he didn't draw attention to his misery. In his final days, one of his visitors massaged his forehead with tender strokes to comfort him. The man who often drove him around Iowa to Healing Masses, acted as a gatekeeper to protect him, and visits were more regulated. Betty Anderson Torey came to visit him. He was awake while she stood by his bed, and they talked quietly. They understood each other so well that few words were needed.

Fr. Mottet knew death was approaching. His funeral was arranged and paid for. Friends came to visit. Some of his Assumption High School students, who were in town for a class reunion, visited him. Until two days before his death, he asked whether there were any more questions for the book when he woke from sleep. He repeated some of his most familiar stories. He gave marching orders to the people in his social justice sphere, particularly emphasizing the imperative to teach and mentor young leaders. He approached death with the same matter-of-fact grace and humility with which he had lived his long and remarkable life. He died peacefully, without struggle, on Friday, September 16, 2016, at Kahl Home. Loxi Hopkins had the privilege of being with him.

Before his death, people waited for the chance to sit quietly with him. It felt sacred. I hated to leave, knowing it might be my last visit, but others deserved their turn too. I wanted to know about Fr. Mottet's death, and Loxi was the one who knew. She worked closely with him for many years, and Fr. Mottet described her as "the most outstanding leader we ever produced in Quad Cities Interfaith." I asked Loxi to share what it was like to work with Fr. Mottet, to be present when he died, and to help fulfill his legacy.

From the start, Fr. Mottet told me what he wanted me to do. I was passing out roses at Sacred Heart on Rose Sunday and collecting money for a right to life organization. He asked why I wasn't Catholic. When I said I didn't know, he said, "I would like you to come to inquiry. It's going to happen in two weeks." My husband and I both came, not intending to become Catholic. Of course, Fr. Mottet was urging me on through the whole thing, and after inquiry, I decided to go to the Rite of Catholic Initiation of Adults. My husband was absolutely positive that he wasn't converting, but he came too. Anyway, we both joined the church.

Within two weeks, Fr. Mottet said, "I want you to go to Gamaliel training and learn community organizing." When I got there, I said, "What has he done to me?" because it was so tough. Fr. Mottet never asked anybody if they would do something. He said, "Here's what I want you to do." I've never heard anybody turn him down. Until the day he died, he was still doing the same thing. He told me he wanted me to make sure young people are trained and make sure the diocese doesn't turn to charity over justice. When Bishop Zincula came, that's the first thing I talked to him about, the importance of justice over charity. I think God leads you to where you are supposed to be.

My first organizing assignment was to go around the area near Sacred Heart with a Quad Cities Interfaith organizer and put red paint on the sidewalks in front of broken-down houses. There were a lot of them and a lot of rental houses. The disparity between Black and White neighborhoods showed up in Davenport schools. One of the worst houses was ultimately torn down. Then Fr. Mottet started Interfaith Housing to clean up the housing around Sacred Heart. I saw the suffering of people in that neighborhood, which I hadn't seen before. They were being taken advantage of, and someone needed to stand with them. I talked with quite a few of them and asked them what they would like to see happen in their neighborhood.

We didn't ask them to be Catholic, but people, including fallen-away Catholics, started to come to Sacred Heart. The church grew like crazy with Fr. Mottet. People with no faith came to the Rite of Catholic Initiation of Adults. He held neighborhood meetings to help neighbors organize and deal with their issues. It was an exciting time, really empowering. You don't need to be a large group to make change. Usually, some people don't like you if you do community organizing, but I never heard anyone say a critical thing about Fr. Mottet.

Early on, people donated houses that needed to be cleaned up. Fr. Mottet recruited people to do the work, and the houses grew in value. He helped people get trained in construction. I became involved on the board of Interfaith Housing and so many other groups. Now, I'm involved in work with the police department in cooperation with the anti-violence groups. If I hadn't met him, I probably wouldn't be involved in community organizing. He rubbed off on people.

I became involved with the Hispanic community thanks to him. He invited me to a Spanish-speaking church for a Life in the Spirit seminar. I didn't speak Spanish, but I helped there.

He had so many ideas. We should do this, or we should be involved in that. He helped inspire so many people to become social justice activists. There is a strong social justice community here. There's still a lot of wrong, but it is never left alone. Fr. Mottet always tried to find the right people to run what he set up. He found that if he turned something over to the wrong person, it fell apart. It was amazing how many people Fr. Mottet knew. He had so many stories.

His influence led me to encourage others to be activists instead of doing things by myself. I'm on so many boards now that sometimes I have six meetings in a day. I'm up at six and get home at nine at night. I tell my husband that I need to do what Fr. Mottet wanted done, even when my husband suggests that I slow down. Fr. Mottet didn't slow down until he could no longer go. I need to keep influencing people to do good.

He had a note Mother Teresa wrote in the front of a book to encourage him. People had to dig like crazy in the diocese archives to find it, but that book is on display in St. Vincent's. He had all sorts of stuff. He had a letter from Mother Teresa. He was so matter of fact. No drama.

It was an ache in his heart when he was required to move from St. Vincent's to a care facility. That was not handled well. He was worried when his family and others came to clean out his room at St. Vincent's. He had to make sure important things weren't pitched into the garbage. I and others did our best to help sort through everything in his room. When he went to the nursing home, it was time. He drove longer than he should have and had several accidents.

I was with him when he died. He said it would be a joyous death. He died just as he lived. He had instructions for me, and he called and met with people in the days preceding his death. On the last day, he was in a coma. Hospice came. I sat alone in the room with him. He just kept breathing. I put my hand on him, and he gasped. I was startled and quickly removed my hand. He died quietly, so peacefully. Two or three people came in to pray for him after he died. One man said rosaries over him. It was a privilege to be there. He told me the day before his death "You don't have to do this." I said, "Yes, I do." I felt I had to be there. He was strong until the last day. His death was with no struggle. That is a wonderful way to die. Death is nothing to be feared.

Just about every day something reminds me of Fr. Mottet. I can't think of any regrets he had or things that didn't work out well, but the scandals in the church really hurt him. At the end, the groups he helped start weren't as respectful of him as they should have been. Young people had taken over, and they didn't recall what he had done. He and the other justice priests weren't treated well.

Fr. Mottet would like Bishop Zincula because he works with immigrants, and he considers it his job to implement Pope Francis' teachings. Justice work is still very strong in Davenport, but it wouldn't be without Fr. Mottet's lasting influence throughout the diocese. Kent Ferris is doing a good job with the Social Action Office.

I don't know where to start to say what I learned from him. As a person, he was so strong, but also so gentle. He was always activated by his faith. He always found ways to gently guide people. He was a beautiful man. I wouldn't be who I am and doing what I am without him. It isn't just me. I see his influence in my grandchildren. It keeps going on through the generations.

I was at the funeral visitation with Dan Ebener and others who knew him well, like Greg Galluzzo. They began discussing his legacy. It came about naturally. In a coffee house, we drew up what would become the Mottet Leadership Institute. Within a year, the Institute was running and had its first class of around fifty students. That was too many, so we cut down to thirty each year after that. It is a nine-month program. We brought in organizers and trainers from Gamaliel Foundation to help with the program. It has no direct connection with St. Ambrose University, though the Institute has three scholarships for St. Ambrose students. All of Fr. Mottet's justice books are at St. Ambrose.

Three classes went through the Institute before the COVID pandemic. Over a hundred students have completed the courses. They are from different backgrounds, not just Catholic. I keep in touch with many of those activists, and I know they are doing what they were taught.

Afterword

Seven years have passed since Fr. Mottet's death. I wish I could ask him a lot more questions. When I think about national and world events as well as personal situations, I often say, "Fr. Mottet was right."

The night before his funeral, a large group of people gathered for a prayer service at the funeral home in downtown Davenport. When I saw his simple, beautiful casket, I remembered him talking about caskets made by Trappist monks. It was a comforting evening. People shared their memories about him. It reminded me of what the priest from Des Moines said about Sr. Concetta's lunches for seniors: "The Kingdom of God is in there." Plans were already underway for the Mottet Leadership Institute, "a training program to engage people of all ages, particularly young adults, in the work of social justice."[55]

As I prepared to write the final chapter, I watched Fr. Mottet's Mass of Christian Burial on YouTube. Bishop Martin Amos celebrated the Mass at Sacred Heart Cathedral on September 21, 2016. Father's beloved cathedral was packed. He had chosen the songs, scripture readings, and speakers. It was one more opportunity to get his message across. Kent Ferris, Social Action and Catholic Charities Director, read from Isaiah 58, which was followed by the responsorial psalm: "The Lord hears the cry of the poor. Blessed be the Lord." The second reading was First Corinthians 2:2-5, the verses that stabbed him like a sword to break down his resistance to the baptism of the Holy Spirit.

Fr. Ed O'Melia's homily focused on the driving force of Fr. Mottet's life rather than his accomplishments. "There was something guiding, driving, moving Marv. That energy was the Holy Spirit and the Word of God…He was a pragmatic person who saw needs and tried to figure out a way to take care of them." For people who weren't aware of all Fr. Mottet accomplished, Fr. O'Melia said, "Read the book. If it's not out, it will be very soon." He was only wrong about the timing. He quoted Bilbo Baggins' famous summation of his relationship with Thorin Oakenshield in The Hobbit: "He was my friend."

Fr. Mottet's funeral was a call to action. He told people what he wanted them to do, and he was fearless in asking for favors or money. Dan Ebener laid this out clearly when he spoke. He said, "Marv's legacy is secure, but his work is not… For Marv, living life was a form of prayer. The gist of what he asked me to say in this address was this: Pray, and act. In his final days, he was praying that somehow, the rest of us would act, or as he put it, 'Pick up the slack'." In their final conversation, Fr. Mottet choked out three words: "Get…to work."

Fr. Mottet was interred in the priest's circle at Mount Calvary Cemetery in Davenport. He had organized a party afterward at the Knights of Columbus Hall with a buffet of simple food and plenty of beer. People talked around tables, and children played, just the way he wanted.

As we sort through the collage of stories he told, we see his steadiness. He was able to recognize basic truths and stick with them as they evolved and deepened. No one will be surprised by the list of his most important life lessons because they are woven through every chapter of his story, and they are interconnected.

I asked Fr. Mottet's for his "top-ten lessons." This was hard for him, and his list grew slowly. Each reader will probably discover different lessons in his book, but here are the ones he chose, not in order of importance:

- Charity can't make up for what is lacking in justice.

- Don't seek reputation for yourself but answer a call from the church.

- Everything important I have achieved came from relationships.

- You have to know people's interest and passion to get them involved.

- You must distinguish between private and public relationships.

- Ignoring the gift of the Holy Spirit is a big mistake. He's the best help we've got. That's how Jesus continues His work.

- Be a contemplative in action.

- Observe, judge, and act.

- Be a citizen lobbyist.

- Be fearless in asking for favors.

Fr. Mottet liked to say, "The world is run by friends." We are thankful for the opportunity to have Fr. Mottet as our friend. Occasionally, I read a biography that makes me love the protagonist. I hope that happens with this book, but even more, I hope Fr. Mottet's lessons stick, and we all get to work.

Endnotes

1 "The Oleomargarine Act," History, Art &Archives United States House of Representatives. Oleomargarine is a butter substitute made from previously wasted animal fat. It is an unappealing gray color and must be bleached before adding artificial colors and flavors to make it butter-like.

2 American Farm Bureau Federation website, fb.org.

3 4-H website, 4-h.org.

4 "St. Martin de Porres," Catholic Online (catholic.org)

5 Denis Hughes and Brian Jordan, "Catholic social teachings call to the dignity of creation," National Catholic Reporter, May 13, 2016. (ncronline.org)

6 Young Christian Workers website (ycwimpact.com)

7 St. John's University website (advancingsaintjohns.org)

8 "Vatican II: A Half Century Later, A Mixed Legacy," October 11, 2012. National Public Radio, WBEZ Chicago. (npr.org)

9 *The Catholic Messenger* is the newspaper of the Diocese of Davenport. It's mission is to inform, educate, and inspire the faithful.

10 Tonsure is a rite of admission to a new stage of religious activity by shaving a portion of the head.

11 The people who formed the Catholic Interracial Council were Fr. Bill O'Connor, Fr. Ed O'Connor, Charles Toney, Ernie Rodriguez, Henry Vargas, Fr. Griffin, Fr. Ruhl, Fr. Jack Smith, and Fr. Kamerick. Dr. McMahon was elected president, and Fr. Mottet was asked to be chaplain.

12 Pitz, Arthur, "Citizen Second Class—and the movement to change that in America's Heartland, details the civil rights history of Davenport, Iowa." This

paper is available at Putnam Museum, the African American Museum of Iowa, or by request from the author.

13 "The Economic Opportunity Act of 1964," Merced County Community Action Agency. (mercedcaa.com)

14 The Knights of Columbus, the world's largest Catholic fraternal service organization, was founded in 1882. The order upholds four key principles as pillars: Charity, Unity, Fraternity and Patriotism.

15 Fr. Mottet's students Pat Deluhrey, Greg Cusack, and Tom Higgins served in the Iowa legislature.

16 The Pacem in Terris Peace and Freedom Award is presented by the Davenport Diocese in collaboratin with other organizations to honor a person for his or her achievements in peace and justice in their country and in the world.

17 Curan, Charles E., "The Teaching and Methodoloogy of *Pacem in Terris, Journal of Catholic Social Thought,* Vol. 1, Issue 1, Winter 2004, 17-34. (villanova.edu)

18 Brecht, Tony, "Power of prayer offers brighter tomorrow," *Quad-City Times,* September, 2005.

19 "Full Gospel Business Men's Fellowship International (FGBMFI) is the largest network of Christian Businessmen in the world. Founded in 1952, we are in over 85 nations - meeting in thousands of chapters." (fgbmfi.org)

20 "The New Evangelization New Steps for a Special Kind of Saint," Saint John Institute. (saintjohninstitute.org)

21 Pope Paul VI, *Evangelii Nuntiand (Evangelization in the Modern World),* no. 41.

22 "United Way mobilizes communities around the world to close gaps and open opportunities so everyone can thrive. Through our global network spanning 37 countries and 1,100 communities, United Way connects partners, donors, volunteers, and community leaders to tackle the root causes of the world's most complex challenges while making a positive impact in the lives of millions of people." (unitedway.org)

23 Family Resources (famres.org)

[24] A photo of Sr. Concetta is available on the Project Renewal website. (projectrenewal.net)

[25] The Center for Active Seniors (CASI) provides services that promote independence and enrich the lives of older adults through socialization, health and wellness, and supportive services. The 40,000 square foot state-of-the-art center has daily activities, classes, community forums, a fitness center, and educational activities. CASI has a professional staff dedicated to the advocacy of seniors and all issues facing an aging population. (casiseniors.org)

[26] Dubb, Steve, "National Network Leader Looks Back on 40 Years of Community Organizing." *Nonprofit Quarterly*," May 2, 2019. (nonprofitquarterly.org)

[27] Thomas Merton Center at Bellarmine University (merton.org)

[28] Request the paper by emailing artpitz@hotmail.com.

[29] Call to Action website (cta-usa.org)

[30] Picchi, Amy, "50 years of tax cuts for the rich failed to trickle down, economics study says." CBS News, December 17, 2020. (cbsnews.com)

[31] Lau, Tim, "Citizens United Explained," Brennan Center for Justice, December 12, 2019. (brennancenter.org)

[32] Byron, Fr. William, S.J. collected a long list of "Baroni principles" that are, in many ways, like Fr. Mottet's operating principles. (eisenhowerfoundation.org)

[33] Gale Cincotta Collection, DePaul University Library. (archives.depaul.edu) Gale Cincotta became so well-known that her story was in the New York Times, the Washington Post, and the Chicago Tribune. She was called "the mother of community reinvestment." She attacked urban redlining and predatory lending. Her organizing efforts resulted in two pieces of groundbreaking legislation that stopped housing discrimination nationwide. A book about her titled *Gale Force* was published in 2011.

[34] The Industrial Areas Foundation is still functioning and is the largest network of faith and community-based organizations.

35 Nuns on the Bus is part of NETWORK, which advocates for justice and is the largest group of Catholic nuns in the U.S. (networkadvocates.org)

36 The federal Housing and Community Development Act of 1974 created Section 8 housing and set up a program of community development block grants. The legislation revitalized areas of inner-cities, but it also led to removal of low-income inhabitants who had their dwellings demolished.

37 The entire *Pastoral Letter on War and Peace* is available on the website of the U.S. Conference of Catholic Bishops (usccb.org). Quotations are from I. A. 4. and I. B. 4.

38 "Project Rachel is a ministry of the Catholic Church in the U.S. to those who have been involved in abortion. It is a diocesan-based network of specially trained priests, religious, counselors, and laypersons who provide a team response of care for those suffering in the aftermath of abortion." (helpafterabortion.org)

39 Fr. Mottet's paraphrase of Ezekiel 37:4-5.

40 Regional Development Authority website. (rdauthority.org)

41 Bowlin, Nick, "Rereading Alinsky in Baltimore: Why broad-based organizing still matters in an age of hashtag activism," *The Nation,* November 8, 2019.

42 "RCIA-Rite of Christian Initiation of Adults," Catholic Parishes of Arlington. (cparl.org)

43 Catholic Charismatic Renewal-Archdiocese of Miami (miamiccr.com)

44 Pierce, Gregory, *Activism that Makes Sense: Congregations and Community Organization,* Ch. 3, "Power: Good Intentions Are Not Enough, pp. 32-43.

45 Sacred Heart School was demolished in the summer of 2017 a few months after Fr. Mottet's death.

46 "Gerald O'Keefe: Bishop Cleared of Sex Accusations," *L.A. Times Archives,* April 15, 2000.

47 Ickes, Barb, "Ambrose to Remove Former Bishop O'Keefe's Name from the Library," *Quad-City Times,* August 3, 2007.

⁵² Turner, Jonathan, "O'Keefe's Name Removed from St. Ambrose Library". (bishopaccountability.org)

⁴⁹ Noble, Greg, "Cardinal Joseph Bernardin helped hide priest abuse in Chicago, documents show." Cincinnati WCPO, January 21, 2014. (wcpo.com)

⁵⁰ Dunklau, Sam, NPR Illinois, "Illinois Catholic Church Didn't Disclose Hundreds of Abuse Cases, New AG Finding Shows," December 19, 2018.

⁵¹ "Iowa Diocese Files for Bankruptcy," October 10, 2006, CBS News. (cbsnews.com)

⁵² Fr. Mottet's speech is on YouTube under the title "Pacem In Terris Peace and Freedom Award 2008: Msgr Marvin Mottet."

⁵³ Beaumont, Douglas, "What Are Ghosts?" *Catholic Answers,* October 11, 2018. (catholic.com)

⁵⁴ Dr. Margaret Schlientz was founder and first executive director of Pope Leo XIII Institute. (popeleo13institute.org)

⁵⁵ Arland-Fey, Barb, "Mottet Leadership Institute fulfills on of priest's last wished," *The Catholic Messenger,* July 6, 2017.

Fr. Mottet's Life in Historical Context

Life Story		Historical Context	
		1929	Great Depressing begins with stock market crash. Herbert Hoover becomes President (1929-1933).
1930	Birth on May 31 in Ottumwa, Iowa		
		1933	Franklin Roosevelt becomes President (1933-1949). New Deal begins (1933-1939).
1936	Attends St. Patrick's Catholic School (1936-1944)		
1937	Mother becomes critically ill. Aunt Katherine teaches him to read.	1937	Wagner Act enables workers to unionize. Congress of Industrial Organizations is founded.
Circa 1939	Brothers Wilbert and Paul leave for military service.	1939	World War II begins.
1944	Attends Central Catholic High School (1944-1948)		
1945	Toney court case begins civil rights movement in Davenport, Iowa.	1945	Harry Truman becomes President (1945-1953). Atomic bomb dropped in Japan ends World War II.
1947	Meets Jeanne Sheehan	1947	Cold War begins (1947-1989).

Interracial Club established at St. Ambrose College.

1948   Plays in Iowa State High School Basketball Tournament.
        Enrolls at St. Ambrose College (1948-1952).
        Participates in Young Christian Students.

1950   Ends relationship with Jeanne.

1950   Korean war begins (1950-1953).
        McCarthyism begins (1950-1954).

1951   Transfers to seminary at St. Ambrose.
        League for Social Justice Founded (1951-1954).
        Jeanne marries Dallas Traxler.

1952   *Citizen Second Class* is published.
        Works on Cooks Point relocation project
        Meets Charles and Ann Toney.
        Enrolls at Mt. St. Bernard Seminary.

1953   Travels to Chicago where he learns from activist priests.
        Clarence Mottet dies.

1953   Dwight Eisenhower becomes President (1953-1961)

1954   Brown v. Board of Education of Toopeka ends school segregation.

1955   Vietnam War begins (1955-1975).

1956   Receives ordination as
        diocesan priest.
        Begins teaching at St.
        Ambrose Academy
        (1956-1958).

1957   Helps start Davenport   1957   Little Rock, Arkansas school
        Catholic Interracial   integration.
        Council (1957-1977).   Civil Rights Act of 1957 is
        Toneys set up barber   passed (first since
        shop in home.   Reconstruction).
        Margaret Gertrude
        Mottet dies.

1958   Continues teaching as St.
        Ambrose Academy
        becomes Assumption
        High School (1958-
        1966).
        Runs extensive Young
        Christian Students
        program.
        Becomes chaplain of
        Catholic Interracial
        Council with Charles
        Toney as president.

1959   Travels to Mexico,
        Columbia, Panama, and
        Peru as papal volunteer.
        League of United Latin
        American Citizens
        established in Davenport
        (1959-present).

1961   Civil rights leaders begin   1961   John F. Kennedy becomes
        planning meetings in   President (1961-1963).
        Toneys' new barber
        shop.

1962   Meets Jack Schneiders.   1962   Vatican II begins (1962-
                                               1965).

Nuclear war narrowly averted during Cuban Missile Crisis.

1963   Studies Spanish at Center for Intercultural Formation in Cuernavaca, Mexico. Participates in civil rights march in Davenport. Participates in March on Washington for Jobs and Freedom. Hears Martin Luther King, Jr.'s "I Have a Dream" speech.

1963   Lyndon Johnson becomes President when Kennedy is assassinated (1963-1969). Iowa legislature passes Fair Employment Practices Act of 1963. Baptist Church bombing in Birmingham, Alabama, kills four young girls.

1964   Plans first Pacem in Terris Peace and Freedom Award presented to John Howard Griffin and posthumously to John F. Kennedy. Receives master's degree in theology from Dominican House of Studies.

1964   Great Society and War on Poverty begin (1964-1968). Freedom Summer brings national attention to African American voting rights issues. Civil Rights Act of 1964 prohibits discrimination. Anti-Vietnam War movement starts (1965-1975).

1965   Martin Luther King, Jr. receives Pacem in Terris Award in Davenport.

1965   Iowa Civil Rights Act of 1965 establishes Civil Rights Commission. March from Selma to Montgomery in Alabama leads to Bloody Sunday on Edmond Pettus Bridge and Voting Rights Act of 1965.

1966   Year-long "dark night of the soul" begins.

1967   Bishop O'Keefe arrives in Davenport.

Enrolls in Graduate
School of Social Work at
University of Iowa.
Attends Saul Alinsky's
class on community
organizing in Chicago.
Marches in Milwaukee
with Fr. James Groppi.

1968   Undergoes cancer
surgery in Houston.
Receives baptism of the
Holy Spirit.
Becomes Associate
Chaplain at Marycrest
College.
Moves to St. Joseph's
rectory and begins
charismatic prayer group.
Starts conscientious
objector program in
Davenport Diocese.

1968   Open Housing Ordinance is
passed in Davenport.
Gamaliel Foundation
founded in Chicago (1968-
present).
Tet offensive begins in
Vietnam.
Martin Luther King, Jr. is
assassinated.
Riots break out in one
hundred cities.
Robert Kennedy is
assassinated.
Fair Housing Act of 1968 is
passed.

1969   Starts Diocese of
Davenport Social Action
Department (1969-
present).
Opens first Catholic
Worker house.

1969   Richard Nixon becomes
President (1969-1974).

1970   Hires Sr. Concetta
Bendicente.
Starts Legal Aid.
Starts Area Board of
Migrants.

1971   Attends meetings of
Catholic Committtee on
Urban Ministry at Notre
Dame.

1972   Helps Sr. Concetta start
        Senior Iowans.
        Social Action
        Department establishes
        an Immigration Office.
        Begins healing ministry
        by praying for baby with
        Downs Syndrome.
        Dorothy Day receives
        Pacem in Terris Award
        in Davenport.

1974   Helps Sr. Concetta start   1974   Davenport Civil Rights
        Project Renewal (1974-   Commission begins (1974-
        present).   present).
                                                President Nixon resigns
                                                following Watergate scandal.
                                                Gerald Ford becomes
                                                President (1974-1977).

1975   Receives MSW degree
        from University of Iowa.
        Develops two feet model
        of social ministry.

1976   Mother Theresa receives
        Pacem in Terris Award
        in Davenport.

1977   Catholic Interracial   1977   Jimmy Carter becomes
        Council disbands.   President (1977-1981).

1978   Becomes National
        Director of Campaign
        for Human
        Development (1978-
        1985).
        Lives in Washington,
        D.C. (1978-1985)

Starts and lives in first of
three Catholic Worker
houses.

1979   Receives five invitations
to the White House.
Witnesses Pope John
Paul II's speech in
Chicago where he praises
the Campaign for
Human Development.

1980   Visits Mondragon
worker-owned coop in
Basque region of Spain.

1980   High inflation and stagnant
economic growth
(stagflation).
Deindustrialization,
economic decline,
population decline, and
urban decay in "rust belt"
region (including
Davenport).

1981   Ronald Reagan becomes
President (1981-1989).

1983   Becomes Chairman of
the Board of Gamaliel
Foundation (1983-1998).

1983   National Conference of
Catholic Bishops publishes
pastoral letter on war and
peace.

1985   Returns to Davenport to
become pastor of Sacred
Heart Cathedral.
Receives Project Rachel
training.

1986   Starts Quad Cities
Interfaith (1986-present).

Circa   Begins healing Masses at
1989   Sacred Heart Cathedral
that spread through the
region.

1989   George H. W. Bush
becomes President (1989-
1993).

Soviet Union collapses
(1989-1991).
Cold War ends.

Circa 1990 — Welcomes Vietnamese congregation to Sacred Heart parish.
Enlarges congregation through Come and See—Go and Tell initiative.

1991 — First Gulf War (100 days).

1992 — Bishop O'Keefe sued for sexual abuse and acquitted.

1993 — Starts Interfaith Housing (1993-present).
Receives permission for exorcism and deliverance ministry.
Enjoys three-month sabbatical in Rome.
Meets Pope John Paul II.
Meets Fr. Amorth (best-known exorcist in the world).
Visits Holy Land and begins leading ecumenical pilgrimages.
Bishop O'Keefe resigns.

1993 — Bill Clinton becomes President (1993-2000).
Seminarian files sexual abuse lawsuit against Cardinal Joseph Bernardin, head of Archdiocese of Chicago.

Circa 1996 — Receives housing grant for Cathedral Heights, and fierce opposition begins.

1998 — Receives kidney transplant.

2001 — Receives title of Monsignor.

2001 — George W. Bush becomes President (2001-2009).

Attack on World Trade Center begins "war on terror."

2002   *Boston Globe* exposes Catholic sexual abuse scandal in the U.S.

2003   Second Persian Gulf War begins (2003-2011). Vatican conference on sexual abuse.

2005   Retires from Sacred Heart Parish.

2006   Diocese of Davenport files for Chapter 11 bankruptcy due to sexual abuse scandal.

2007   Serves as sacramental minister at St. Mary's parish in Davenort.

2007   Subprime mortgage crisis leads to Great Recession (2007-2010).

2008   Receives Pacem in Terris Award.

2009   Barak Obama becomes President (2009-2017).

2010   Affordable Care Act is passed.

2014   Moves to Kahl Home. Works to get funding for worker-owned coop to benefit veterans. Prepares for eternity.

2016   Celebrates sixtieth anniversary of ordination. Dies on September 21 at age eighty-six.

2016   Donald Trump is elected President.

Suggested Reading

Chambers, Edward T. *Organizing for Power, Action, and Justice.* New York: Bloomsbury Publishing, 2003.

Costello, Mary. *Monsignor Mottet Stories.* Davenport, Iowa: Costello Creations, 2017. Print.

Day, Dorothy. *The Long Loneliness.* San Francisco: Harper & Row, 1981.

Doherty, Catherine. *Poustinia: Encountering God in Silence, Solitude and Prayer.* Combermere, Ontario: Madonna House Publications, 1993.

Frisbie, Margerie. *An Alley in Chicago: The Life and Legacy of Monsignor John Egan.* Franklin, Wisconsin, 2002.

Griffin, John Howard. *Black Like Me.* New American Library, 2004.

Harrington, Michael. *The Other America: Poverty in the United States.* Harmondsworth, Middlesex: Penguin Books, 1981.

Merton, Thomas, Giroux, Robert, and Shannon William H. *The Seven Storey Mountain.* New York: Harcourt Brace, 1998.

Pierce, Gregory F. Augustine. *Activism that Makes Sense: Congregations and Community Organization.* Chicago, Illinois: ACTA Publications, 1984.

Skerrett, Ellen, Kantowicz, Edward R., and Avella, Steven M. *Catholicism, Chicago Style.* Chicago: Loyola University Press, 1993.

Van der Meersch, Maxence. *Fishers of Men.* translated from the French by Rev. John Fitzsimmon. New York: Shed & Ward, unknown publication date.[55]

Authors

Suzanne Pitz taught psychology, conducted business training, and helped faculty design online college courses. She is co-founder and Director of Operations of White Field Partners, a non-profit corporation that does development work in Sierra Leone, West Africa. After retiring, Suzanne taught in universities in Slovakia and conducted workshops in several countries in Central Europe. She now specializes in grandmothering, writing, gardening, and volunteering. Suzanne and her husband Art Pitz have a longstanding commitment to their Christian faith and to working for a more just world. They have been married for over fifty-five years and live in Elmhurst, Illinois. They relish international adventures and still claim that the best is yet to come.

Dr. Arthur Pitz is an award-winning history professor, museum exhibit curator, avid reader, public speaker, Rotarian, storyteller, and sports enthusiast. His teaching career spans over 55 years. He has taught courses and conducted workshops in multiple countries and served as a Fulbright Senior Specialist in Finland, Macedonia, and Slovakia. He talks about history and politics whenever he can because history helps make sense of our choices for the future. Check out his "History Behind the News" blog at artpitz.com. Art serves as President of White Field Partners.